ORIGIN AND GROWTH OF TOWNS

ORIGIN AND GROWTH OF TOWNS

A.K. SINGH 'ANAL'

CONCEPT PUBLISHING COMPANY, NEW DELHI 110059

ISBN 81-7022-322-9

First Published 1990

Published and Printed by
Ashok Kumar Mittal
Concept Publishing Company
A/15-16, Commercial Block, Mohan Garden
NEW DELHI 110059 (India)

Lasertypeset by
Microtech Advance Printing Systems (Pvt.) Ltd.
H-13, Bali Nagar
NEW DELHI 110015

PREFACE

URBANISATION IS one of the most striking features of contemporary civilisation. Researchers have readily recognised the varying processes and rates of urbanisation in various parts of the world, both in the pre-industrial and industrial periods. Economic progress, technological efficiency and industrial growth are symbolised by the prosperity of towns. The town not only provides meaningful clues about the economic and social health of its region but also reflects transformation of the physico-socio-cultural landscape. It is a source of change in its own right. Davis and Casis (1946, p. 141) have noted the importance of city as a centre for diffusion of modern civilisation, thereby providing a milieu in which social ferment and innovation can take place. Its expansion, therefore, helps to determine the trend towards more modern conditions.

Recently, the number and size of towns have increased greatly in most of the developed and developing regions of the world. Introduction of modern means of transportation, changing cultural outlook and industrial expansion have given rise to many new problems. Consequently, urban geography has come to assume greater importance, both as an academic discipline and as a practical science for tackling the manifold problems of urban areas, including their planning. Location, area, extent and interaction among the urban functions are the prime concern of the urban geographer (Mayer and Kohn, 1967, p.1). Evaluation of economic and physical patterns in urban areas, tackling of problems arising therefrom, and appropriate allocation of various land-uses largely depend upon a pre-knowledge of the above-mentioned facts.

There are two major approaches, namely, the demographic and morphological, in the study of towns. The demographic approach lays emphasis on the study of the distribution, size, function and the rate of growth of the town's population, whereas the morphological approach is primarily concerned with the build of the town, including its layout plan, both internal and external, as expressions of its manifold functions. The two approaches are so overlapping in nature that it becomes difficult to maintain a clear differentiation. In the present investigation, however, an attempt has been made to adopt the second approach. Thus, it becomes imperative to examine more closely the various connotations of morphology, including its usage in the interpretation of town's form and structure.

The term 'morphology' has been derived from two Greek words, *morphe* (form) and *logos* (discourse), which literally mean description of form. Though the essence of the idea of morphology was initially expressed in the writings of the great poet and philosopher Goethe (1790), the term as such was first used in bio-science. Recently, it is being increasingly used in geography, geology, philology and other subjects. In bio-science, it is defined as the science of organic form, or simply the development of the form of living organisms. The term, however, is used not only to study the shape and structure in plants, animals and microorganisms but also of the size, shape, structure and relationship of the parts comprising them (*Encyclopaedia Britannica*, 1974, p. 451). Morphological analysis has been widely used in geography as well. According to Stamp (1961, p. 326), it is defined as the science of form and structure, including developments which influence the form. In humanities, the concept of morphology has been applied in the study of social institutions phenomenologically; these institutions are inter-related with socio-economic norms and bonds and various functional as well as interactional system supporting decision, transformation and communication among the complex structures of various groups or cultures within the spatial matrix (Singh, R.L. and R.P.B. Singh, 1978, p.5). Morphology of settlement, however, is the expression of various functions of physical and cultural variables which can be identified in the building fabric of build-up area.

Morphology of plants and animals is quite distinct from those of settlements. The form and function of a living organism can be easily distinguished, but in settlement these are inter-fused together. Consequently, the biological domain is rather more distinct than the geographical sphere. Another difference is noticed in regard to pattern weaving and structural behaviour. An organism is always governed by the norms set by a particular reproductive group, which goes on producing a particular form, but this is not so in case of town development. For example, two towns sited either on river banks or at rail-heads do not possess identical morphological characteristics.

Thirdly, an organism is short-lived, whereas the town, with the passage of time, transforms itself into different structural forms and continues to exist even afterwards. A town may grow into a city or it can degenerate into a rural settlement.

Under morphology of settlements, Dickinson (1951, p. 8) considers the plan and build of the habitat as viewed and interpreted in terms of its origin, growth and functions. Morphological studies, according to Murphy (1966, p.4), generally deal with the development of form and pattern of the present city or other urban area through time, in short, with evolution. The morphology of a town may be, therefore, considered as the reflection of its manifold functions as a consequence of either planned or unplanned growth. In fact, evolution, functions and morphology of a settlement are so closely inter-related that their separation is somewhat difficult. Nevertheless, the morphology of a town relates to its anatomy, i.e., its physical form and structure, including the layout of streets, spacing and size of buildings and their architectural designs. Evidently, there is a lot of variation in the physical form, street pattern, type and design of buildings in the towns of North Bihar to merit a scientific investigation. Such an investigation is necessary not only from academic point of view but also for planning economic development and expansion of the town in future.

Numerous studies have been made, in the past, pertaining to site and situation of towns both in India and in Western countries. Recently, these studies have tended to become more rigorous and, certainly, more focused upon specific problems of the urban community, to which urban geographers have given high priority.

Morphological study of town was first initiated by Dickinson (1945) in Europe. Urban geographers, like, William-Olsson (1940-52), Smailes (1953), Jones (1960), Conzen (1960) and Whitehand (1977), have also contributed to the study of the morphological aspects of towns. Among notable contributors to the morphological aspects of the towns in U.S.A. are Harris (1945), Bartholomew (1955), Mayer and Kohn (1959), Berry (1959, 1963), Murphy (1966) and Northam (1975). In the last two decades, some serious attempts have been made to provide a conceptual framework or model for urban development. In this regard, the social scientists of the Chicago school, particularly Burgess (1925), Hoyt (1939) and Ullman (1945), have adopted a more balanced stance in their studies. In fact, the present theoretical frame-work of urban geography is largely based on their contributions.

Among various urban studies made by Indian Geographers, the

initial contributions were by E. Ahmad (1950, 1965), R.L. Singh (1955), U. Singh (1958), M.P. Thakore (1962), A.B. Chatterjee (1964), S.M. Alam (1965) and H.H. Singh (1965). Thus, cities, like, Varanasi, Allahabad, Kanpur, Delhi, Howrah, Hyderabad and Secunderabad, have been studied in detail with special reference to their growth and evolution and determination of their demographic and functional structures as also their *umlands*. These investigations were followed by a host of identical works. The functional classification of towns and the trend of urbanisation based on demographic statistics have been attempted by A.S. Jauhari (1957), A. Ramesh (1964), K.K. Dube (1965), M. Mukherjee (1966), S.M. Karimi (1967), P. Pandeya (1968), P.S. Tiwari (1968), Onkar Singh (1968), N.B.K. Reddy (1969), D. Thapan (1969), O.P. Singh (1969) and B. Thakur (1980). Special mention has to be made of the study entitled 'Morphology of Indian Cities' by K.L. Taneja (1968). It is an important contribution in the field of town morphology wherein the author applies the biological concept of morphology to urban ecological growth processes and obtains some meaningful generalisations based on a sample study of eight cities of India.

The present investigation is to identify various morphological characteristics of the towns of North Bihar and to show how these have evolved through time. Application of the concept of developmental biology is made use of to analyse the developmental pattern and morphogenesis of towns. The functional structure of the town, in fact, reflects in large measure the developmental processes in biology. It has been recognised that the various organs of a town act in an orderly way under the impact of certain push and pull factors. The transport arteries and various functional zones, including the built-up area, constitute the principal organs of a town; their size, form, proportion and arrangement are subject to most varied developments and modification.

The morphological characteristics of the towns of North Bihar are typical of a predominantly agrarian society of the developing world with low rates of urbanisation. Development of the road and rail transports has made deep inroads into the traditional subsistence pattern of living and has engendered commercial activity, resulting in the growth of a network of urban centres which, though small by size, have accentuated certain characteristics of town development. An attempt has been also made to examine the impact of various physical and cultural influences upon the evolution and morphology of towns. This analysis is largely based on similar studies made earlier by Colby

(1933), Dickinson (1945), Conzen (1960), Murphy (1966), Whitehand (1977), Ahmad (1950-1976), Singh (1955-1979) and Taneja (1968). Meaningful explanations have been obtained for variations in the morphological characteristics of the towns in North Bihar.

North Bihar forms a distinct physical and cultural region in Bihar. The economic base of the region has been analysed variously at block, sub-division and district levels, depending on the availability of data. Most of the analysis, including mapping, has been done on the basis of the old district boundary, namely those of Saran, Champaran, Muzaffarpur, Darbhanga, Saharsa, Purnea and parts of Monghyr and Bhagalpur lying north of the Ganga. Since the reorganisation of the districts in 1972, North Bihar has 15 districts, namely Saran, Siwan, Gopalganj, East Champaran, West Champaran, Muzaffarpur, Vaishali, Sitamarhi, Darbhanga, Samastipur, Madhubani, Begusarai, Saharsa, Purnea and Katihar. Besides, Khagaria and Naugachhia sub-divisions of Monghyr and Bhagalpur districts respectively also lie in North Bihar. In the text, however, the sub-divisions of Begusarai and Khagaria have been, sometimes, denoted as North Monghyr. Most of the information has been gathered from published and unpublished maps and records, census statistics, government and semi-government publications. But there is a general lack of systematic publication of statistics and proper maintenance of records. In spite of persistent efforts, maps of a few small towns could not be obtained, as these have not been published yet. In view of the general lack of source materials for the study of the towns, field investigations were undertaken several times in the region.

The study has been divided into ten chapters. Chapter 1 makes an appraisal of the physical and economic background of urban settlements in the region, under sub-titles of physiography, drainage, floods, land-use, agricultural typology, industries and communication. Chapter 2 analyses the population characteristics of the region with special reference to its growth, distributional pattern, density, occupational structure, besides the processes of urbanisation, growth of urban population in various size-classes of towns and urban zones. It also includes an analysis of the spatial distribution of towns. Chapter 3 attempts to trace the origin and growth of towns in the historic past. This has helped to bring out the dominance of historical as well as physical factors on the growth of towns in the region. The general morphological characteristics of towns, including the layout plan, morphological zones and the developmental pattern are described in

Chapter 4. Chapter 5 presents a detailed analysis of the functional structure of 11 sample towns with their geographical setting, spatial shape, population growth and occupational and functional structures. Occurrence of the varying proportions of the urban space under various functional uses in different categories of towns has also been critically examined. Chapter 6 deals with the morphology of residential areas, including their general characteristics and distributional pattern, nature and causes of slum formation, and the design and type of residential accommodation available. Chapter 7 analyses the morphology of commercial areas. It also includes identification and description of the type of retail structure available, such as the central business area (C.B.A.), neighbourhood shopping centre and isolated shopping nucleation. Chapter 8 gives an account of the morphology of other functional areas, viz., industrial, administrative, educational, medical and recreational. Chapter 9 deals with the problems and planning associated with various morphological areas. Summary and Conclusion of the study given in Chapter 10. It also includes suggestions for comprehensive planning of urban areas, so that the towns could prosper in future as well. The study is illustrated with 45 maps and figures, mostly drawn first hand, and 19 plates.

This work seeks to make the following original contributions:

1. A detailed study of the morphology and general characteristics of the towns of North Bihar has been presented for the first time. In this context, the physical and geonomic personality of the region has been presented with the help of earlier published or unpublished literature, economic statistics and maps.
2. Recent changes in the distribution of population, including the processes of urbanisation and their relationship with physico-cultural landscape, have been vividly portrayed and interpreted. Spatial pattern of town distribution has been obtained through statistical indices. Though the network of streams has been the chief determinant in the spread of towns in the past, the recent growth of rail and road transports has also affected their distribution.
3. The evolution and origin of towns, traced from historical records and archaeological findings, have provided an insight into the processes of town growth during historic and recent times.
4. The histogenesis of the towns of North Bihar has been obtained

after evaluating the traditional theories of urban growth and application of the concept of developmental biology. Town plans have been interpreted with the help of cadastral maps, topographical sheets and field investigation. The external form and the internal structure of the urban fabric have been explained as consequence of certain physical or cultural phenomena.

5. Functional analyses of 11 sample towns have been obtained and their spatial shape measured by using circular geometric techniques. Analysis of the occupational structure of towns has revealed a large dependence on primary activities. It also shows a complex mosaic of inter-woven land-use.
6. Morphological analysis of residential, commercial, industrial and other functional areas has helped to reveal the internal complexes of the town's structure. A distinct impact of historical antecedents, physical build of site and the economic and social climates prevailing in the region have been noticed on the town morphology.
7. The morphological problems of the various components of the town have been systematically anatomised through model design, and a model plan for town development has been suggested for a decent urban living.

REFERENCES

Davis, K. and Ana Casis (1946): "Urbanisation in the Latin America", In P.K. Hatt and A.J.R. Jr. Ed. (1963), *Cities and Society*; New York, pp. 141-56.

Dickinson, R.E. (1951): *The West European City*, London. *Encyclopaedia Britannica* (1974), Chicago.

Goethe, J.W. Von (1970): Kersuch die Metamorphose der ptlanzen zu erklaren, Gotha Work cited in A.S. Foster and E.M. Gifford Jr. Ed. (1967) *Comparative Morphology of Vascular Plants*, Bombay, p. 2.

Mayer, H.M. and C.F. Kohn Ed. (1967): *Readings in Urban Geography*, Allahabad.

Murphy, R.E. (1966): *The American City: An Urban Geography*, McGraw Hill Book Co., New York.

Singh, R.L. and R.P.B. Singh (1978): Concept of Morphological Analysis: Some Theoretical postulations, *National Geographical Journal of India*, 24, pp. 1-16.

Stamp, L.D. (1961): *A Glossary of Geographical Terms*, London.

ACKNOWLEDGEMENTS

I EXPRESS my sincere thanks to the University Grants Commission for awarding me a fellowship, the Department of Geography, Banaras Hindu University, for providing me research facilities and the Government of India and the Administration in Andaman and Nicobar Islands for granting me study-leave to complete my present study.

I offer my heartfelt gratitude to Dr. N.K.P. Sinha, for providing me sound critical comments and inspiring guidance in preparation of the manuscript.

My thanks are also due to Prof. A.S. Jauhari, Head of the Department, Prof. Kashi Nath Singh, Prof. S.L. Kayastha, Dr. K.N. Singh, Dr. D.N. Singh, Dr. Onkar Singh and Dr. V.K. Kumra of the Department of Geography, Banaras Hindu University, for their advice and suggestions in various ways.

I am grateful to the officials of Municipal bodies and police stations, located in various towns, for providing me maps and statistics and to many other departments of the Government for their help in several ways. I am also indebted to the authorities of *Zila Khadi Bhandar*, who graciously provided me accommodation in most of the towns of North Bihar in the course of my field-work.

I owe a lot to my teachers, particularly Prof. E. Ahmad and Prof. P. Pandeya, for stimulating my interest in research and under whom I took my post-graduate degree from Ranchi University. Special mention has to be made of Prof. R.L. Singh, Vice-Chancellor, Meerut University, who initially provided me with the frame-work of the study and whose concept of urban geography has greatly influenced my thinking.

I wish to record my deep sense of gratitude to Dr. A.V.V. Iyer, Principal, Government College, Port Blair, for his inspiration and encouragement at all times.

My sincere thanks are also due to Sarvashri V.C. Jha, G.S. Singh, J. Singh, B.N. Singh, S. Singh and Dr. H. Prasad, Research Scholars in

Geography Department, B.H.U., who ungrudgingly provided help in the course of the completion of the study.

I am thankful to Shri S. Prasad for re-producing the maps to required size and to the Typing Centre, Durgakund Road, Varanasi, for typing the manuscript in a short time.

Lastly, but not the least, I would like to thank my wife, Krishna, for her patience and forbearance throughout the preparation of this book.

AWADHESH KUMAR SINGH 'ANAL'

CONTENTS

LIST OF FIGURES

LIST OF PLATES

LIST OF TABLES

1

GEOGRAPHICAL BACKGROUND

PHYSICAL SETTING

Location

NORTH BIHAR stretches approximately from 25°10′ N to 27°31′N latitudes and from 83°58′E to 88°17′E longitudes (Fig. 1.1). It measures 53,796 sq. km which is about one-fourth of the total area of the State of Bihar. Its maximum length, along the E-W axis, is about 440 km and its width, along the N-S axis, is about 170 km. It is demarcated by the Ganga in the south, the Ghaghra in the south-west, Saran-Deoria district boundary in the west, the Siwalik hills in the north-west, the Nepal Tarai in the north and the Bengal plains in the east. The shape of the region somewhat resembles a trapezoid with its northern and southern boundaries being more or less parallel while its eastern and western boundaries are irregularly aligned either N-S or NW-SE. Its general slope is towards the south and east.

Physiography

Physiographically North Bihar, with the sole exceptions of the Sumeshwar Range and the Ramnagar Dun in Northern Champaran, is a featureless plain. Its general elevation is less than 75 m above the mean sea level (Fig. 1.2A). Monotony of its landscape is broken by the existence of a large number of stream channels — some discarded ones, others active round the year and a few during the floods. These streams flow in southerly or south-easterly direction until they meet the Ganga whose channel elevation is 60 m in the west and 30 m in the east. The hilly tract of Sumeshwar and the Ramnagar Dun, in Bihar,

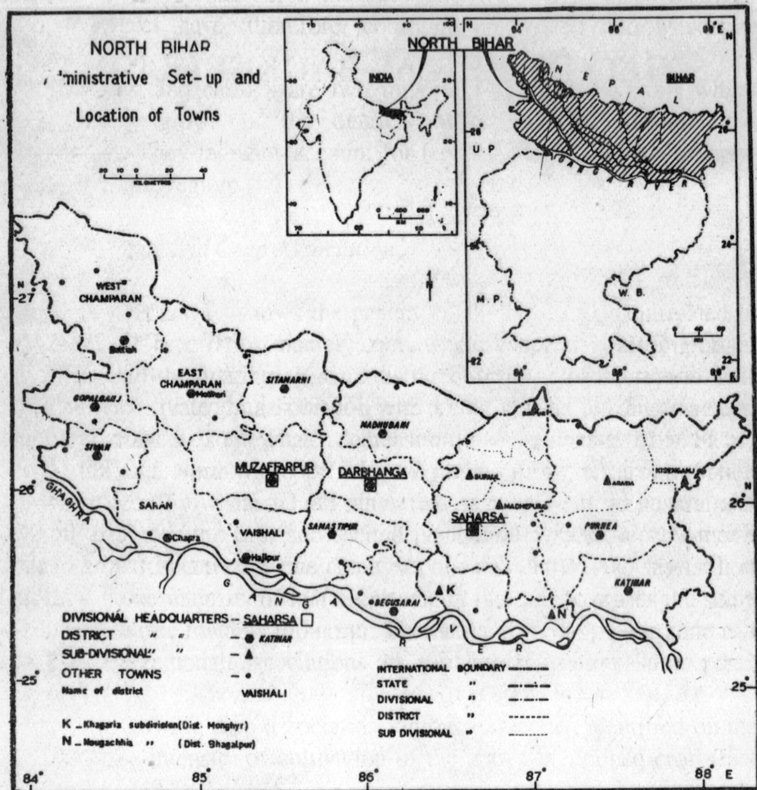

Fig. 1.1: Administrative set-up and location of towns.

measure about 943 sq. km; they vary in elevation from 150 m to 460 m. The imperceptible general slope of the North Bihar plain, as shown by stream courses, is from the north-west to the south-east, descending about 30 m in an expanse of about 600 km. Its descent from north to south, towards the Ganga, along the longitudes of 85°, 86°E and 87°E is 1/5,200, 1/4,400 and 1/2,800, respectively, which shows that the slope is steeper in the east than in the west (Ahmad, 1965, p. 21). Thus, considering relief and slope variations, the region can be divided into the following physiographic units:

(a) The Himalayan foot-hills, in the extreme north-west,
(b) The moist Tarai belt, in the north,
(c) The vast Gandak-Kosi plain, and
(d) The scattered marshy low lands and depressions.

The Himalayan foothills, comprising the hilly tracts of Sumeshwar and Ramnagar Dun, form the outer margins of the Siwaliks whose major part lies in Nepal. These hills, overlooking the Gandak-Kosi plain, have been worn down by the fluvial process of river action into a series of steep ravines and almost inaccessible summits (Chaudhury, 1960, p. 10). This hilly tract extend for about 30 km in south-westerly direction on the north-western margin of the district of Champaran. Between the Sumeshwar ranges lies the Ramnagar Dun which includes places of natural beauty such as Bhikhna Thori, Kapan and Harha.

The Tarai region lies to the south of the Siwalik foothills and stretches in a W-E belt all along the northern margin of North Bihar plain. It is supposed to be comparatively unhealthy and consists of marshy grassland and forest land (Chaudhury, 1960, p.11). The Tarai belt is characterised by re-emergence of water that percolates into previous synclinal strata in the upper foothills. This results in seepages and makes the area moist and marshy.

The Tarai belt is followed, towards the south, by the fertile Gandak-Kosi plain which occupies the largest area of the region. This plain is divided into three well-defined tracts by the Great Gandak, the Burhi Bandak and the Kosi rivers. Its level slopes make it the playground of numerous Himalayan rivers, namely, the Ghaghra, Gandak, Caghmati, Kamla, Balan, Kosi and Mahananda and other minor streams. These rivers, before draining into the Ganga, have quite frequently changed their courses, owing to heavy deposition of silt in the stream courses. They generally flow on raised beds or 'river ridges'

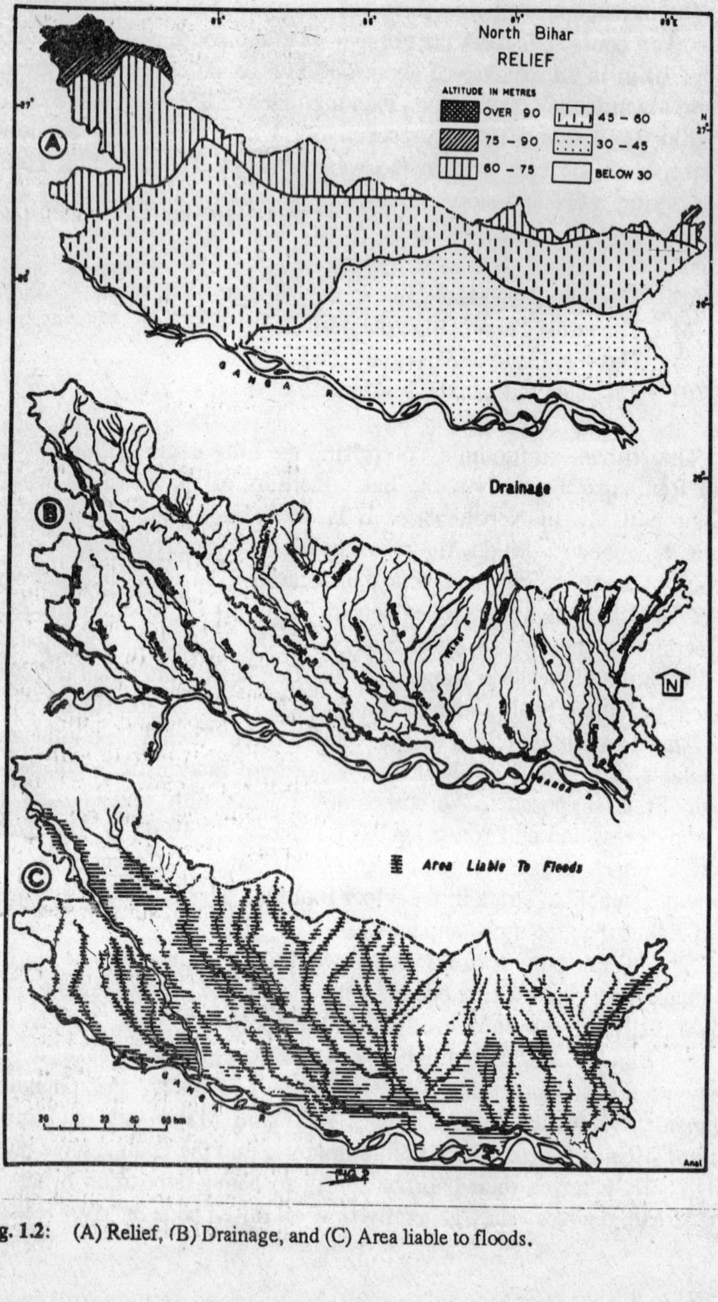

Fig. 1.2: (A) Relief, (B) Drainage, and (C) Area liable to floods.

that lie slightly above the general level of the plains and frequently inundate the low-lying lands on either side during the monsoons. The Kosi and the Gandak, in particular, have formed alluvial 'cones' in the process of their former oscillation (Singh, 1973, p. 18). Other streams, originating in the snow-fed Himalayas, have formed smaller cones. Sometimes 'inner cones' or 'cone within cone' have been formed by the tributaries of larger streams.

There are also a large number of swamps and marshes scattered over the plain region. The most remarkable among these is a chain of 43 lakes in the district of Champaran. It includes the important lakes of Lal Saraiya, Sugaon, Tinkulia, Motihari, Pipra, Siraha, Nawada, and Tetaria, which together extend over an area of about 30 sq. km (Chaudhury, 1960, p. 36). They represent the former off-shoots of the old bed of the Great Gandak. Several other 'Chaurs', 'Tals' and shallow marshy depressions also occur in the districts of Muzaffarpur, Darbhanga and Begusarai. The most important among these are Baraila Tal in Muzaffarpur, Bahera Chaur in Darbhanga and Kabar Tal in Begusarai. These low-lying depressions receive the local run-off as also overflows from numerous streams in the area. Areas adjoining the 'Chaurs' and 'Tals' and the 'diara' tract along the Ganga are most fertile in the whole region.

Geology

The surface geology of North Bihar, except the Sumeshwar range, relates to pleistocene and later times. The Sumeshwar range, composed of sandstones and conglomerates, forms a part of Siwalik system of fresh-water deposits of late Tertiary times; this system accounts for the foothills ranges along the entire length of the Himalayas west of Darjeeling. The fore-deep of the Himalayas, south of the Siwaliks, has received sedimentary deposits by the Ganga and its numerous tributaries over a long period of time. The filling up of this depression by alluvial deposits resulted in the formation of the Gangetic plain of which the North Bihar plain is just a part. It is presumed that the basement of the plain is formed by a part of the ancient continent of Gondwana land, supposed to be composed of Archaen granites and gneisses (Diwakar, 1959, p.5).

There is lack of information regarding the thickness of alluvial deposits in North Bihar plain. After a few borings, made in this area, it was assumed that the alluvium was 300 m to over 1500 m thick. The whole expanse of the plain is covered with invarying monotony of pleistocene and recent alluvial deposits (Wadia, 1953, p. 385). Its northern part is largely made up of older alluvium of *Bhangar* of pleistocene times, comprising coarse sand, gravels and surface *Kankar*. In contrast, its southern part is mostly composed of newer alluvium or *Khadar*, which includes depositions of sand, silt and clay in the flood-plains of rivers, during recent times.

The North Bihar plain lies in the active seismic zone of India. It is liable to severe earthquakes. For example, the earthquake on 15th January, 1934, had severely affected the whole of North Bihar when cracks had developed in the earth, out of which spread sand and water. A large quantity of sand was also thrown up the beds of rivers and wells which affected the surface configuration in some parts of the region. Some of the severest shocks felt in the towns of Motihari, Madhubani, Darbhanga and Purnea badly damaged them. In case of Motihari and Sitamarhi, the damage was so great that the administrative infrastructures of these towns were altogether shifted to new locations. It is presumed that movements associated with faults or cracks in the basement, underlying the alluvium, may be the cause of this or any other earthquake in future.

Drainage

The drainage system of North Bihar has played a dominant role in the evolution of urban settlements and their patterns since the historic times. The Ghaghra (Saryu), the Gandak (Narayani), the Burhi Gandak, the Kosi and the Mahananda, all draining into the Ganga, are the trunk streams of this region. These and their tributaries form the drainage system of the region (Fig. 1.2B). The rivers emerging in the High Himalayas are perennial in nature; they cause floods due to heavy rainfall in their catchments during the rainy season. All these streams are snow-fed, they are able to maintain their flow even in the lean months of summer season.

The Ghaghra River, which flows for about 100 km along the western boundary of North Bihar, is liable to overflow its channel and inundate large area adjoining its banks during the monsoons. The Gandak and the Kosi have large catchments in the Nepal Himalayas where they flow through narrow and deep gorges characterised by innumerable waterfalls and rapids. However, soon after entering the North Bihar plain, they begin to flow through tortuous meandering courses with broad and shallow valleys.

The Gandak, which is a snow-fed stream, is one of the largest feeders of the Ganga. It carries an enormous volume of water and detritus material. Its formerly disastrous floods have been now contained by the construction of an embankment, extending downstream from Bagaha to its confluence with the Ganga near Hajipur town.

The Burhi Gandak, like the Gandak, flows from north-west to south-east and joins the Ganga near Khagaria. It has a long meandering route over the plain and is liable to produce both floods and changes in stream course. Though it is not a snow-fed stream, it is able to maintain considerable flow in the dry season, largely due to the availability of seepage water in the sub-mountainous tract of the Sumeshwar range.

The Baghmati River, having source in Nepal Tarai, follows a course nearly parallel to that of the Burhi Gandak which it ultimately joins near Rosera town. It is fed by numerous hill streams and torrents, its water level rises rather quickly after downpours. Consequently, it inundates large areas in the plains. The towns of Sitamarhi and Darbhanga, located close to this stream, are frequently affected by its floods. In the dry season, however, the water level in the Baghmati goes as low as knee-deep at some places. The rate of siltation along the channel of this stream is quite high.

The Kosi is notorious because of its freak nature of changing its course quite frequently. Having its sources near the Mt. Everest in the Himalayas, it enters the region in Saharsa district and flows along the eastern boundary of Darbhanga district. It receives a large amount of water from its tributaries, namely, the Kamla, the Balan, the Tiljuga and the old channels of the Baghmati River. The river makes a bow-like bend near Kusheshwarasthan in Darbhanga district and then, following the old bed of its former tributary — the Ghughri — flows in easterly direction parallel to the Ganga which it ultimately joins at Kursela in the district of Katihar. With the construction of the Kosi Barrage at Bhimnagar and embankments to contain its vagaries, the river has developed more or less permanent and deep channel. But over a wide stretch of the plain, it still breaks into numerous capricious channels having shallow depths.

The river, including its seven tributaries, has a vast catchment area of about 61,400 sq. km in the Himalayas. It brings a large amount of boulder, sand and silt which are largely deposited along its channel. Consequently, the river bed lies a little above the general level of its flood plain. In the past, the river used to change its course quite frequently. Authentic records indicate that in 1736, the Kosi flowed about two km to the west of the present town of Purnea and joined the Ganga opposite Sahibganj. But during 1800-39, it flowed east of Dhamdaha and joined the Ganga near Kursela. Still latter, during 1873-92, it migrated further west and, since then, it has moved westwards at an average transitional rate of about one-and-half km per year and is now moving towards Darbhanga (Diwakar, 1959, p. 31). Though the vagaries of this stream have been stopped with the recent construction of protective embankments, it still carries on considerable erosion and shifting in the area lying between the two embankments. Nevertheless, mention has to be made of the fact that the growth of urban settlements in the districts of Saharsa and Purnea has been adversely affected, in the past, by the disastrous floods in the Kosi and its migratory nature.

The Mahananda flows in a meandering channel through the districts of Purnea and Katihar in the eastern part of North Bihar, and runs somewhat parallel to its eastern boundary. It also inundates large tracts during the rainy season. Numerous ox-bow lakes and swamps have developed along the former (abandoned) channels of this river.

Floods

An examination of the drainage system of North Bihar clearly reveals that large areas adjoining the major rivers are liable to inundations during the monsoon season (Fig. 1.2C). Rivers, like, the Gandak, the Burhi Gandak, the Baghmati, the Adhwara, the Kamla, the Balan, the Kosi and the Mahananda and their numerous tributaries drain this saucer-shaped plain, between the Himalayan foothill and the northern bank of the Ganga, in long tortuous and often uncertain courses. The drainage of excess rain water becomes almost impossible through these streams, particularly when the Ganga River is in floods. This creates a bottleneck and, consequently, large areas in this vast plain of North Bihar are submerged.

Periodic occurrence of floods in the region is due to the availability of an enormous quantum of run-off during the months of July-September. In times of high floods, rivers and their tributaries and distributaries disappear under an endless sheet of fast moving currents. In 1954, the deluge that descended upon North Bihar from the hills covered three-fourths of its countryside under one to two metres of water. Flowing across soft alluvial tracts, the streams have formed tortuous and meandering courses with a high degree of sinuosity. Stream oscillation is the most dangerous phenomenon in this region, results in the abandonment of old channels and cutting of new ones under the stress of heavy discharges. This process continues from monsoon to monsoon, the heavier the flood, the greater is the stream oscillation. Smaller depressions and 'Chaurs' abound in every river basin; their development has taken place as a consequence of stream oscillation. Even floods of normal magnitude in the region have been known to wash away embankments, roads, railways, bridges and culverts, to say nothing of crops, and the peasants' homesteads and livestock. Flood-water often enters into the towns of Siwan, Chapra, Sitamarhi, Bairgania, Muzaffarpur, Darbhanga, Samastipur, Khagaria and Katihar, causing great damages to urban property. This has adversely affected the morphology of these settlements.

Climate

North Bihar lies in a belt of transition between the comparatively most parts of Bengal in the east and the drier parts of Uttar Pradesh in the west. Hence, the heat in the summer is generally not as intense as in the drier west. The climate of the region can be analysed under the following three seasons into which the year has been divided.

The Cold Weather Season (November-February)

This season experiences a warm and sunny weather. There is a steady fall in temperature since the beginning of the cold weather season in early November. January is the coldest month of the year which has a mean monthly temperature varying between 15°C and 19°C. The wind generally blows from north-westerly direction. Cyclonic storms, caused by westerly disturbances, sometimes visit this region and account for the occasional winter rains of the area. Periodic cold waves also occur in the month of January. Morning dew drops and fog are particularly experienced in the months of December and January.

The Hot Weather Season (March-May)

This season is characterised by ever-increasing temperatures and aridity. Hot westerly winds begin to blow in March; they increase in intensity with the progress of the season. The temperature starts to rise in March and continues through April. May is the hottest month of the year when the mercury rises as high as 42°C. Hot winds, locally known as *loo*, particularly blow in the western part of this region. A notable feature in the months of April and May is the occurrence of afternoon storms which burst after the heat of the day and form the chief source of rain. This rain is often accompanied by hale. The intensity of these storms, associated with the 'Norwesters', decreases westwards in the region. This rainfall, usually termed as 'mango showers', is useful for mango and *lichhi* fruits. It also helps in the timely cultivation of '*bhadai*' crops. Occasional duststorms visit the western part of the region.

The Rainy Season (June-October)

The season of general rains begins with the burst of monsoon, generally in the second week of June. It brings immediate fall in temperature and causes widespread rain throughout the region. The rainfall of this period is largely derived from the Bay of Bengal branch of the S.W. Monsoon. Purnea (1,699 mm) records the heaviest rainfall in the region. The amount of annual precipitation decreases from east to west, e.g., Darbhanga (1,202 mm), Muzaffarpur (1,180 mm) and Saran (1,093 mm), and from north to south, e.g., Champaran (1,356 mm), Sitamarhi (1,266 mm) and Samastipur (1,166 mm).

Regional Distribution of Rainfall

The amount of annual rainfall in North Bihar generally varies from about 100 cm to 200 cm (Fig. 1.3). It is noted that the rainfall decreases from east to west and from north to south. Saran and the lower Gandak plain (comprising the districts of Samastipur and Vaishali) get less than 125 cm rainfall. Uncertainty regarding the timely onset of the monsoon and variations in the amount of rainfall received from year to year badly affects agriculture. Failure of the summer rain adversely affects the standing 'kharif' crops as also the sowing of 'rabi' crops.

Soils

The soils of North Bihar are mostly alluvial in nature; these have been brought and deposited by rivers originating in the Himalayas. A patch of colluvial soil is found in the foothill region of the Sumeshwar range

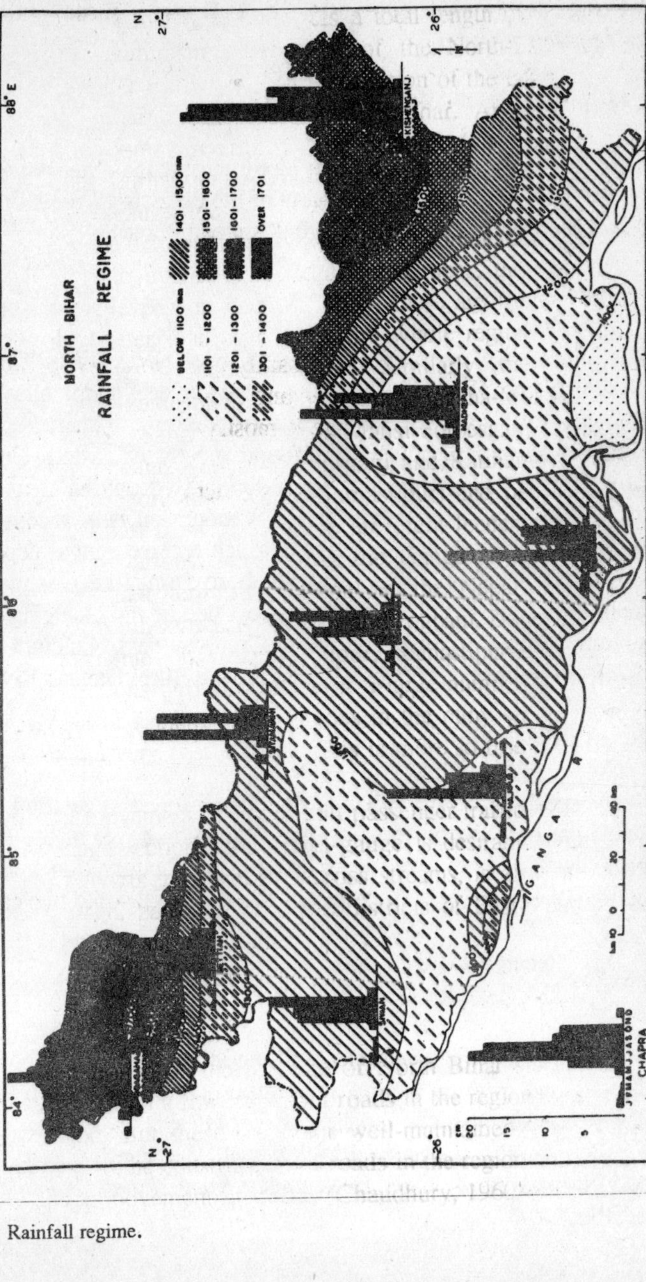

Fig. 1.3: Rainfall regime.

and Ramnagar Dun. The most typical soil of the plain is loam with varying proportions of sand, silt and clay. These soils can be categorised as under:

The Sub-Himalayan Soil

This soil is found in a E-W belt along the international boundary with Nepal, including the northern parts of the districts of West Champaran, East Champaran, Sitamarhi, Madhubani and Purnea.

The Alluvial Soil

The alluvial soil occurs predominantly over North Bihar. This may be classified into older or *Bhangar* and newer or *Khadar* alluvium. The *Bhangar* soil of pleistocene age is mostly loamy in character but often contains *Kankar* nodules; it is found mostly in eastern Champaran, Muzaffarpur, Darbhanga and Saran districts, occupying areas generally above the present flood levels. The *Khadar* soil is of recent age; it is found in the flood-plains of rivers which receive annual deposition of silt. Large areas in Saharsa and Southern Purnea have sandy loam or loamy sand soils. This is as a consequence of the changing nature of stream courses experienced in the remote past. Calcium rich soil occurs in patches, particularly along the old Burhi Gandak River.

Natural Vegetation

Truly speaking North Bihar is devoid of forest vegetation, except a small patch in the north-west. The vegetation cover of the region has been destroyed as a result of extension of cultivation and reckless cutting of forest trees. The forest of the region falls into two categories:

(i) moist deciduous, and
(ii) dry deciduous.

The moist deciduous forest is found in the Himalayan foothill zone. The *sal* and *shisham* are the most important tree species in this forest. The secondary growth consists of *Narkat* and reed. *Sabai* grass and bamboo are also widespread in this area. The northern parts of Purnea and Saharsa have large areas under *Kans*, *Pater*, *Sabai* grass and bamboo.

Patches of dry deciduous vegetation occur associated with waste and unreclaimed lands of the region. Vegetations of grass, reeds, scrub and bushes are commonly met in the riparian tracts.

Orchards and groves of mango, palm, bamboo, *Mahua*, *Shisham*, *Jamun* and other trees, including *Babul* and *Khair*, are quite common near village habitations.

ECONOMY

Cultural and economic considerations, besides the physical attributes of terrain, have important bearing on the location and growth of towns. Towns are generally dependent upon the agricultural surplus of the region which they dominate. Consequently, there is positive correlation between urbanisation and agricultural density (number of males engaged in agriculture per sq. km of cultivated area). Cities demand more agricultural products and, hence, require a dense population in rural areas (Davis and Golden, 1954, p. 120). Increasing pace of economic activity during the modern times, has led to urbanisation and the two together have tended to make agriculture more efficient. Development of modern means of transport and communication has not only accelerated the pace of economic activity, trade and commerce but it has also led to increased urbanisation. It is, therefore, pertinent to examine the various facets of the economy of North Bihar which might have affected the evolution of urban settlements in the area.

Agriculture

Land-use

Agriculture is, by far, the most dominant sector of the economy of North Bihar. It provides livelihood to about 92 per cent of the region's population. The entire region, except a small patch in the north-west, is a plain land, composed of fertile alluvial deposits, which has attracted people to take to agriculture. Broadly speaking, 66.8 per cent of the region is under crop cultivation. Land put to non-agricultural uses and current fallow account for 13.2 per cent and 7.5 per cent, respectively, (Table 1.1). The share of cultivable waste is only 0.9 per cent. Barren, uncultivable land, pastures and other grazing land account for 4.6 per cent, 2.8 per cent and 0.6 per cent, respectively. The area under forest is only 1.6 per cent. Practically the entire region, except the Siwalik foothills in the extreme north-western part of Champaran district and scattered patches in Purnea district, is devoid of forest worth its name. It is noted that even this small area under forests seems to be undergoing diminution with the ever-increasing extraction of commercial timber and fuelwood.

Table 1.1: Land Utilisation in North Bihar (1975-76)

Land category	*Area ('000 ha)*	*Area (%)*
1. Forest	83	1.6
2. Barren land	243	4.6
3. Land put tó non-agricultural uses	709	13.2
4. Permanent pastures and other grazing lands	21	0.6
5. Cultivable waste other than fallow lands	41	0.9
6. Land under miscellaneous trees and groves	148	2.8
7. Other fallow lands	112	2.0
8. Current fallow	401	7.5
9. Net area sown	3,574	66.8
Total area	5,432	100.0

Source: Data extracted from Bihar Statistical Handbook, 1978

The distribution of cultivated area in North Bihar is a reflection of the influence of relief, soils and water supply conditions (Ahmad, 1965, p. 17). Mention has to be made of the fact that the cultivated land, including fallows, has varied from year to year, depending upon the monsoonal conditions and the extent of flood ravages. Figure 1.4A reveals that the net area sown, in 1975-76, ranged from 55 per cent to 76 per cent in the various districts of North Bihar. The districts with relatively lesser percentages of land area under crops have been Vaishali (58 per cent), West Champaran (55.5 per cent), North Monghyr (54 per cent), Katihar (57.3 per cent) and Saharsa (59.5 per cent). This may be accounted due to the occurrence of hilly tract in Champaran, greater proportion of *diara* lands in Vaishali and North Monghyr, and greater flood ravages in Saharsa and Katihar. Floods not only cause damages to standing crops and habitations situated in the riverine belts but, sometimes, also lead to depositions of sand, thereby converting fertile farms into wastelands. This has happened particularly in parts of Ghanshyampur and Kuseshwarsthan blocks of

Darbhanga district and Bihpur and Gopalpur blocks of Naugachhia sub-divisions.

The net area sown is highest in the district of Gopalganj (76 per cent). This is mainly because of the fertile soils and better availability of irrigational facilities, provided by the Gandak canal and other sources. The percentage of net area under cultivation is also high in other districts of North Bihar.

Large areas of wasteland in the districts of Katihar, Purnea and Saharsa, formerly affected by the vagaries of the Kosi River, are now being reclaimed for agriculture. It is presumed that the net area sown in these districts is likely to increase considerably in the near future as a result of the reclamation process, introduction of mechanised cultivation and provision of irrigational facilities.

Crop Cultivation

The agricultural economy of the region is dependent upon the intensity of agricultural practices and type of crops cultivated, amount of rainfall received, absence of flood and availability of irrigation water. From the point of view of crops grown, there are three main categories of harvests, namely, the *Aghani*, the *Bhadai* and the *Rabi*. The *Aghani* crop is sown in June-July and harvested in the month of *Aghan* (December-January). Rice is the most important crop of the season. The *Bhadai* is the early autumn crop reaped in the month of *Bhadon* (August-September). It includes coarse rice, *marua*, maize, millets and other less important grains including pulses, like, *moong*. The *Rabi* includes the cold weather crops, like, wheat, barley, gram and pulses, like, *arhar*, *urad*, etc. Acreage-wise, the *Aghani*, *Rabi* and *Bhadai* crops account for 43 per cent, 31 per cent and 26 per cent of the net cropped area, respectively. Thus there is predominance of the *Aghani* crops in the region.

The agricultural operations, like, digging, ploughing, pulverising, manuring, irrigation, protection of crops from pests, cattle and floods, besides harvesting, threshing and storage, vary from crop to crop. Most of these operations are performed manually with the help of draught cattle and outdated implements. Mechanised cultivation is practised only by rich land-holders with large holdings, particularly in Purnea, Champaran and the Tarai region.

Cropping Pattern

The crops of the region are grouped into two categories: (a) food crops and (b) non-food crops. The principal food crops are paddy, wheat, maize and barley. Other cereals include pulses such as *khesari, arhar, moong, masoor, kelai, urad*, gram and peas. Among the non-food crops, the most important are sugarcane, jute, tobacco, chillies and oilseeds (mustard, linseed, *til* and rapeseed). Cultivation of potato, on a commercial scale, is a recent development.

North Bihar primarily has a food crop economy with more than 86 per cent of its cropped area devoted to the cultivation of cereal crops. Cash crops, like, jute, sugarcane, tobacco and spices — chillies and turmeric — account for another 7 per cent.

Rice is the most dominant crop of the region. It covers 49 per cent of the net cropped area. This rice crop, which is sown with the onset of the rainy season and harvested during the winter months of November-December, is known as *Aghani* rice. The acreage of paddy varies from district to district. The most important producers of *Aghani* paddy are Madhubani (78%), Sitamarhi (63%), Darbhanga (63%), Purnea (63%), West Champaran (55%), East Champaran (54%), Muzaffarpur (54%) and Katihar (53%). Poor acreages of paddy in the district of Begusarai (7%) and the sub-divisions of Khagaria (11%) and Naugachhia (12%) are largely due to poor soil conditions and flood ravages. Paddy cultivation is substantial, but below the regional average in the districts of Saran (31.7%), Siwan (34%), Gopalganj (35%), Samastipur (27%) and Saharsa (48%). Large areas in these districts are devoted to other crops, particularly maize for which conditions are more suitable.

Wheat is next to rice in importance. It accounts for 23 per cent of the net cropped area of the region (Fig. 1.4C). The crop is largely cultivated in the districts of Begusarai (41%), Saran (36%), Siwan (36%), Gopalganj (35%) and Samastipur (22%). A substantial increase in the acreage under wheat has taken place in the last 30 years or so because of special efforts, including provision of irrigation facilities, improved varieties of seeds, manures, fertilisers and other energy inputs. Also, loss of paddy crop due to floods in the rainy season has fostered the cultivation of the more dependable wheat in such areas.

Maize, accounting for 11.2 per cent of the region's net cropped area, is the third important crop of the region. It was formerly sown a little after the cultivation of the *Rabi* crops. But with the introduction of high-yielding varieties and availability of irrigation facilities and other inputs, maize is grown almost throughout the year. The district of Begusarai and the sub-division of Khagaria are the most important maize producing areas, where it accounts for 41 per cent and 39 per cent of the total net cropped area, respectively. Other districts are Saran (18%), Gopalganj (16%), Vaishali (21%), Samastipur and Saharsa (14%). Presence of well drained sandy loam soil has particularly favoured its cultivation in the *diara* tracts and natural levels of streams in the districts of Saran, Vaishali, Samastipur and Begusarai. The yield is generally high in areas which receive fresh deposits of silts.

Barley, which accounts for only 2.3 per cent of the net cropped area of the region, is mainly grown in the districts of East Champaran and Saran. It is mostly cultivated on unirrigated land.

Khesari is widely grown as a cash crop on rice lands in the districts of Sitamarhi, Darbhanga, Samastipur and Saharsa where it accounts for 11 per cent, 8 per cent, 6 per cent, and 5 per cent of the net cropped acreages, respectively. It is sown as a *Rabi* crop on rice lands while the paddy is still standing. Among other pulses, arhar occupies portions of Siwan and Saran districts. It is sown in the 'Kharif' season, generally along with maize. Potato, which accounts for 1.4 per cent of the net cropped area of the region, is widely cultivated. However, unsuitable soil and moisture conditions do not favour its cultivation in the districts of Begusarai and Saharsa.

Sugarcane is the most important non-food crop, accounting for 2.5 per cent of the region's net cropped area. It is grown as a cash crop in the western districts (Fig. 1.4E). The districts of West Champaran (9%), Gopalganj (7%), Siwan (4%) and East Champaran (1%) are the largest growers of sugarcane. It is also grown in the districts of Samastipur and Madhubani where it covers 2 per cent and 1 per cent of the net cropped acreages, respectively. Recently, the farmers of Purnea and Saharsa districts have taken up the cultivation of sugarcanc on a large scale with the establishment of a sugar factory at Banmankhi Bazar. The overall increase in the acreage under sugarcane, during recent years, is largely because of the ready money it brings to the cultivator and the ever-increasing demand of sugar and its by-products in India and abroad.

Jute is another important cash crop accounting for 7.4 per cent of the net cropped acreage of the region. This fibre crop is particularly grown in the eastern districts of Purnea, Katihar and Saharsa where it accounts for 12 per cent, 9 per cent and 2 per cent of the net cropped acreage, respectively. Some jute is also grown in the districts of Samastipur and East Champaran. Low-lands and swampy areas in the *Khadar* belt, along riverine tracts, with sufficient amount of precipitation have favoured the cultivation of jute in these districts. Jute factories have, therefore, come up at Katihar and Muktapur (Samastipur).

Tobacco and chillies are two important commercial crops which are mainly grown in the districts of Samastipur, Vaishali and Begusarai. They together account for 0.5 per cent of the net cropped acreage of the region.

Crop Intensity and Crop Association

Figure (1.4B and E) shows the general intensity of crops cultivated in the region. Three crops, namely, rice, wheat and maize, are important in almost all the districts. But rice is the chief crop of the region. It is generally cultivated in association with wheat, maize, jute and *Khesari*. Its importance, somewhat, decreases in the districts of Saran, Begusarai and North Monghyr where it ranks second or third. In Saran, it is replaced by wheat which ranks first. Similarly, in Begusarai and North Monghyr the first and second positions are occupied by maize and wheat, respectively; rice comes a poor third in these districts. It is noted that the intensity of maize cultivation increases towards the south and that of rice towards the north. The two cash crops, sugar cane and jute, have regional associations in the western and eastern parts, respectively.

The following crop association regions have been identified on the basis of the intensity of cultivation of the above-mentioned crop (Fig. 1.4F).

Rice-Wheat-Maize Regions (RWM): This region includes six districts, namely, East Champaran, Siwan, Muzaffarpur, Vaishali, Gopalganj and Saharsa. In Gopalganj and Siwan, the fourth ranking crop is sugarcane whereas in East Champaran, Vaishali and Muzaffarpur, it is barley. Interestingly, a large area is devoted to *Khesari* in Saharsa which is often affected by flood ravages. Consequently, the soil and moisture conditions favour the cultivation of this crop in the winter season.

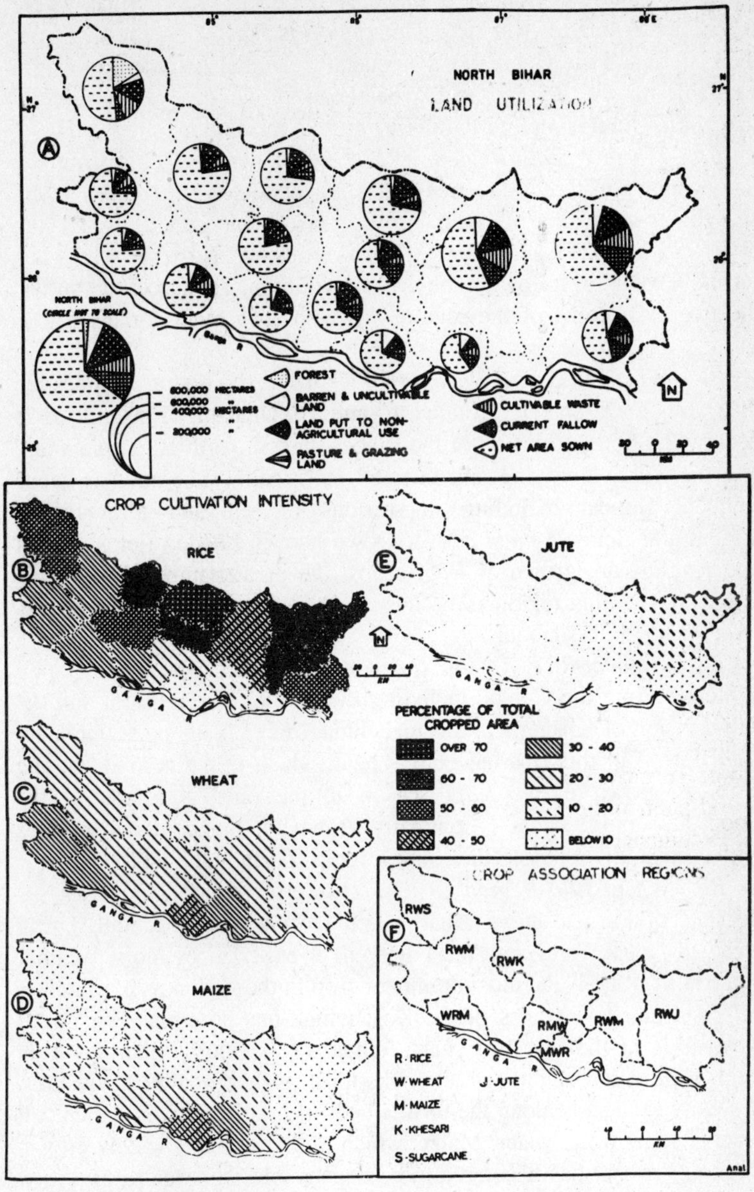

Fig. 1.4: (A) Land utilisation, (B) Crop cultivation, intensity (Rice), (C) Wheat, (D) Maize, (E) Jute, (F) Crop association regions.

Wheat-Rice-Maize Region (WRM): The district of Saran forms the wheat-rice-maize region. It is the only region in North Bihar where wheat predominates over rice. This region is flanked by the Ghaghra, the Ganga and the Gandak. Consequently, there is sufficient moisture available in the soil so that wheat can thrive here even without irrigation. Gram is the fourth ranking crop in this region.

Rice-Maize-Wheat Region (RMW): Likewise, the district of Samastipur constitutes the rice-maize-wheat region. The *diara* tracts and the flood plains of rivers provide favourable conditions for the cultivation of maize and rice as 'Kharif' crops, respectively. Wheat is a recent newcomer, following the green revolution. Tobacco and chillies, the two cash crops of the region, vie with each other for the fourth rank.

Rice-Wheat-'Khesari' Region (RWK): This crop region includes the districts of Darbhanga, Sitamarhi and Madhubani. These districts occupy the bottom portion of the saucer-shaped North Bihar plain and are, therefore, low-lying and infested by streams. The streams cause frequent floods, including depositions of silt and alluvium in agricultural fields. *Aghani* rice in grown here in flooded fields. Wheat and *Khesari* are grown as *Rabi* crops; the greater importance of the latter crop in this region is because it is sown broadcast and, hence, requires much less labour.

Maize-Wheat-Rice Region (MWR): The maize-wheat-rice region stretches along the Ganga, including the district of Begusarai and the sub-division of Khagaria and Naugachhia. Maize is the most dominant *Kharif* crop in this riparian belt. Wheat, which is the second ranking crop, is grown in the *Rabi* season in the out-lying parts of the flood-plain only. Arhar is generally grown on higher *diara* grounds with comparatively desiccated soil; it ranks fourth in the region.

Rice-Wheat-Jute Region (RWJ): This crop region comprises the districts of Purnea and Katihar which receive heavy rainfall. Lying close to Nepal Tarai and West Bengal, it experiences moist weather conditions. Rice is the most dominant crop in the region as it no longer suffers from the ravages of the Kosi which has progressively moved westwards in the last 100 years. Wheat is the most important *Rabi* crop. Cultivation of jute, which ranks third, is favoured on sandy loam to loamy sand soils along the former beds of the Kosi River, which still receive some flood-water. Maize, which ranks fourth, is widely grown. Recently, wheat has become a more dependable crop due to provision of irrigation facilities from the Eastern Kosi canals.

It is noted that, in spite of the region being frequently afflicted by floods, intensive cultivation is in vogue throughout the region. Certain parts of Purnea and Saharsa districts are considered more favourable for the cultivation of sugarcane. But its cultivation has been undertaken on a modest scale only because of the labour intensive nature of its cultivation and lack of sugar factories in the area. Nevertheless, its economy derives substantial strength by the cultivation of commercial crops. The development of agriculture in an area cannot be uniform because the socio-economic factors influencing the development are not spread uniformly throughout (Joshi and Dube, 1979, p. 585).

Therefore, application of scientific methods of cultivation, including selective land-use, and provision of irrigation facilities, better seeds, manures and other energy inputs, besides an improved transport system, is sure to increase the productivity of the crops cultivated. New innovations in agriculture are necessary not only for increasing productivity but also for finding food for the increasing numbers and for bettering the lot of people of the region who are almost wholely dependent upon agriculture. The aim of agricultural planning in the region should be towards achieving self-sufficiency in food-crops and gaining sufficient ground in the cultivation of cash crops. This can be achieved through community development programmes undertaken at micro-level.

Horticulture

Horticulture occupies an important place in the economy of North Bihar. Mango, *lichhies*, guava and banana are the principal commercial fruits grown in the region; they occupy large areas in the districts of Vaishali, Muzaffarpur, Darbhanga and Samastipur. These fruits have widespread market both in the State and outside (Chaudhury, 1964, p. 159). Among the aquatic vegetable products, water-chestnut (*singhara*) and *makhana* are widely cultivated in the districts of Darbhanga, Katihar, Saharsa and Madhubani. These districts have numerous ponds, water pools, tanks and other reservoirs of a temporary nature which provide sufficient space for these aquatic crops to grow.

Industries

Power and minerals are the essential pre-requisites for the development of industries. North Bihar, being an alluvial plain, lacks these facilities. There is a total lack of heavy industries in the area. Recently, a few industries have been established, but it still has a predominantly agricultural economy. In 1975, there were 8,042 registered factories, employing 49,149 workers. In addition there were 1,468 small-scale industrial units which engaged 10,898 persons. Under the later category, 293 small units were registered as factories. According to the census of 1971, only 3.1 per cent of the gainful workers were engaged in manufacturing, household or otherwise, as against 66 per cent in agriculture. Thus, it is obvious that the economy of the region does not have a sufficiently wide industrial base. Moreover, the greater bulk of the industrial employment is confined to the household sector which accounts for 56 per cent of the workers engaged in industries.

Though the region does not have mineral resources to feed big industries, it has still developed a few small and medium sized industries. These industries are mostly agro-based, namely, sugar, jute, paper and rice processing (Fig. 1.5A). The important industries of the region are briefly described as under:

Sugar Factory

There are, at present, about 28 sugar factories working in the region employing an average of 12,266 workers. These are mostly situated near the rail tracks in the cane-growing areas of Gopalganj, Siwan, West Champaran and Madhubani districts. Sugar factories are also located at Hasanpur (Samastipur) and Banmankhi Bazar (Purnea). There are great prospects for the development of sugar industries in these areas as the alluvial soil and climatic conditions are most conducive to the cultivation of sugarcane.

Jute Industry

Jute manufacturing, like sugar, is confined to the jute growing areas. There are at present three jute mills; two of these are located at Katihar and the third one at Muktapur (Samastipur). These mills are employing persons ranging from 1,400 to 3,300 per day. These factories manufacture jute ropes, jute twines, gunny bags and hessian. Most of these products are exported. The packaging needs of the sugar factories of the region are met from these jute mills. In addition, jute bailing press, its subsidiary industry, is numerous in the region. These are

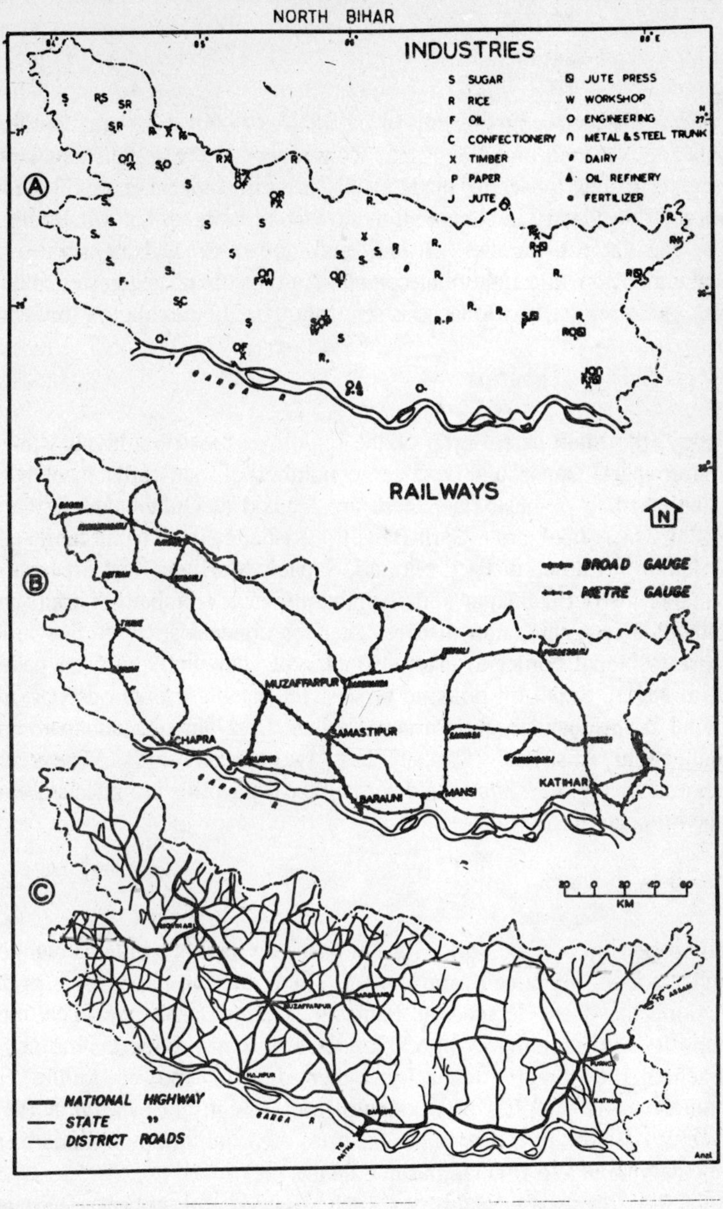

Fig. 1.5: (A) Industries, (B) Railways, (C) Roads.

mostly located at Forbesganj, Purnea, Garh Banaili, Kasba and Kishenganj.

Tobacco Industry

Tobacco is grown intensively in the districts of Samastipur, Katihar, Saharsa, Vaishali and Begusarai. Consequently, the region is a large supplier of raw tobacco. This is mostly used for *bidi* making which is a household industry in almost all the towns. It is noted that Muzaffarpur has the largest number of *bidi* making units. Dalsinghsarai and Mahanar Bazar are important centres. As there is no cigarette making unit in the region, raw tobacco is sent for cigarette making to Monghyr.

Rice, Flour and Oil Mills

Paddy, the main cereal crop of the region, is mostly cultivated in its eastern part. Consequently, a large number of rice mills have been established to de-husk rice; these are located at Gulabbagh, Jogbani, Forbesganj, Jalalgarh, Garh-Banaili, Kishenganj, Thakurganj, and Galgalia in Purnea district; Nirmali, Sapaul, Murliganj and Saharsa in Saharsa district; Jainagar and Jhangharpur in Madhubani district, and Chanpaia in Champaran district. There is concentration of rice mills close to Nepal border to take advantage of easy availability of paddy from Nepal. Small oil mills, to process the locally grown oilseeds, are found at various places in Purnea, Katihar, Darbhanga, Madhubani and Samastipur districts. Katihar has two flour mills. They are manufacturing *atta*, *maida* and *suji*. Other flour mills are attached with rice mills at various places.

Paper Industry

The paper industry in North Bihar is based on locally available bamboo and woodpulp obtained from Assam. There are two paper mills in the region; these are located at Samastipur and Darbhanga. The total capacity of these mills is 16,500 tonnes. But their production has never reached the targeted capacity either due to 'power failure' or non-arrival of supplies of woodpulp from Assam (*The Indian Nation*, Oct. 17, 1980). Two new paper factories are coming up at Kumarbagh in Champaran and Baijnathpur in Saharsa.

Other forest-based industries, such as, wood and timber, are located at Jogbani, Madhubani, Raxaul, Katihar and Hajipur. Sawn timber is marketed on a large scale at these places.

Engineering Industry

The engineering industry has largely developed at Muzaffarpur, Katihar and Barauni. The Arther Butler & Co. of Muzaffarpur manufacture bolts, nuts, and other metal parts needed in sugar factories. Manufacture of cycle parts takes place at Katihar. Aluminium kitchen wares, agricultural implements, buckets, trunks, wire nails and G.I. pipes are made at Chapra, Siwan, Hajipur, Purnea, Darbhanga, Barauni, Begusarai, Samastipur, Motihari, Forbesganj and Katihar.

The Khadi and Village Industries

The Khadi and handloom are small-scale household industries which are widely distributed in the entire region. Muzaffarpur, Madhubani, Darbhanga, Biraul and Siwan are large collecting and distributing centres of the Khadi industry. Besides, manufacture of soap, fibre, hand-made paper, leather, pottery, non-edible oil, *Gur* and *Khandsari* takes place, on a small-scale, both in villages and towns. These products have good market not only in the State but also throughout India.

Other Industries

Establishment of the Indian Oil Refinery with a capacity of 3 million tonnes, at Barauni, in 1963 has fostered the development of a few important industries in its neighbourhood. This includes a giant-sized thermal power plant and a fertiliser factory, besides other ancillary industries with petroleum as the feed stock. Among other industries being established in Barauni-Begusarai-Samastipur belt are a drum and wagon factory, and a factory for the manufacture of barrels to meet the requirements of the refinery. Besides, a host of other petro-chemical industries can be set up in this belt, utilising the refinery gases and its by-products.

Food-based industries, like, flour, bread, biscuit and bakery, are found in almost all the urban centres. A large confectionary unit is located at Marhowrah (Saran) whose products have market in the whole country.

Prospects for Industrial Growth

Both poverty and unemployment are most rampant in North Bihar. Their impact on the pattern of urbanisation in the region is most evident. Recently, there has been some significant advancements in agriculture, but the developments in industry are not equally matched. Recent construction of the rail-cum-road bridge over the Ganga, proposed conversion ot the metre-gauge railway line into broad-gauge, establishment of a super thermal power station at Muzaffarpur and location of a paper factory at Kumarbagh in Champaran are expected to give a boost to industrial growth in the region. A medium or small scale agro-based industry, besides the petro-chemicals, can be set up in Samastipur-Barauni-Begusarai industrial belt. Similarly, small-scale agro-based industrial units can profitably function at Darbhanga, Muzaffarpur, Purnea, Ramnagar, Kishenganj, Marhowrah, Hajipur and Murliganj.

The *Khadi* and Cottage industries, with villages as base units, have great employment generating possibilities. These have to be fostered in all earnestness. Construction of the road-bridge across the Ganga at Patna is expected to clear the transport hurdle between North and South Bihar. This will also help the development of agro-based industries at Hajipur in Vaishali district. Easy availability of bagasse *Kans*, *Pater* and other grasses, besides hard-woods obtainable from the forests in Nepal and Champaran, favour the establishment of paper mills in the region. Likewise, sugar and jute factories can be set up in the eastern districts of Purnea and Katihar.

Transport

The economic prosperity of a region is inescapably related to the 'structure and pattern of the existing transportation arteries which establish economic links with other areas' (Singh, 1969, p. 43). The rail and the road network constitute the main arteries of transport in North Bihar. Existence of a large number of streams with capacity to inundate large areas during floods have greatly affected the layout of the transport network.

Railways

The railway network in North Bihar has a total length of 2,400 km, falling under the administrative control of the North-Eastern and North-Eastern Frontier Railways. The jurisdiction of the latter railway lies only in the district of Purnea and Katihar. At present, the broad-gauge line joins Semaria with Sonpur (via Samastipur-Muzaffarpur) and Katihar with Kumedpur only. All other areas are served by the metre-gauge lines.

The rail network exhibits both N-S and W-E orientation (Fig. 1.5 B). In their effort to avoid the flood-affected areas, they generally follow the natural levees of streams. Thus, there are trunk, branch, loop, chord and feeder lines traversing the whole region. The only important trunk line is Mairwa-Katihar. Similarly, the important branch lines are Samastipur-Narkatiaganj, Bagaha-Muzaffarupur, Nirmali-Darbhanga, Saharsa-Katihar, Mansi-Forbesganj, Sonpur-Barauni, Purnea-Jogbani, Katihar-Thakurganj and Katihar-Kumedpur. There is only one chord line (Mansi-Samastipur) and one loop line (Siwan-Chapra). Apart from these, there are eight feeder lines which either terminate at various *ghats* along the Ganga or at the Nepal border. The important terminal stations on the Nepal border are Bhikhna Thori, Raxaul, Jainagar, Nirmali and Jogbani. Double haulage facilities are available on Chapra-Sonpur, Samastipur-Barauni and Mansi-Katihar sections only. Existence of a large number of drainage channels, capable of causing flood havocs in the rainy season, makes the railway track a very costly affair. This is more so true of the Kosi region.

For efficient movement of goods and passenger traffic, conversion of the metre-gauge sections into broad-gauge is desirable. Similarly, conversion of culverts into bridges, across streams, is also called for dependable haulage, particularly in the districts of East Champaran, Sitamarhi, Darbhanga and Saharsa.

Roads

Roads have functioned as the life line of North Bihar since historic times. There have been a few important roads in the region even in the pre-British period. But these were not well-maintained. The British gave top priority to the construction of roads in the region with a view to facilitate quick movement of troops (Chaudhury, 1960, p. 250), and officials on administrative assignments. As trade grew, goods traffic also developed on these routes. The development of roads, however, has taken place at a tremendous pace since independence, under successive Five-Year Development Plans.

The total road length in North Bihar is about 40,372 km (1976). Of this, about 7,722 km is metalled and 32,650 km unmetalled. National and State Highways and P.W.D. roads are all metalled but large sections of D.B., Block Highways, project and village roads are unmetalled. The National Highways — N.H. 31 — runs W-E from Barauni to Thakurganj (Purnea). N.H. 28, originates at Barauni, runs up to Gorakhpur via Muzaffarpur, Motihari-Gopalganj. A branch from this highway — N.H. 28A, goes north up to Bhikhna Thori on India-Nepal border, linking it with Kathmandu. These highways form the backbone of the road system in North Bihar. Besides, there are trunk roads, also known as State highways and lateral roads, which provide links with the various district headquarters.

The road network is comparatively denser in the western and central parts of North Bihar (Fig. 1.5C). Lesser density of roads in the districts of Saharsa, Katihar, Purnea and the eastern part of Darbhanga is due to the existence of a large number of stream channels with flood potentials. The village roads are invariably unmetalled. During the monsoons, the village and District Board roads are generally submerged under the flood water. Consequently, large stretches of these roads are washed away.

Water Transport

River transportation was quite common in North Bihar before the coming of the railways. In those days, a large number of towns had grown up at ferry points on rivers which were used for handling merchandise. However, subsequent development of the road and rail transports led to a decline in river transportation. Neglect of river transport, particularly after A.D. 1900, resulted in the decline of settlements, established earlier, at ferry points on river banks.

As the cost of rail and road haulages has increased recently, there is a lot of scope for developing this cheap medium of transport. The Gandak and the Kosi are navigable throughout the year. They provide scope for the movement of grains, timber, jute and other commodities from one place to the other. The Burhi Gandak, Baghmati and Balan are navigable during the rainy season only. The Ganga and the

Ghaghra are quite important from navigational point of view. There is regular movement of men and merchandise on steamers across the Ganga at Pahlezaghat, Mahnar, Semaria, Mahadeopur Ghat and Manihari. Erosion of river banks and oscillation of stream course during floods greatly affect river transport.

Lack of proper maintenance of water-ways has stood in the way of the development of river transport during recent times. Nevertheless, movement of bulk cargo, like, jute from Kosi region and timber from Champaran, can be profitably undertaken through rivers.

REFERENCES

Ahmad, E. (1965): *Bihar A Physical, Economic and Regional Geography*, Ranchi University, Ranchi.

Chaudhury, P.C.R. (1960): *District Gazetteers, Saran*, Secretariat Press, Bihar, Patna.

Chaudhury, P.C.R. (1960): *District Gazetteers, Champaran*, Secretariat Press, Bihar, Patna.

Chaudhury, P.C.R. (1964): *District Gazetteers, Darbhanga*, Secretariat Press, Bihar, Patna.

Davis, K. and H.H. Golden, (1954): "Urbanisation and the Development of Pre-industrial Area", In P.K. Hatt and J.R.J. Albert, Ed. (1963), *Cities and Society*, New York, pp. 120-39.

Diwakar, R.R. Ed. (1959): *Bihar Through the Ages*, Orient Longmans, Bombay.

Joshi, Y.G. and J. Dube, (1979): "Measurement of Regional Disparities in the Level of Agricultural Development", *The Deccan Geographer*, XVII, pp. 609-15.

Singh, D.N. (1969): "The North Bihar: A Study in Transport Geography", B.H.U., Varanasi.

Singh, S.C. (1973): *Changes in the Courses of Rivers and their Effects on Urban Settlement in the Middle Ganga Plain*, N.G.S.I., Varanasi.

The Economic Times, April 12, 1965, Bombay.

The Indian Nation, August 15, 1979, Patna.

The Indian Nation, October 17, 1980, Patna.

Wadia, D.N. (1953): *Geology of India*, London.

2

POPULATION

GROWTH AND DISTRIBUTION OF POPULATION

ECONOMIC ACTIVITIES have meaning only in the context of the human factor. The nature and scale of economic activity, in a region, is generally influenced by the size and character of its population. North Bihar, being a predominantly agricultural region, has 94.87 per cent of its population residing in rural habitations. Most of its present-day towns have developed from villages. Hence, an analysis of the growth and distribution of its population, during historic and recent times, is likely to reveal the processes and patterns of urbanisation in the region.

Growth of Population

The growth of population in North Bihar is related to its terrain conditions, including variations in physiographic, climatic and soil conditions, migration since the early historic times. There are few authentic records regarding ancient settlements in North Bihar, except some accounts left by early travellers. This vast alluvial tract, according to folklore, was first Aryanised by 'Mathav Videha', who is said to have dried up the marshes, cleared the jungles and established a kingdom known as 'Videha' (Pandey, 1963, p. 10). Archaeological excavations as well as Puranic and Epic renditions give us the names of numerous kings of 'Videha' who ruled the region since long. It seems that the first Aryan settlers, in this area, were most attracted by the existence of vast stretches of a featureless plain, composed of newer alluvium. Later, this region of highly fertile soils and bountiful climatic conditions came into prominence as the kingdom of 'Vaishali'.

It is evident through the accounts of travellers, like, Fai-Hien, that this alluvial tract was quite prosperous. In the medieval times, successive phases of war and peace led to a virtual stagnation in its population. But some important migration took place in this period, particularly from the west. For example, the Rajputs of Malwa, harassed by frequent Muslim incursions, migrated to this region where a scramble for land and agrarian settlements followed. This ultimately led to the establishment of these Rajputs as the landed aristocracy in the districts of Saran, Darbhanga and Saharsa (Ahmad, 1965, p. 210). In the reign of emperor Akbar, this region was divided, on the basis of population, into *'Sarkar'*, *'Mahal'* and *'Parganas'* for revenue collection. The growth of population in the early years of British colonisation was quite modest. Several attempts were made, during 1826-71 to have an enumeration of the population of the region. But these attempts proved to be futile. Ultimately, the first official census of 1872 revealed a population of 11.5 million for North Bihar which gave it a density of 333 persons per sq. km. Thus, it is noted that the region had a moderately dense population even in the latter half of the 19th century.

Table 2.1 shows the growth of population in North Bihar from the first census in 1872 to the last census in 1971 (Fig. 2.2B). It reveals that there has been a steady growth in population during 1872-1891 when the average growth rate happened to be 1.38 per cent per year. But, the population during 1891-1901, actually declined by about 0.19 per cent per annum.

Table 2.1: Growth of Population in North Bihar (1872-1971)

Year	*Population*	*Year*	*Population*
1872	1,15,47,768	1931	1,53,21,497
1881	1,31,51,451	1941	1,66,28,996
1891	1,39,64,835	1951	1,81,22,170
1901	1,36,86,998	1961	2,18,63,388
1911	1,40,12,092	1971	2,63,04,409
1921	1,39,74,957		

Source: Census of India, Bihar, 1931, 1951, 1961 and 1971.

The decline in population in this period was due to higher mortality owing to the outbreak of plague, cholera and other epidemics. A famine also took place in 1897 which adversely affected the population of the region. It is pertinent to mention here that the Censuses of 1872, 1881 and 1891 have suffered from under-enumeration, in the region, by not less than 10 per cent (Census Report, 1961, p. 99). The census of 1901, in fact, makes the beginning of more reliable population enumeration. Hence, it may be treated as the base for measuring the subsequent growth of population.

Table 2.2 gives the comparative growth rates of population for North Bihar, the State of Bihar and India as a whole for seven decades from 1901 to 1971. It reveals that the growth has been low during 1901-21, moderate during 1931-51, but remarkably high during 1951-71.

Table 2.2: Comparative growth rates of population (1901-1971)

Decade	*North Bihar*	*Bihar*	*India*
1901-11	+2.37	+3.67	+5.75
1911-21	–0.26	–0.66	–0.31
1921-31	+9.63	+11.45	+11.00
1931-41	+8.53	+12.20	+14.22
1941-51	+8.98	+10.27	+13.31
1951-61	+22.60	+19.77	+21.51
1961-71	+20.31	+21.33	+24.57

Source: Census of India, 1971.

Period of Slow Growth or Actual Decline (1901-1921)

The first decade of the century shows a low growth rate of only 0.23 per cent per year for North Bihar as compared to 0.36 and 0.57 per cent per year for the State of Bihar and India, respectively. A decline in population actually took place in the country as a whole, during 1911-21, when North Bihar recorded a negative growth of 0.02 per cent per year. This has been attributed to excess of mortality over births, resulting from poor economic conditions and bad state of public health. The region was also affected by floods which caused considerable damage to crops. Outbreak of epidemics caused heavy loss of life, particularly in the districts of Muzaffarpur, Saharsa and North Monghyr, where the fall in population was of the order of 4 per cent to 7 per cent in the decade. The district of Darbhanga, which was only marginally affected by epidemics, experienced a fall in population by only 0.6 per cent. On the contrary, increase in population took place in the districts of Saran, Champaran and Purnea, which remained unaffected by those ravages.

Period of Moderate Growth (1921-51)

There has been a moderately rapid growth of population during 1921-51; the growth rate in this period has varied from 0.85 per cent to 0.96 per cent per year. This increase in growth rate was due to some improvement in public health conditions since 1921. But the earthquake of 1934 caused considerable damage in the region, with the result that some very fertile lands were covered with sand. Thus, the average growth rate of population in North Bihar, during 1931-41, was only 0.85 per cent per annum as compared to 1.2 per cent per annum for Bihar and 1.42 per cent per annum for India. It is noted that this steady growth of population (0.89 per cent per annum) continued even during 1941-51, in spite of several natural calamities like severe floods in 1943 and 1944 and drought and famine in 1940. The increase in population of Purnea district, particularly, took place after 1948 when Bengali refugees from East Pakistan (now Bangladesh) started pouring in. It is noted that in spite of influx of refugees from Pakistan, the economy of the region gained in strength in the post-independence period.

Period of Rapid Growth (1951-71)

The period 1951-71 was of rapid growth when the increase in population varied from 2.03 per cent to 2.26 per cent per annum. It appears that availability of better health care led to a steep decline in mortality rates, resulting in greater life expectation. Besides, implementation of successive Five-Year National Plans and construction of the Kosi barrage and embankments led to greater agricultural prosperity which, in turn, fostered higher growth rates.

Growth of Population by Districts

Figure 2.1 shows decade-wise variation in population for various districts in North Bihar during the century. The growth of population, in the first quarter of the century, has been rather slow. It is noted that during 1911-21 the districts of Muzaffarpur, Darbhanga, Saharsa and North Monghyr, recorded population losses, whereas those of Purnea,

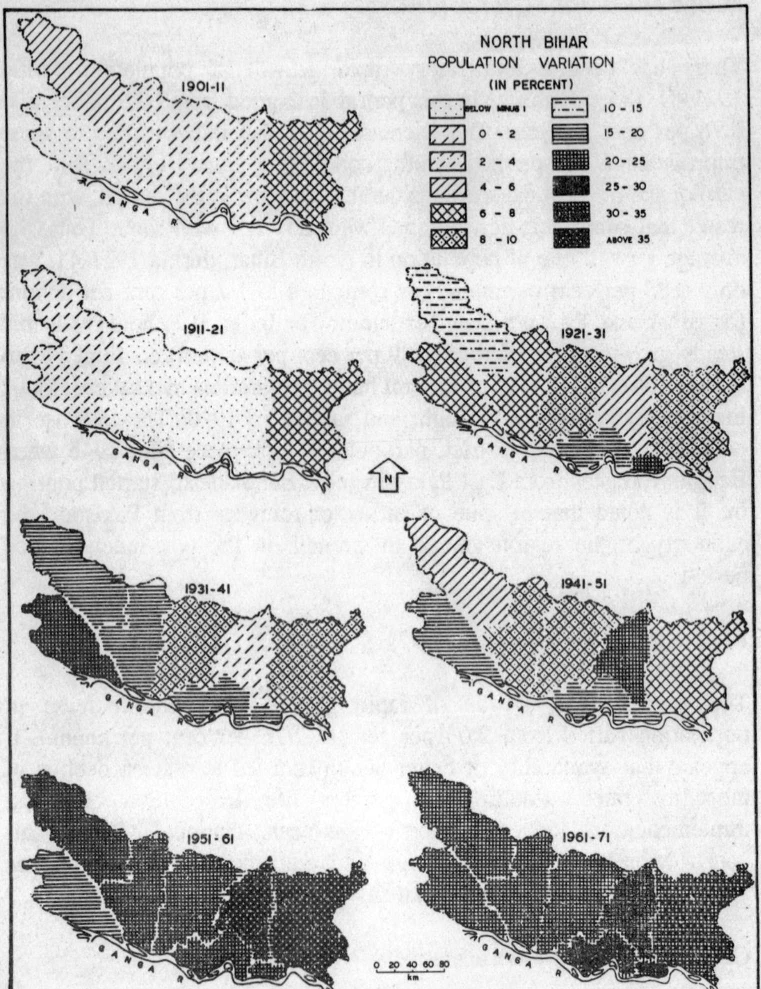

Fig. 2.1: Population variation; 1901-11, 1911-21, 1921-31, 1931-41, 1941-51, 1951-61, 1961-71.

Champaran and Saran recorded slight increases in population. This was because of the fact that the former districts were more severely affected by natural calamities, like, plague, cholera and floods, than the latter districts.

There has been a remarkable rise in the population of almost all the districts since 1921, except Saharsa which, in the past, has suffered from the vagaries of the Kosi River. Frequent occurrence of floods and droughts and a sense of insecurity, generated due to the Second World War, resulted in a temporary slowing down in the rate of population growth during 1941-51. But after 1951, a sharp increase in the growth rate has been noted in almost all the districts.

Analysing the growth of population for the entire period of 1901-71, it is noted that the districts with higher densities of population have recorded slower growth rates than the regional average and *vice versa* (Fig. 2.2A). For example, the absolute growth in population, in this period, has been comparatively lower in the districts of Darbhanga (79.7%), Saran (77.5%) and Muzaffarpur (75.6%) because they, together, constitute one of the densest tracts in Bihar. It appears that the population of these districts has almost reached saturation level as the land is unable to sustain any greater numbers with the present level of technology. In contrast, the rate of population growth has been more than the regional average in the districts of Saharsa (99.5%), North Monghyr (98.3%) and Champaran (97.8%). This increase has taken place largely due to natural growth as a result of general improvement in public health conditions and the lowering of death rate.

The most spectacular increase in population, however, has taken place in Purnea district (150.7%) where the population has more than doubled itself during this period. It has experienced a remarkably uninterrupted growth during the last seven decades although initially it had low pressure of population.

Freedom from floods and endemic malaria due to westward migration of the Kosi River and availability of large tracts of fertile land at low rates, attracting people to settle, have been important factors contributing to this spectacular increase in the population of Purnea district. Thus, large tracts of land on a barren and sandy and left high and dry with a rich layer of silt deposited by the retreating Kosi River have been brought under intensive cultivation. The big spurt in population of the region in the last two decades (1951-71) has taken place due to a combination of factors, including implementation of the Kosi Project and Five-Year Development Plans, general improvement

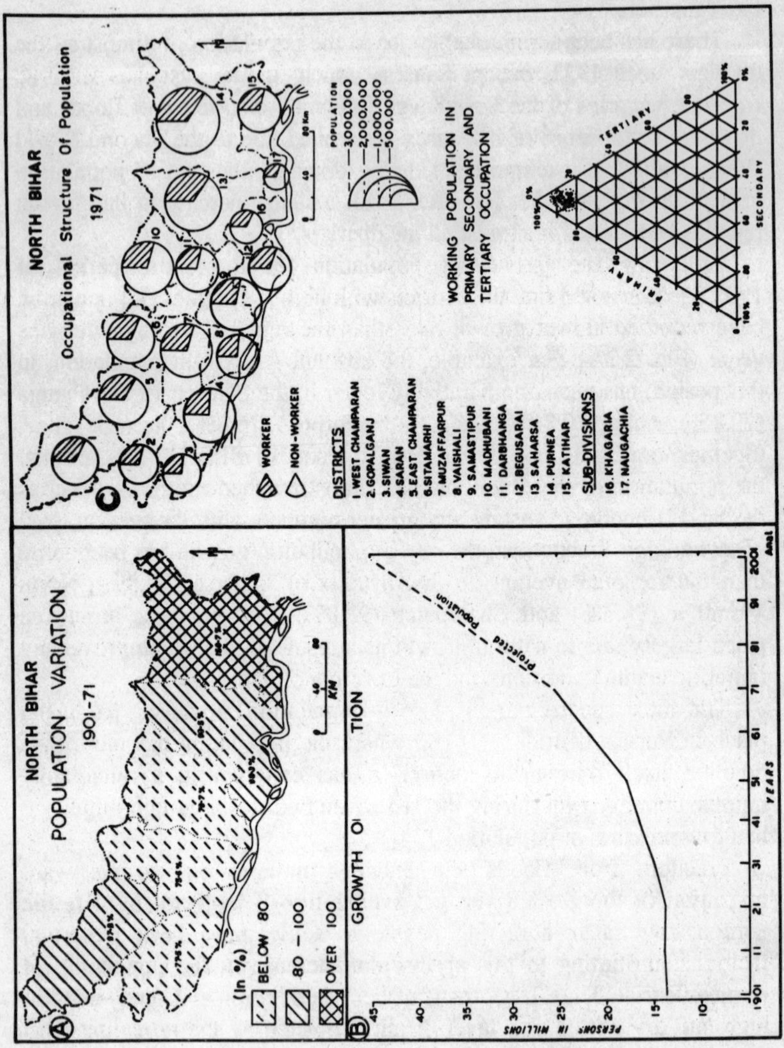

Fig. 2.2: (A) Population variation, 1901-71, (B) Growth of population, (C) Occupational structure of population, 1971.

in public health and large-scale immigration of displaced persons from East Pakistan (now Bangladesh).

Summing, up, the population growth in North Bihar, during recent times, can be attributed to the following factors:

(a) immigration of refugees from East Pakistan (Bangladesh),
(b) taming of many notorious rivers, like the Kosi, the Kamla, the Balan and the Gandak,
(c) construction of canals to irrigate the agricultural land and to discharge the flood-water,
(d) introduction of scientific methods of cultivation and farm practices,
(e) rural electrification,
(f) implementation of National Community Development Projects,
(g) development of transport and communication facilities, and
(h) availability of modern medical facilities.

Distribution of Population

North Bihar, with a population of 2,63,04,409 persons in 1971, accounted for about 44.6 per cent of the total population of the State. An even distribution of population is noted in the North Bihar plain, except the Kosi belt (both present and former) and the hilly tract in North-Western Champaran (Fig. 2.3). Dense population characterises the central part of the region, comprising the districts of Darbhanga, Muzaffarpur and Begusarai, because of intensive agriculture and comparatively lesser impact of floods. However, the riparian ribbons, in this part, are sparsely populated, because of water-logging caused by flood-water and pressure of infertile sandy soils. The population is less dense in the eastern part of the region, comprising the districts of Saharsa, Purnea and Katihar, which has been once the playground of notorious streams, like, the Kosi and the Mahananda. The extreme north-western part of the region with undulating topography, infertile soils and lesser accessibility, is also sparsely populated. Thus, a general decrease in population density is noted from west to east. Recent development of the rail and road transports has also greatly influenced the distribution of population in the region. Areas with low density of roads and placed far away from urban centres, generally, have population concentrated in large and medium size villages.

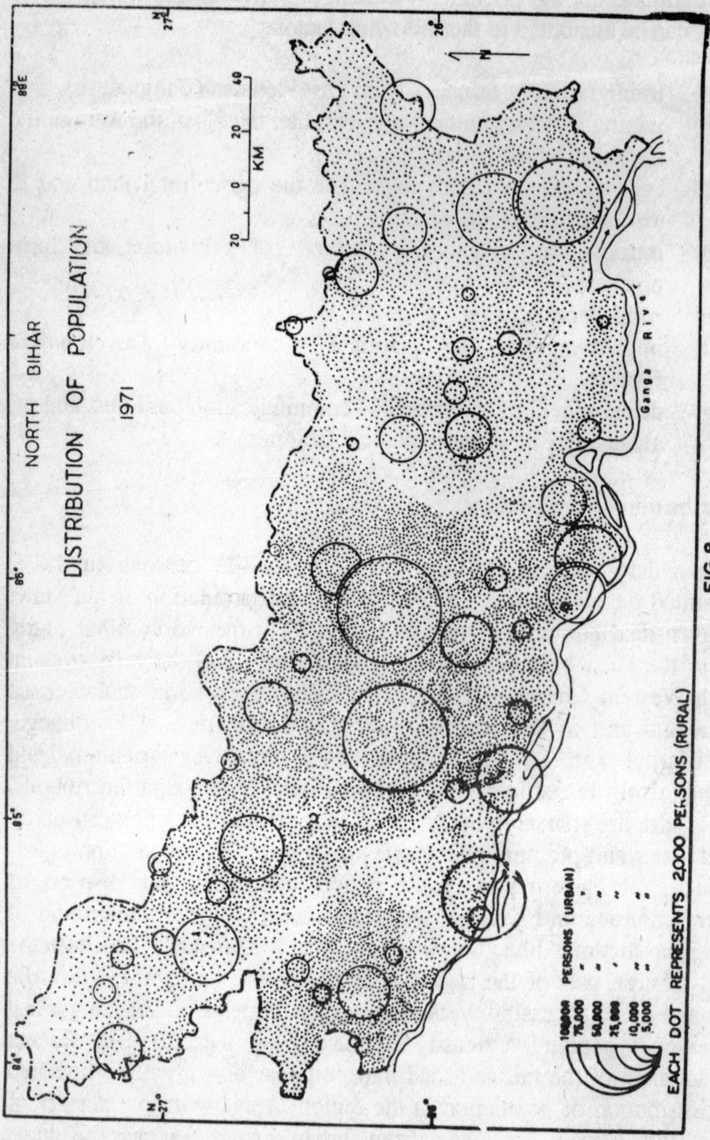

Fig. 2.3: Distribution of population, 1971.

Density of Population

North Bihar has an average density of 507 persons per sq. km, which is nearly double than that for the State of Bihar and India as a whole. The region has an exceptionally high density than most countries of the world. It is noted that the areas adjoining the main rivers, namely, the Ganga, the Kosi and the Gandak, have a comparatively lower density of population (Fig. 2.4). These areas are liable to inundate in the rainy season and have suffered from floods year after year, causing loss to the standing crops and turning fertile fields into barren sandy tracts and swamps. The density of population increases towards the inter-stream divides that lie at some distance from the river banks. Thus, it is evident that the density is higher in areas which are either free or less affected by floods.

Identification of six population density types have been made on the basis of calculation of population density, by dot method, of individual square grids of 10 sq. km units, into which the region has been divided (Fig. 2.4). These are described as follows:

Areas of Exceptionally High Population Density (Over 1,000 Persons sq. km)

This density type characterises the blocks of Mushari, Darbhanga and Chapra. Occurrence of large urban centres accounts for the exceptionally high density of population in these blocks.

Areas of Very High Population Density (800-1,000 persons sq. km)

The areas of very high population density occur as concentric rings around the three main urban centres, namely, Darbhanga, Muzaffarpur and Chapra. This density type is also found in and around the townships of Madhubani, Siwan, Bettiah, Purnea, Katihar, Begusarai and Barauni and the block of Rajnagar in Madhubani district. These areas are generally free from floods and water-logging, and have non-calcareous and non-saline alluvial soils which are quite suitable for intensive cultivation. Also, the dry season water-table remains at a comparatively higher level in these parts.

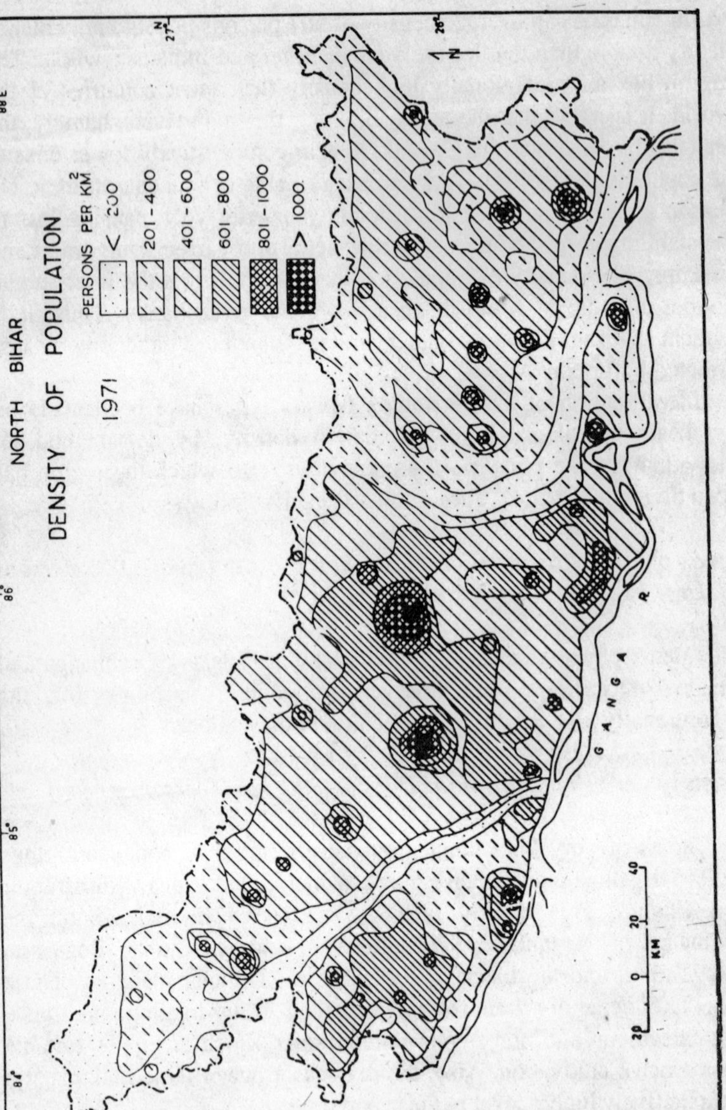

Fig. 2.4: Density of population, 1971.

Areas of High Population Density (600-800 Persons sq. km)

The high density areas occur in the central part of the region, comprising parts of the districts of Darbhanga, Muzaffarpur and Vaishali. Parts of the districts of Siwan, Gopalganj and Begusarai also have high densities. In addition, small patches occur as concentric rings around urban centres. These areas of high density are only marginally affected by floods. Provision of irrigation facilities, during the dry season, ensures higher crop yields in these areas.

Areas of Moderately High Population Density (400-600 Persons sq. km)

Moderately high population density characterises the long tract between the western Kosi embankment and the Gandak River (excluding north-western Champaran), the districts of Saharsa, Purnea and Katihar, and the peripheral parts of the high density zone in Saran district. These areas are frequently affected by floods. Consequently, the economic and health conditions of their inhabitants are generally poor. A large number of small-size towns occur in this density zone.

Areas of Medium Population Density (200-400 Persons sq. km)

Medium population density is noted in the districts of Saran and Champaran, the areas adjoining the Gandak, the Kosi and the Mahananda rivers, and the "Tarai" region along the international border with Nepal. Besides, small pockets of medium density also occur in the districts of Saharsa and Purnea. These areas are liable to severe floods almost every year. This results in water-logging and poor agricultural yields. Economic backwardness and poor transport facilities in these areas account for the absence of large urban centres, except Bettiah in Champaran district.

Areas of Low Population Density (Below 200 Persons sq. km)

The north-western hilly tract of the region, comprising the blocks of Sidhaw, Ramnagar, and Gaunaha in West Champaran district, has low population density. This sub-Himalayan belt of poor forest soils generally has poor yields from agriculture, Other areas of low population density include long strips close to the Gandak and the Kosi rivers and along the Ganga in Khagaria sub-division. These riverine tracts are not only affected by infertile sandy and calcareous soils, inadequate water-supply in the dry season and poor transport facilities. The proportion of arable land is also low in these areas.

Perspective

High population density, in the predominantly agricultural milieu of North Bihar, is typical of areas generally free from floods and bestowed with fertile soils on which intensive farming is commonly practised. Other factors favouring higher density of population are urbanisation following the growth and development of industries, commercial activities and transport facilities.

Occupational Structure

The working population in North Bihar is about 30.81 per cent of its total population. Cultivators and agricultural labourers, who are directly dependent upon agriculture and allied pursuits for their livelihood, account for 38.31 per cent and 40.35 per cent respectively, of this work-force. Tending livestock, fishing, plantation and allied services engage another 10.20 per cent. The lowest employer is mining and quarrying with 0.01 per cent only. A very small proportion of the working population is engaged in secondary productions. Thus, household and other industries account for only 1.88 per cent and 1.35 per cent respectively. The remaining 7.57 per cent of the working population finds employment in tertiary occupations, including trade and commerce (2.78%), transport and communication (0.95%) and other services (3.84%).

Figure 2.2C shows the total and working populations in various districts of North Bihar. A district-wise plot of working population engaged in primary, secondary and tertiary sectors has been also made on a triangular graph. It reveals a predominance of the primary occupation, namely, agriculture and allied activities, which account for about 84.13 per cent to 91.56 per cent of the labour force in various districts. The secondary and tertiary activities, including industries, are much less developed.

Sex Ratio

'A clear knowledge of sex ratio helps to explain the employment and consumption patterns, social needs of the people and, perhaps, the psychological characteristics of a community' (Franklin, 1956, p. 162). The sex ratio is said to be favourable if the number of females exceeds that of males and adverse if the opposite holds good.

In 1961, the sex ratio in North Bihar was 1,011 females per 1,000 males. But this position was reversed in the census of 1971 which, on an average, revealed the existence of only 966 females per 1,000 males. The decline in the sex ratio has taken place in almost all the districts. However, the females still outnumber the males in the western districts of Saran (1,053), Siwan (1,077), Gopalganj (1,018) and Vaishali (1,016). This apparent surplus of females is explained by large-scale migrations of male labourer from these districts, only for short periods, to far-flung places, like, Calcutta, Bombay and tea gardens in Assam.

The sex ratio is generally adverse in towns than the adjoining rural areas, because more male members migrate to towns than females either for seeking employment as labourers or professionals or for other purposes. The only town having favourable sex ratio in North Bihar is Mahnar Bazar (1,007), located in Vaishali district. The well-to-do among the villagers also prefer to have residences in towns for the education of their children and for other amenities. But even these persons leave the women folk, particularly the aged ones, to look after the village property. This necessarily results in greater imbalance in the larger town.

Population Projection

'Population projection attempts to outline the size or composition of a population at a future date' (Goode and Hatt, 1952, p. 313). Estimation of population is generally a risky affair because it is often based on certain assumptions, which, in course of time, may prove wrong. For finding out the population of a region, at a future date, the rate of population change is first calculated by the following formula (Gibbs, 1965, p. 108):

$$r = \frac{(P_2 - P_1)/t}{(P_2 + P_1)/2} \times 100 \qquad \text{(a)}$$

where r, the rate of change, is a function of the mathematical relationship among the population size at one point in time (P_1), population size at later point in time (P_2), and the number of years over the period (t). This average arithmetical formula expresses change in numbers on an annual basis $(P_2-P_1)/t$ as a per cent of the average population size $(P_2+P_1)/2$ over the period of time.

Once the rate of population change is known, the projected population can be calculated by using the compound interest formula as under:

$$A = P\,(1 + r/100)^n \qquad \text{(b)}$$

where A stands for projected population,
P for present population,
r = rate of change and n for number of years.

The population of North Bihar in 1971 was 2,63,04,409 persons. So the rate of growth during the decade 1961-71 will be

$$r = \frac{(2{,}63{,}04{,}409 - 2{,}18{,}63{,}388)/10}{(2{,}63{,}04{,}409 + 2{,}18{,}63{,}388)/2} \times 100$$

$$= 1.84 \text{ per cent}$$

Considering the growth rate (1.84 per cent) till 1981 and at the end of century, the population projection of the region has been calculated (Table 2.3). Thus, it is estimated that the population of North Bihar will increase to 43.65 million by A.D. 2001.

Table 2.3: Population projection for North Bihar (1981-2001)

Year	*Projected population (in millions)*
1981	3.3
1991	36.80
2001	43.65

Source: Calculated by the author.

It means an increase of 65.96 per cent on the present population. This phenomenal increase in population will further aggravate the acute problems of finding food, clothing and shelter for the region's population. It will also add to unemployment, which is already running very high. Population explosion is, in fact, racking the region's economy. It needs to be contained by drastically reducing the birth rate. This is most essential for providing a decent standard of living for the region's population.

TREND OF URBANISATION

Population and space are two important variables of urbanisation. "The process of urbanisation is typically said to involve the movement of people out of agricultural communities into other and generally larger non-agricultural communities" (Hauser, 1966, p. 519). This process, in fact, leads to concentration of population in a limited geographical area by which villages turn into towns and towns develop into cities (Sinha, 1979, p. 211). The study of urbanisation, therefore, includes consideration of the urban locale and complex, its growth and development, its characteristics and influences (Saxena, 1970, p. 2). Urbanisation is both a social as well as a cultural process. It is closely related with the pace of economic development of a region.

Although a few urban centres existed in several parts of the world even during the ancient times, the growth of modern urbanisation is the gift of industrial revolution which swept Europe in the later part of 19th century and other parts of the world subsequently. In recent decades, the rate of urbanisation has advanced at a tremendous pace not only in advanced countries but also in developing countries of the world. North Bihar provides such an example of rapid urban growth in a predominantly agrarian society of the developing world. The study also attempts to bring our regional and sub-regional variations in urbanism under geographical purview.

Growth of Urban Population

Authentic records of the enumeration of urban population are available since 1901 only. Earlier enumerations were neither very accurate nor did they provide detailed information regarding the urban population in North Bihar. The total urban population of North Bihar was 3,53,924 in 1901 with 18 urban centres (Fig. 2.5), this increased to 13,60,673 in 1971. Thus, the increase in the last seven decades has been by 284.4 per cent. The corresponding increase in the general population of the region in the same period has been of the order of 88 per cent only.

The pre-1921 pattern of urban growth in the region is quite different from the one in the post-1921 period. In fact, the first two decades of the century (1901-11 and 1911-21) recorded a fall in the urban population of the region by as much as 5 per cent. Most of the towns declined except Katihar, Bettiah, Motihari, Samastipur and Sitamarhi. But a steady increase in urban population has been recorded since 1921. Consequently, the number of towns increased from 21 in 1921 to 24 in 1941 (Fig. 2.6). The increase in urban population during 1921-31 has been rather slow but subsequently it increased rapidly so much so that during 1931-71 it increased by 269 per cent. This period had been the most favourable one for the town growth, the number of urban centres went up to 32, 43 and 49 in 1951, 1961 and 1971, respectively (Figs. 2.6, 2.7). Thus, keeping in view the changing pattern of growth of total urban population, we can divide the study into two periods, 1901-31 and 1931-71, for analysis. The pattern of growth since 1931 has been entirely different from that in the previous decades (1901-31). This variation can be studied in relation to the growth of rural population.

Table 2.4: Growth of urban and rural population in North Bihar (1901-71)

Year	*Urban population*	*Decade-wise variation (%)*	*Rural population*	*Decade-wise variation (%)*	*Urban population to total population (%)*
1901	3,53,924		1,36,36,392		2.5
1911	3,33,913	–5.6	1,36,78,183	+3.0	2.3
1921	3,20,496	–4.0	1,36,54,571	–1.71	2.2
1931	3,69,217	+15.2	1,47,17,407	+7.7	2.4
1941	4,73,634	+28.3	1,61,55,362	+9.7	2.9
1951	6,41,414	+35.4	1,71,91,217	+6.4	3.6
1961	10,47,291	+63.2	2,08,16,097	+21.2	4.8
1971	13,60,673	+29.9	2,49,43,736	+19.8	5.2

Source: Data computed from Census of India, 1931, 1951, 1961, and 1971.

Table 2.4 shows variation in both rural and urban growth in North Bihar during 1901-71. It is noted that the per cent decadal variation in urban population, since 1921, has been always more than double than that of the rural population, except during 1961-71. The rural population in the last decade (1961-71) has increased by 19.8 per cent whereas the urban population by 29.9 per cent only. This is largely a reflection of the changed definition of urban area in 1961, which

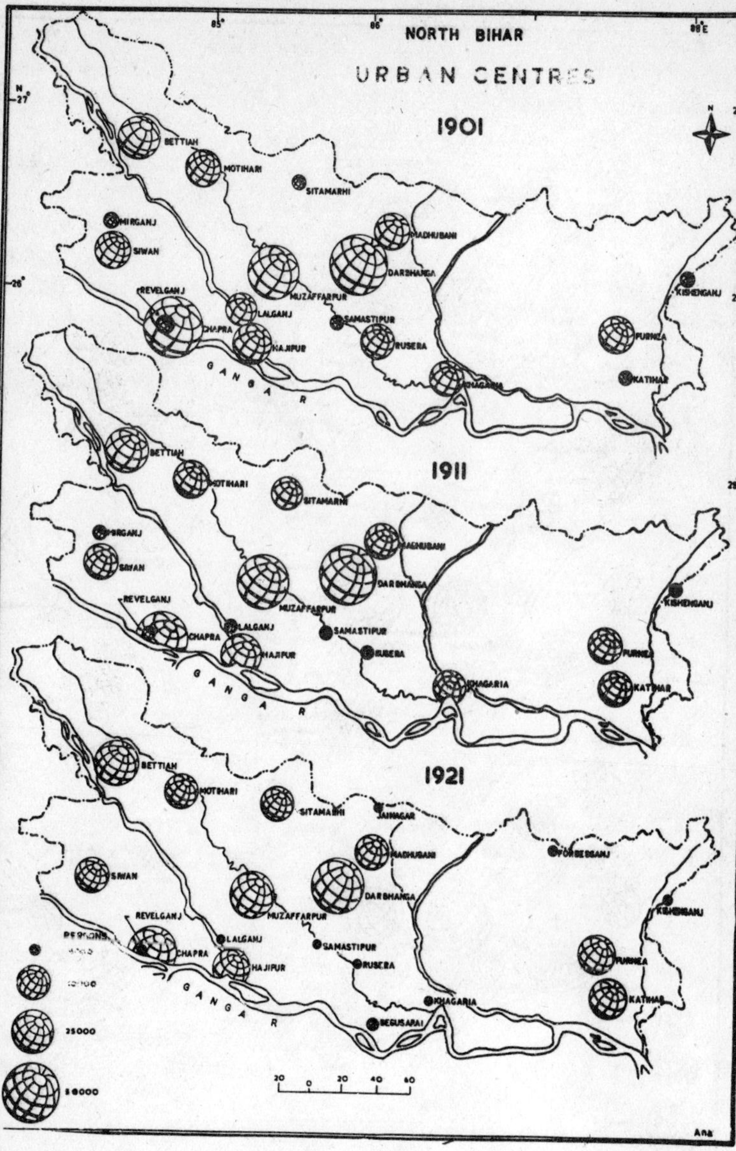

Fig. 2.5: Urban ce·tres; 1901, 1911, 1921.

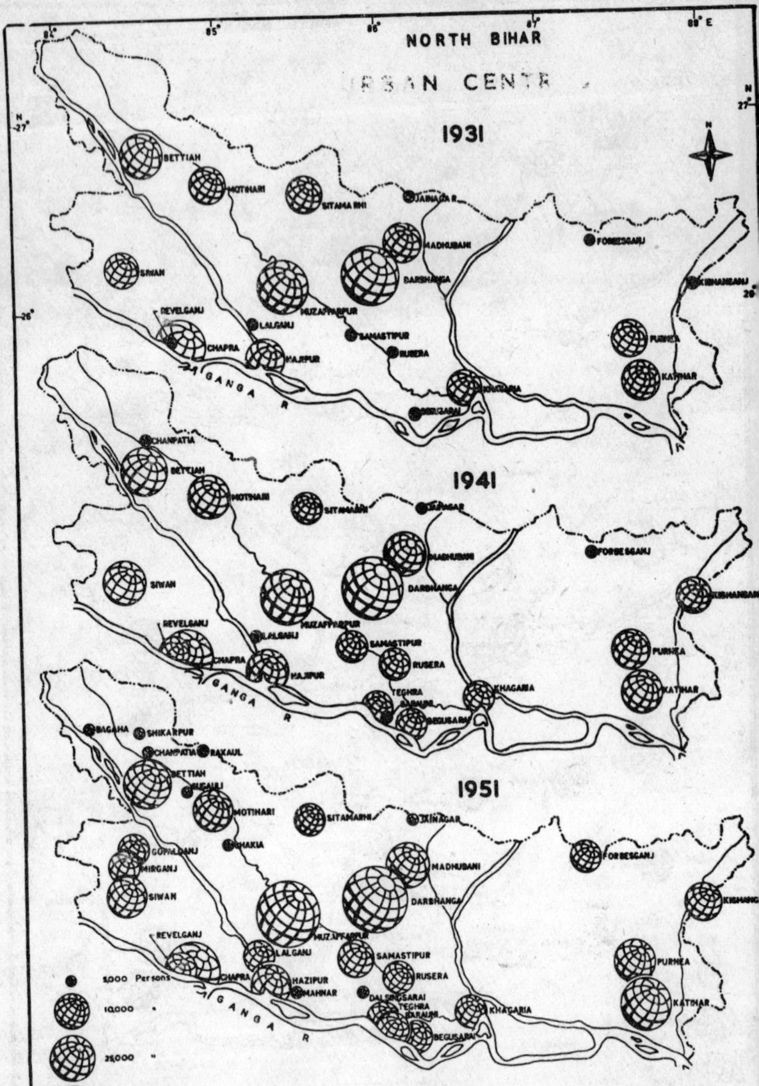

Fig. 2.6: Urban centres; 1931, 1941, 1951

resulted in de-classification of a few towns. Thus, some centres which could have been classed as urban according to 1961 classification were left out in 1971 census.

The trend of urban growth has been examined under (i) period of slow growth and (ii) period of rapid growth.

Period of Slow Growth (1901-31)

It is evident from Table 2.4 that the pace of urbanisation in North Bihar has been rather painfully slow during 1901-31. In fact, there was a slight decline in urban population in the first decade (1901-11), even though the general population showed a small increase (0.15%). This was occasioned by a fall in the population of most of the towns in the region, including Chapra, Revelganj, Muzaffarpur, Hajipur and Rosera. The main reason for the decline for urban population in this period has been attributed to the prevalence of plague and other epidemics in most of the towns during this period. Nevertheless, a slight increase in the population of Bettiah (4.4%), Motihari (8.3%), Sitamarhi (6.1%), Purnea (5%) and Katihar (5.5%) has been noted. Most of these towns were generally free from these diseases and, hence, experienced accretion of population.

The population of the region experienced a moderately slow growth during 1921-31. The rate of urban growth, in this period, was almost double than that of the general growth of population.

Period of Rapid Growth (1931-71)

The urban population of the region increased at a faster rate since 1931. The rate of urban increase was not only sustained but it gained further accelerated momentum and was nearly three to five times higher than the corresponding rate of general growth up to 1961. However, this pace of accelerated urban growth seems to have slowed down by 1971 as the increase in urban population during 1961-71 was 29.9 per cent only as compared to 63.3 per cent in 1951-61.

Various factors seem to have influenced the rapid growth of urban population in this region. "One important factor is the steady stream of migration from villages to towns in pursuit of business, occupation, education, trade and various kinds of employment following the increasing pressure of population on agriculture in the countryside." In the eastern part of the region, quite a few towns emerged from villages

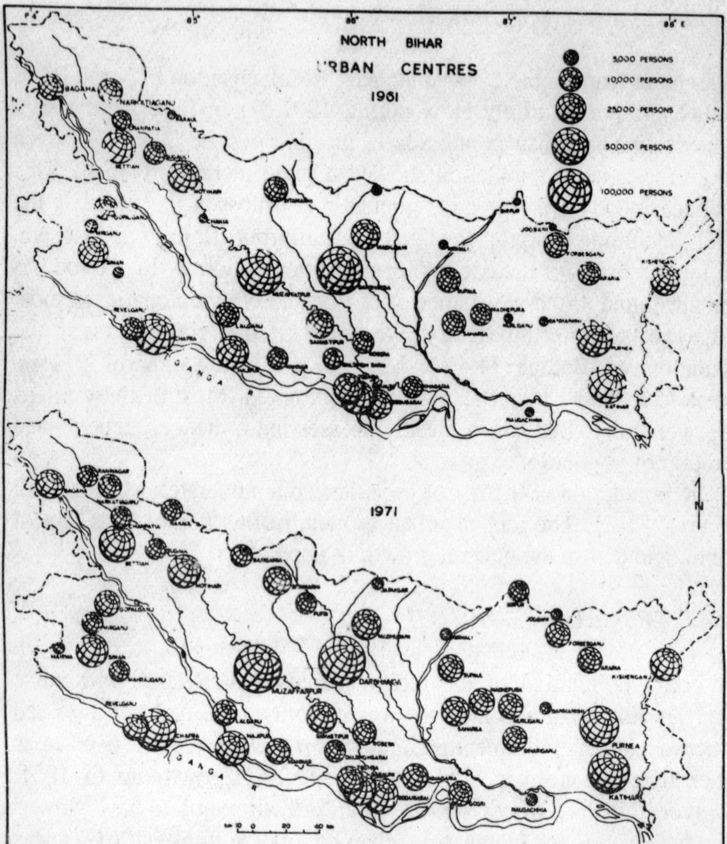

Fig. 2.7: Urban centres; 1961, 1971.

following industrial, commercial, administrative and other developments.

Growth of Urbanism in Size-class of Towns

Table 2.5 shows the percentages of urban population residing in various classes of towns during the period 1901-71. Also, the changes in the respective position of various classes of towns have been noted since 1901.

Table 2.5: Percentage of urban population in various size-classes of towns in North Bihar (1901-71)

Class	*1971*	*1961*	*1951*	*1941*	*1931*	*1921*	*1911*	*1901*
I	19.0	20.3						
II	21.0	26.3	34.8	37.8	16.5	16.7	18.7	18.8
III	34.3	23.8	27.2	24.3	32.0	31.2	33.5	38.8
IV	21.7	21.9	28.2	30.3	33.7	30.6	32.6	26.7
V	3.8	7.7	9.8	5.8	17.8	20.0	15.2	15.7
VI	0.2			1.8		1.5		

Source: Computed from Census of India, 1971, Bihar.

There has been a general tendency for a lower class town to grow into a higher class town. This trend is clear from Fig. 2.9A,B which shows both the number of towns and the percentages of total urban population residing in various classes of towns during the past seven decades. It also reveals that the two Class I towns, accounting for 20.3 per cent of the total population, emerged in 1961 only. Though the population of the two cities increased by 21 per cent during 1961-71, their share in the region urban population, in fact, decreased to 19.0 per cent.

The case of Class II towns is quite different. Only one town, namely, Darbhanga, came in this category during 1901-31. This town has experienced several setbacks, but its share in the region's urban population has been maintained between 18.8 per cent and 16.5 per cent during 1901-31. In 1941, the number of Class II towns increased considerably. Thus, the percentage of population residing in these towns suddenly increased to 37.8 per cent. Its proportion decreased slightly in 1951. But a marked downward trend in the proportion of population living in Class II towns has been noted during 1961-71, mainly because of the upgradation of two Class II towns (Muzaffarpur and Darbhanga) into Class I cities.

A continuous increase in the number of Class III towns has been observed during 1901-71. But the proportion of urban population residing in Class III towns has continuously decreased from 38.8 per cent in 1901 to 23.8 per cent in 1961. This anomaly is explained by upgradation of a few towns in the population range of 40,000–49,999 while inclusion of more towns with population range of 20,000–25,000 in this category during these decades. The proportion of urban population residing in Class III towns again jumped to 34.3 per cent in 1971. There has been also a continuous increase in the number of Class IV towns since 1901. However, the proportion of urban population residing in these towns has decreased from 33.7 per cent in 1931 to 21.7 per cent in 1971. It is noted that North Bihar had a maximum number of towns (22 in 1971) in this category. Towns of Class V category indicate an almost similar trend as Class IV towns. But some variations may occur due to the upgradation of towns in the last few decades. The proportion of population residing in Class IV, V and VI towns has decreased abruptly during 1951-61. This may be due to de-classification of three Class VI towns and changes in the urban areas of the rest. It is also noted that most of the towns of the region have been upgraded with the general increase in population during 1901-71.

General Distribution of Urban Population

North Bihar has a predominantly agricultural economy. It has lagged behind the State of Bihar in urban development. In 1971, the region had a total population of 2,62,94,865 of which only 13,67,322 persons (5.2%) were enumerated as urban-dwellers, living in 49 towns (Fig. 2.7). It is noted that the towns of the region are mostly small-sized. A few urban agglomerations, associated with transport network, also exist. Most of the towns are located along the rail routes. A greater concentration of urban centres is noticed in the central part of North Bihar, along Muzaffarpur-Darbhanga axis. The urban centres of Muzaffarpur and Darbhanga, classed as big towns, have dominated the trade and commerce of the entire region. Their hinterlands or urban-fields are quite large; this has helped them to attract large number of immigrants from rural areas. Being administrative headquarters of Darbhanga and Tirhut Divisions, these centres have also witnessed rapid expansions in administrative and educational functions. Expansion of small-scale industries has taken place in and around their urban fringes. Recently, there has been a growing tendency among the well-to-do farmers and ex-zamindars to shift their residences from the countryside to towns. It is also noted that existence of urban amenities in large measure, at these centres, has hindered the growth of satellite towns around them.

The second urban belt is ribbon-like in the district of Begusarai; it includes the towns of Begusarai, Barauni and Teghra. This belt has grown rather rapidly, within a short span of time, due to the establishment of Indian Oil Refinery, Indian Fertilizer Factory and other ancillary industries in and around Barauni. This industrial complex has engulfed large rural areas. It has assumed urban status because of the unprecedented industrial development in the area during recent times.

Other urban centres have grown mostly from villages which, in course of time, developed into local markets or rurban centres. Some of these centres were initially selected as district or sub-divisional headquarters which gave them opportunity to grow. Later, with the development of rail network and location of sugar refineries that brought economic prosperity to the region, these and other urban nuclei got further impetus to grow. Thus, various socio-geographical factors account for the growth of these urban centres.

Distribution of Urban Population by District and Size-class of Towns

Table 2.6 gives district-wise percentages of urban population to total population, urban population to total urban population and urban area to total urban area in North Bihar.

It is evident from the Table 2.6 that only 5.2 per cent of the population of the region lives in towns. This indicates a poor level of urbanisation in the area as a whole. Neverthcless, some regional variations are noted. For example, North Monghyr (including Begusarai and Khagaria) and Purnea districts, with 8.1 per cent and 6.3 per cent of urban population, respectively, are relatively more urbanised. The district of North Monghyr accounts for 10.6 per cent of the total urban population and about 8.5 per cent of the total urban area of North Bihar. Purnea surprisingly has the maximum share of both urban population (18.3%) and urban area (28.9%) in the region. The districts of Champaran, Muzaffarpur and Darbhanga, with an urban population ranging from 4.2 per cent to 5.2 per cent, are less urbanised. Saharsa had no urban population prior to 1961, but subsequently its urban growth has been so well-marked that in 1971 it had an urban population of 4.5 per cent.

Table 2.6: Distribution of urban population and urban area in North Bihar (1901-1971)

District/ Sub-division	*Urban population to total population (percentage)*	*Urban population to total urban population (percentage)*	*Urban area to total urban area (percentage)*
Saran	4.2	13.2	10.4
Champaran	5.2	13.1	16.5
Muzaffarpur	5.2	18.7	12.9
Darbhanga	4.4	17.5	5.5
Saharsa	4.5	7.8	16.5
Purnea	6.3	18.3	28.9
North Monghyr	8.1	10.6	8.5
Naugachia	2.9	0.8	0.8
North Bihar	5.2	100.0	100.0

Source: Computed by the author.

It is noted that the number of towns vary from district to district. The pace of urbanisation in the district of Purnea and North Monghyr has been rather fast during recent times. This is due to economic and industrial developments in the area in the post-independence period. Thus, "urbanisation has tended towards its highest point wherever economic productivity has been the greatest, i.e., where the economy is industrialised and rationalised" (Davis, 1955, p. 65).

The process of urbanisation in North Bihar can be examined according to class and size of towns. Table 2.7 gives the distribution of urban population by size-classes of towns in North Bihar. It reveals that the total urban population residing in towns varies from one class of town to the other. The two cities of Muzaffarpur and Darbhanga, forming Class I towns, account for a little less than one-fifth (19.0%) of the total urban population of the region.

There are four Class II towns which account, for 21.0 per cent of the urban population. A maximum of 34.3 per cent urban population resides in Class III towns which are 15 in number, Similarly, Class IV towns are 22 in number. They contain 21.7 per cent of the urban population and are in this respect, at par with Class I and II towns. The shares of Class V and VI towns are rather low; they account for only 3.8 per cent to 0.2 per cent of the urban population of the region, respectively.

Table 2.7: Distribution of urban population in various size-classes of towns in North Bihar (1971)

Class	*Population range*	*No. of towns*	*Population*	
			Persons	*Percentage*
I	1,00,000 and over	2	2,58,438	19.0
II	50,000-99,999	4	2,85,551	21.0
III	20,000-49,999	15	4,66,972	34.3
IV	10,000-19,999	22	2,95,498	21.7
V	5,000-9,999	5	51,244	3.8
VI	Below 5,000	1	2,970	0.2

Source: (Based on Census of India, Bihar, 1971).

It is evident from the above analysis that the fewer number of Class I towns in North Bihar is primarily due to its predominantly agricultural economy. A majority of towns (36 out of 49) belongs to the population range of 10,000–50,000. Most of these towns are district and sub-divisional headquarters.

Urban Concentration

An analysis of the proportion of urban population to total population in 21 sub-divisions of North Bihar brings out a more clear picture of the state of urbanisation in the area (Fig. 2.8A). Urban concentration zones have been delimited after drawing isopleths on the basis of the percentage values of urban to total population in each of the 21 sub-divisions of the region. Thus, the following zones of urban concentration are identified:

(i) Zone of High Urban Concentration,
(ii) Zone of Medium Urban Concentration,
(iii) Zone of Low Urban Concentration, and
(iv) Zone of Least Urban Concentration.

Zone of High Urban Concentration

Sub-divisions with more than 8 per cent of urban population have been included in the zone of high urban concentration. This zone includes Darbhanga Sadar and Begusarai sub-divisions. The sub-division of Darbhanga has only one city and no towns, whereas that of Begusarai possesses three towns only.

Zone of Medium Urban Concentration

Eight sub-divisions, having 6 per cent to 8 per cent of urban population, have been included in the zone of medium urban concentration. This zone appears to be scattered over the entire region. From west to east, it includes the sub-divisions of Saran Sadar, Bettiah, Muzaffarpur, Khagaria, Madhepura, Katihar, Purnea and Kishenganj. The urban population of this zone is concentrated in the city of Muzaffarpur and 16 other classes of towns. This zone occupies more than half of the total urban area and about half of the total urban population of the region.

Zone of Low Urban Concentration

The zone of low urban concentration comprises only four sub-divisions, namely, Siwan, Hajipur, Supaul and Araria. It has about 4 per cent to 6 per cent of urban population. This zone is quite extensive; it includes 11 towns. The rural population, in this zone, is high and dense.

Zone of Least Urban Concentration

The zone of least urban concentration, with 2 per cent to 4 per cent of urban population, comprises the northern sub-divisions of Champaran Sadar, Sitamarhi and Madhubani along the Nepal border, besides Gopalganj, Samastipur, Saharsa and Naugachhia. This zone is also very extensive and includes 16 medium and small urban centres. It has a greater proportion of rural population than all other zones. The progress of urbanisation in this zone is very slow because of the ravages of floods that take place almost every year.

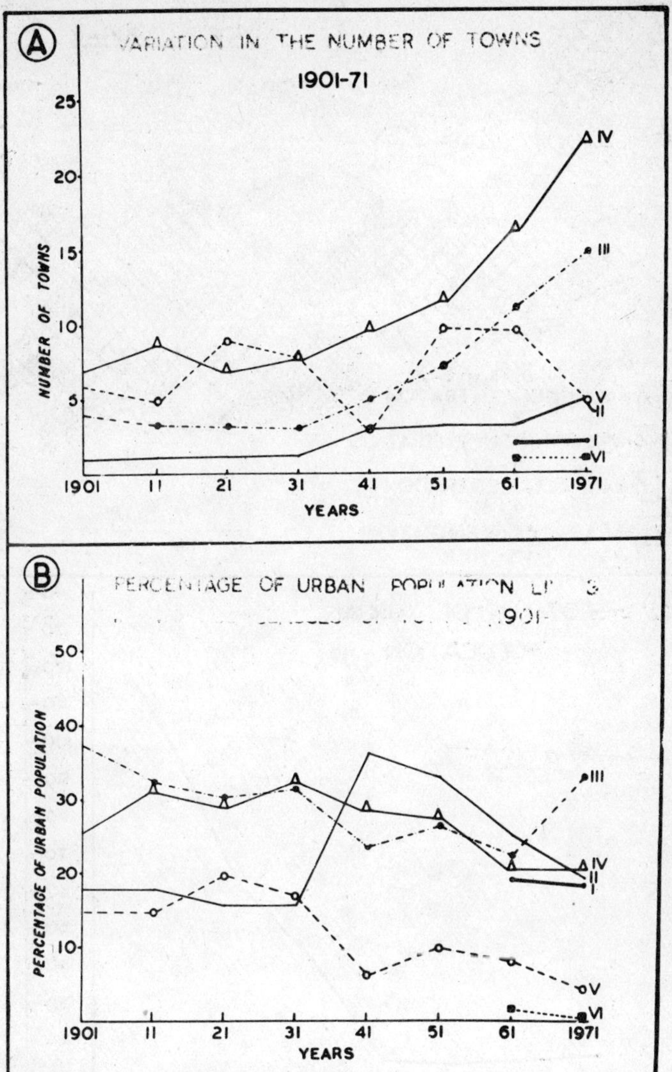

Fig. 2.8: (A) Variation in the number of towns — 1901-1971, (B) Percentage of urban population living in various classes of towns 1901-1971.

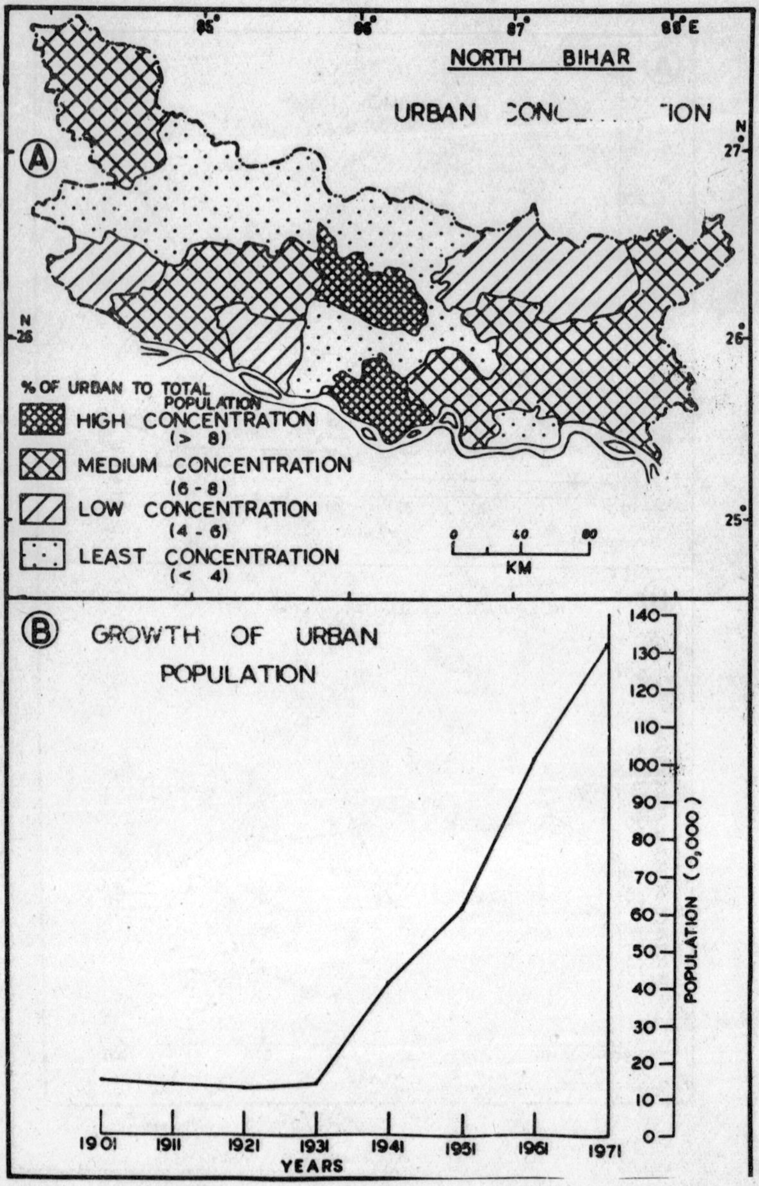

Fig. 2.9: (A) Urban concentration, (B) Growth of urban population.

Spatial Distribution of Towns

Figure 2.10 shows the spacing of a total of 49 towns of various orders in North Bihar. The nature of dispersal of these towns has been analysed by 'Nearest-neighbour technique' (Clark and Evans, 1954) which requires calculation of four attributes, namely, mean observed spacing (*Ro*), hypothetical spacing (*Hs*), nearest neighbour statistic (*Rn*) and index of randomness (*Di*).

The hypothetical spacing is calculated as

$$Hs = 1.0746/\sqrt{d},$$

where *d* is the density of points, in this case towns/km².

The deviation and association between (*Ro*) and (*Hs*) are measured in the light of two assumptions: (a) *Rn* shows the level of association between mean observed spacing (*Ro*) and expected spacing in random situation (*RE*) as

$$Rn = Ro/RE,$$

where RE = 0.5 $\sqrt{A/N}$ (*A* = Area of the region, *N* = number of towns.

Rn has a value range of 0.0 to 2.149), (b) *Di*, showing *Ro* as percentage of *Hs*, i.e.,

$$Di = (Ro/Hs)^{100}$$

(it has a value range of 1 to 100) (Singh and Singh, 1978, p. 14).

Table 2.8 gives the values of these variables for each class of towns. It is noted that the Hs values range between 53.14 km for class IV towns to 175.25 km for Class I towns, whereas the Ro values vary between 28.41 km for Class IV towns to 72.50 km for Class II towns. It reveals that the hypothetical distances are more than the actual distances in case of almost all the towns.

The analysis shows dispersed nature of distribution, wherein the towns are not equally spaced. This trend is further supported with the nearest neighbour statistics.

Considering the nature of dispersion (Rn and Di), the towns of the region can be categorised into three groups:

- (i) loosely clustered (0.4 to 0.8),
- (ii) random (0.8 to 1.2), and
- (iii) low uniformity (1.2 to 1.6).

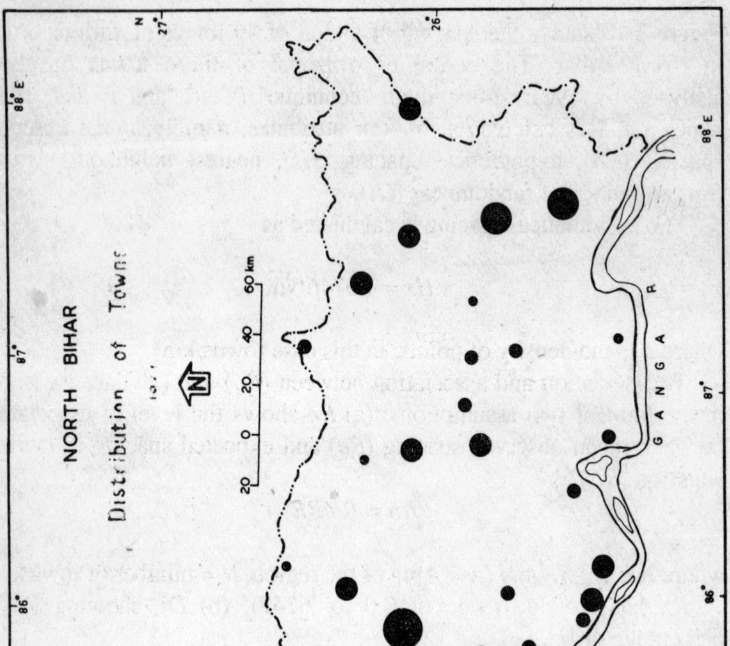

Fig. 2.10: Distribution of towns 1971.

Table 2.8: Spatial characteristics of towns in North Bihar, (1971)

Class of towns (according to population size)	*No. of towns*	*Spacing of towns in km*			*Nature of dispersion*	
		Ro	*RE*	*Hs*	*Rn*	*Di(%)*
Class I	2	50.00	82.007	176.25	0.61	28.37
Class II	4	72.50	57.98	124.62	1.25	58.17
Class III	14	46.57	30.99	66.61	1.50	69.91
Class IV	22	28.41	24.72	53.14	1.16	53.46
Class V & VI	7	64.86	43.83	94.20	1.48	69.00
Entire region	49	21.85	16.56	35.61	1.32	61.36

Source: Based on author's computation.

The *Rn* values of these categories correspond with *Di* values which is observed as 18 per cent, 37 per cent, 55 per cent and 74 per cent respectively. Thus, the two Class I towns exhibit loosely clustered distribution (*Rn* 0.61, *Di* 28.37 per cent). These towns grew as administrative centres on strategic sites along river banks during the medieval times. Random nature of dispersion (*Rn* 1.16, *Di* 46.54 per cent) characterises the 22 Class IV towns found in the area. These small-sized towns, with a few exceptions, are found either along the railway tract or closer to larger towns.

All other Class II, III, V and VI categories, with *Rn* and *Di* values as (*Rn* 1.25, *Di* 58.17 per cent), (*Rn* 1.50, *Di* 69.91 per cent), (*Rn* 1.48, *Di* 69 per cent) and (*Rn* 1.32, *Di* 61.36 per cent) respectively, exhibit a distribution pattern of low uniformity. The development of this pattern has taken place largely due to the physical attributes of the terrain, including existence of a large number of streams causing floods, besides insufficient development of the transport network and industries.

REFERENCES

Ahmad, E. (1965): *Bihar A Physical, Economic and Regional Geography*, Ranchi University, Ranchi.

Census of India, 4, Bihar, General Report 1961.

Clark, P.J. and F.C. Evans (1954): "Distance to nearest neighbour as a measure of spatial relationships in population", *Ecology*, 35, pp. 445-53. Work cited in P. Hagget, A.D.

Cliff and A. Frey Eds. (1977): *Location Methods*, London.

Davis, K. (1955): "The Origin and Growth of Urbanisation in the World" In H.M. Mayer and C.F. Kohn (Eds.) (1967): *Readings in Urban Geography*, Allahabad, pp. 59-68.

Franklin, S.H. (1956): "The pattern of sex ratio in New Zealand", *Economic Geography*, 32, pp. 162-76.

Gibbs, J.P. (1961): *Urban Research Methods*, New Delhi.

Goode, W.J. and P.K. Hatt (1952): *Methods in Social Research*, New York.

Hauser, P.M. and L.F. Schnore (1965): *The Study of Urbanisation*, New York.

Pandey, M.S. (1964): *Historical Geography and Topography of Bihar*, Varanasi.

Saxena, S. (1970): *Trend of Urbanisation in U.P.*, Agra.

Singh, R.L. and R.P.B. Singh (Eds.) (1978): *Transformation of Rural Habitat in Indian Perspective: A Geographic Dimension*. N.G.S.I., Varanasi.

Sinha, V.C. (1979): *Dynamic of India's Population Growth*, New Delhi.

3

ORIGIN AND GROWTH OF TOWNS

NORTH BIHAR has passed through the initial phases of urbanisation which resulted in the transformation of rural settlement into the urban centres. Geographical factors, like, location, natural and cultural resources, besides technological and administrative advantages, give economic identity to urban centres.

Towns are generally regarded 'Mirrors of their age and they often reflect their antecedental fabrics' (Taneja, 1971, p. 21). A study of North Bihar towns is, therefore, likely to reveal the impact of physical and cultural landscapes on the townscape through time and experience of ages. Both geographical and historic events have been discussed to obtain the motivations that led to the origin and growth of individual towns. The history of urban growth in the region may be divided into five periods.

Ancient Period

Our knowledge regarding the origin and characteristics of towns during the historic period is quite limited. Archaeological discovery of pre historic and proto-historic material have not been plentiful in the region and we have very few indications of the early urban settlements. Puranic and Epic traditions, however, give us the names of numerous kings of Videha (Pandey, 1964, p. 11); who ruled the region and founded numerous townships. It is generally believed that when the 'Aryans descended the region, they found a blazing civilisation, rich with plough agriculture, in the surplus products of which lived a society of non-agriculturists forming the kings, ministers, priests, military man and their supporting professionals' (Singh, 1973, p. 85). With the growing number of Aryan immigrants and their natural increase by assimilation with non-Aryan people, they established townships. The origin of 'Janakpur' and 'Sitamarhi' (Chaudhury, 1958, p. 235) is associated with various activities of Lord Ramachandra, the hero of *Ramayana* (Plate 1)

In addition to political, strategic and economic factors, cultural and religious factors played almost exclusively independent roles in the origin and growth of towns. Religious fairs, associated with sacred bath in the Ganga and the Gandak at favourable river bank sites, led to development of township like 'Barauni' and 'Semaria' (near the present Barauni). Ritual rites have been practised at Semaria on the northern bank of the Ganga opposite Mokameh. Similarly, Sonpur also developed as urban site, the place is famous for Hariharkshetra fair (Plate 2).

Colonisation and territorial expansion by the Aryans in the initial phase resulted in the origin of politico-administrative and economic-cultural centres. Development of trade and commerce accelerated the process of urbanisation as is evident from the accounts of ancient centres like 'Vaishali', 'Cherund' and 'Pundra' in North Bihar (Fig. 3.1). Vaishali and Cherund, being the seats of 'Lichhavi' and 'Kusan kings', were particularly more prosperous. Roads ran in almost every direction from these centres, thus connecting them with Taxila and parts of Central Asia where lay the famous silk routes. Political turmoil not only led to the decline and assimilation of these empires but also to the decline and decay of these centres (Prasad, 1975, p. 48). Thus, both Vaishali and Cherund were deserted by their inhabitants as the seat of administrative power shifted to Patliputra (the present Patna). Settlements, which lay on trade routes, also suffered from the decline in trade, both inland and foreign. Consequently, these towns declined rapidly and some were phased out of existence.

Urbanisation was rather slow in the Mauryan period, largely due to the political considerations. Nevertheless, a large number of new towns appeared in North Bihar in this period. These towns generally enjoyed river side location and functioned as collecting and distributing centres. 'Lauriya Areraj', 'Lauria Nandangarh' and 'Kesaria' (Chaudhury, 1960, p. 566) were initially Budhist sites, founded by Ashoka, which soon grew into market towns but were lost subsequently with the decline of the Mauryan power.

It is noted that towns acting as religious or educational strongholds generally survived through the political turmoil while those that grew only as seats of power, or due to their strategic importance, generally succumbed.

Plate 1: A view of Jankiasthan temple at Sitamarhi.

Plate 2: A view of Hariharnath temple, sited at the confluence of the Ganga and the Great Gandak rivers.

There is little historical record to indicate town growth in North Bihar after the decline of the Mauryan power. In the 8th century, however, Gupta – the founder of Pala dynasty in Bihar and Bengal – established his sway westward over North Bihar which favoured town growth. North Bihar experienced similar phase of relative stability in 11th century when Tirhut, including Mithila, formed part of the kingdom of Senas (Chaudhury, 1958, p. 144). Town growth in this period was rather slow.

Muslim Period

The process of urbanisation was accelerated during the Muslim period which is characterised by rapid change of regimes from time to time. Under this political structure, a few established towns grew in size while new towns were founded by local administrators and vassals. Keeping in view the danger from marauding invaders, the towns of this period generally grew around forts which formed the seat of the ruler or chieftains. Some settlements also came into prominence because of their selection for administrative and defence by the ruler and chieftains.

Muslim conquest swept North Bihar between A.D. 1211 and A.D. 1226 during the time of Ghyasuddin Illias, Governor of Bengal, and the 'invasion' of Ghyasuddin Tughluque in 1323 finally put an end to Hindu rule in Tirhut (Chaudhury, 1964, p. 35).

Trading locations and market sites formed the nuclei of early medieval towns, (Dickinson, 1948, p. 14), which gradually grew up adjacent to a stronghold, generally fort, which the developing urban communities eventually wrested their independence. There are authentic evidences to prove that the towns of 'Tughlaqpur' (Darbhanga), 'Samsuddinpur' (Samastipur), Hajipur, Muzaffarpur and Purnea (Diwakar, 1957, p. 51) were established in a similar fashion (Fig. 3.1). These towns came into prominence as seats of Muslim Governors. In addition, some strategically located older centres were fortified and garrisoned, such as 'Jalalgarh' (Chaudhury, 1963, p. 711) and 'Jainagar' (Chaudhury, 1964, p. 718). In case of Jalalgarh, the Muslim ruler re-built its forts and held them. Estimates for fortifying and garrisoning these forts, are still in existence.

While garrison towns came up at Samsuddinpur (founded by Illias Samsuddin) and Hajipur (founded by Haji Illias) in the manner stated above, a few more towns carrying other functions were also founded

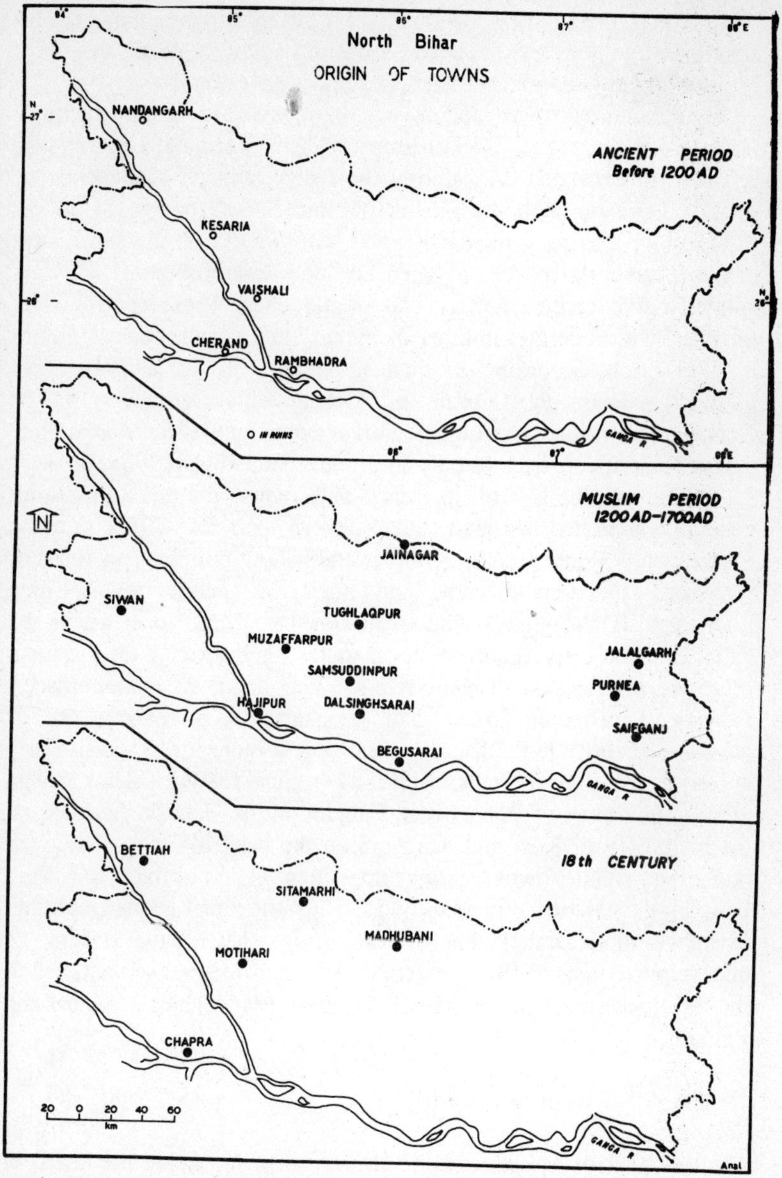

Fig. 3.1 Origin of towns; ancient period before A.D. 1200, Muslim A.D. 1200 A.D. 1700 and 18th century.

by the then rulers. For example, 'Saifganj' (Katihar) was founded as a marketing centre by Nawab Saif Khan, a Fauzdar of Purnea (Chaudhury, 1963, p. 720). Similarly Muzaffarpur was established for administrative purposes by one Muzaffar Khan, a local vassal of Hajipur Sarkar (Chaudhury, 1958, p. 232).

A maximum growth and revival of towns, during the medieval time, took place in the reign of Emperor Akbar (Ahmad, 1956, p. 44); this growth exceeded only during the British and post-independence periods. Division of the Mughal empire into *Subah* (province), *Sarkar* (division), *Dastur* (district) and *Mahal* (sub-division) for administrative purposes resulted in the establishment of new administrative centres and revival of old ones. These centres were provided with a certain number of infantry and cavalary and a fort of mud or brick, according to their importance in the administrative hierarchy. Thus, the *Sarkar* of Tirhut, with Darbhanga as its Headquarters formed the biggest *Sarkar* containing 102 *Mahals* while that of Hajipur consisted of only 11 *Mahals* (Chaudhury, 1958, p. 144).

Taking advantages of its roads and rivers, the Muslim armies generally marched through the southern part of Tirhut *Sarkar*. Consequently, local granaries, *sarais* and halting points along roads or river-road junctions became the nuclei of future towns, like, Lheriasarai, Dalsinghsarai and Begusarai, etc. These *sarai* towns are situated at the convergence of local routes; their spacing on the main routes is a reflection of their relative importance as resting places. Advent of economic peace and prosperity as a consequence of increased security led to the growth of a few more towns, particularly at ferry-points on river banks with road terminal facilities. Thus, Siwan grew on the bank of Daha River, Lalganj on the Gandak, Saifganj on the bank of Kali Kosi and Karagola on the bank of Kosi. Moreover, numerous small towns sprang up, often at cross-road locations, between the existing principal towns. Thus, the nodal towns came into existence. It is noted that allocation, by the Mughal rulers, of undeveloped areas to Hindu chieftains or other imperial servants led to the development of towns like Kishenganj, Madhubani, Motihari and Bettiah.

Origin of Towns in 18th Century

The downfall of Mughal empire in the years, following the death of Aurangzeb, led to the erosion of the central authority so that some of the *subedars, sirdars* or rulers declared their territories independent or semi-independent. Consequently, Darbhanga and Bettiah raj developed as separate entities. Their administrative headquarters, namely, Bettiah and Darbhanga, developed into large trading centres (Fig. 3.1). The other important trading centres developed in that period were Motihari, Sitamarhi and Hajipur. The local chiefs built their fortresses near the pre-existing urban centres. Such a fortress is noted at Subhankarpur near Darbhanga; the settlement here also functioned as an industrial and trading centre. Later, the growth in trade and commerce favoured a few villages to outgrow into towns. A few others were developed on the ruins of former sites on river bank in order to exercise greater administrative hold over the far-flung territories of the *Subah*. Thus, the *Sarkar* headquarters of Muzaffarpur, Purnea and Samastipur, at their former sites, flourished enormously.

The British Period

The scope for trade and commerce had greatly increased in the region by the last quarter of the 18th century. Feeder roads terminating on river banks provided the most advantageous sites for town growth in this period. Thus, a large number of towns were established or developed on river banks by the Britishers on European pattern (Fig. 3.2).

North Bihar came under direct British rule in 1858. This led to several improvements in the region which directly or indirectly helped in the growth of a large number of towns, but adversely affected others. The volume of trade increased greatly with the increase in the attention paid to the safety of traders and the trade routes. Steamer traffic also increased in the Ganga with the result that there was a regular plying of steamer between Patna and other parts of North Bihar. Thus, the towns of Revelganj, Chapra, Manihari, Karagola, Naugachhia, Lalganj, etc., appeared as trading centres in this period. Similarly Rosera and Khagaria developed on the bank of the Burhi Gandak River. Most of the towns of this period were engaged in the trade of indigo.

Introduction of Railways and Growth of Towns

Two most notable developments that paved the way for urban growth, during this period, were the introduction of railways and improvement

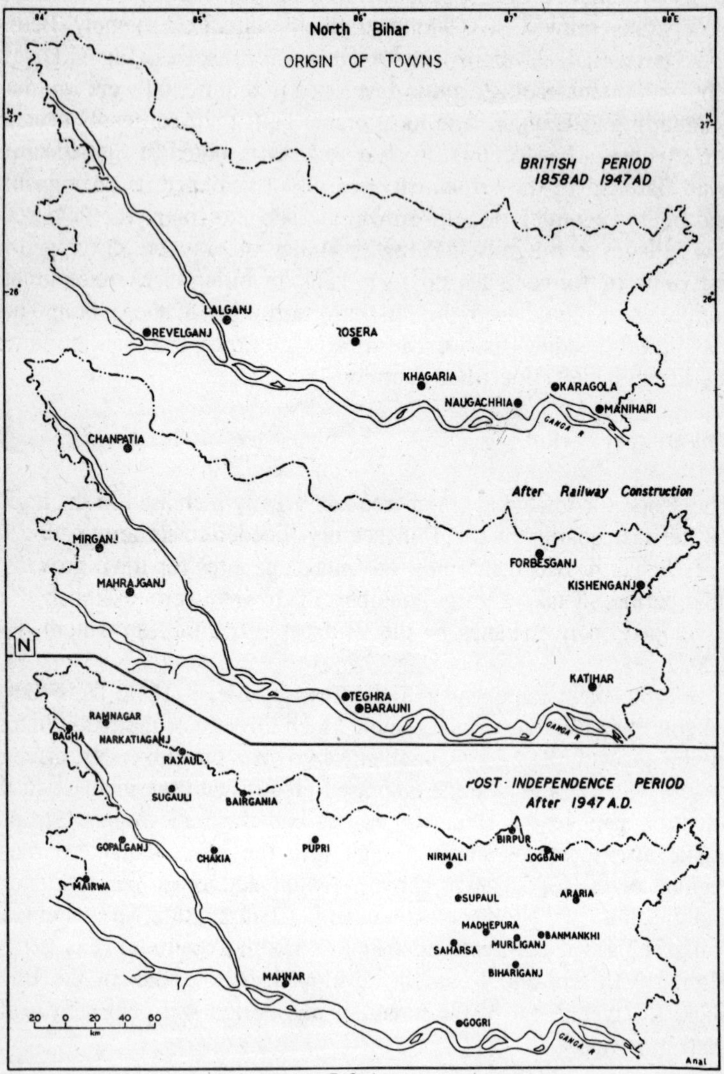

Fig. 3.2: Origin of towns; British period A.D. 1858, A.D. 1947; after railway construction, and post-independence period after A.D. 1947.

of the existing roads. The impact of the railways has been of considerable significance. They not only interlinked the pre-existing established towns but also attracted town development at sites with rail facilities. Also, a gravitational change in the location of commercial centres from inland marts to railway sites took place. As the rail-net expanded, branch feeder lines were provided with the sole objective of the maintenance of law and order so that a better administrative control can be had over the region. The phenomenal growth in trade and commerce, following the construction of the rail network, was not foreseen at that time. Thus, new administrative centres, preferably with rail facilities, were established which attracted trade and commerce. The development of towns, like, Katihar, Barauni, Mahrajganj, Mirganj, Siwan, Chanpatia, Teghra, Narkatiaganj and Forbesganj, has taken place in this manner (Fig.3.2).

A number of both small and large scale industries, including rice, oil, flour, sugar, jute mills, taking advantages of cheap and efficient rail haulage of raw materials, were soon established at these centres. This favoured the further growth and expansion of these towns. The former trade centres of Revelganj, Lalganj and Mahrajganj located on river banks declined in importance as they lay far off from rail communication which had overtaken river traffic.

Among the various measures taken to improve the civic amenities in urban centres, in the British period, mention may be made of the creation of civic bodies, such as municipalities and Notified Areas and town area committees. The residential needs of the people engaged in civil administration led to the establishment of the civil lines at district and sub-divisional headquarters; these were generally developed outside the town limits as the Britishers wanted to keep the civil administration aloof from the town folk. Limitation of space in the older core of the town besides its congestion and unhygienic conditions were other factors which also favoured the separate growth of the civil lines. Better civic amenities in the civil lines later attracted several rural-rich of the adjacent villages to build their residences there. Sometimes villages in close proximity of the civil lines were put under one urban unit. All these factors favoured the growth and expansion of the district and sub-divisional headquarters. A few British officers under whom the municipal organisation worked took keen interest in the prosperity of the town and have left their imprint in the form of markets, such as Revelganj, Forbesganj, Lalganj, Rosera and Kishenganj.

Growth of Towns in Post-Independence Period

This period can be characterised as one of active urban developments in North Bihar. The factors that led to the origin and growth of towns in the part now became more active and vigorous. The phenomenon of urban growth has undergone marked change in the form and size of town, whereas a number of new towns have also been added. Before, independence, only the market centres favourably located on railways were showing a marked growth, but the development of road transport in the post-independence period led to a phenomenal growth in long-distance haulage of goods and merchandise by trucks and passenger movement in buses over long and short distances. This necessarily required development of facilities of various kinds, including repairs, food and drink, besides re-fuelling at way side stations or halting places. Consequently, a few villages located along the roads or at road junction acquired urban characteristics. It has not only helped to withdraw some of the pressure that would have been otherwise put on the already over-burdened railways but also led to some de-centralisation of the urban growth.

A large number of new towns, namely, Saharsa, Madhepura, Araria, Supaul, Dumara, Luthaha and Naugachhia, have developed as a consequence of rapid increase in rural population as a consequence of agricultural prosperity and better medical facilities and establishment of block-offices, besides development of sub-divisional and district headquarters (Fig. 3.2). In the wake of the green revolution, a number of villages with road or railway facilities developed into service centres, providing various inputs for agriculture, repair of agricultural implements, banking and credit facilities as also outlets for their surplus products. They soon became centres of trade and commerce. Thus, in the last two decades have grown the new towns of Raxaul Bazar, Ramnagar, Bagaha, Bairgania, Puri, Chakia, Mairwa, Saharsa, Supaul, Gopalganj, Sugauli, Mahnar Bazar, Nirmali, Birpur, Kasba, Banmankhi Bazar, Bihariganj, Murliganj and Gogri. These towns also fulfil certain administrative functions.

With the construction of the rail-cum-road bridge over the Ganga, near Mokameh, North Bihar has developed direct links with the mineral-rich belt of South Bihar and it is expected that both Barauni and Begusarai will have large industrial complexes in a few years. Also construction of the Kosi barrage has accelerated the growth of Nirmali and Birpur as important urban centres. However, the most important factor favouring growth and expansion of towns in North Bihar, in the post-independence period has been the establishment of agro-based industries, particularly sugar, jute, rice and oilseeds. Towns, like, Katihar, Samastipur, Forbesganj, Banmankhi Bazar, Jainagar and Jogbani, have experienced rapid growth after the establishment of these industries. The older towns of Bettiah, Chapra, Motihari and Purnea, which are industrially backward, have experienced relatively slower growth.

The facilities for higher or technical education in the pre-existing towns have attracted young men and women from the villages to these centres but the charm of urban life has been so great that once they complete their education they almost do not want to return to their rural habitat. It is noted that the towns of Darbhanga and Muzaffarpur have grown in size subsequent to the establishment of fulfledged universities at these places. It is evident that spread of the build-up areas has generally made a far greater contribution than has physical re-organisation of the urban space. Re-development or re-generation of town often results in changes in its built-up area. The natural factors generally remain static or inactive, but these are subject to modification by human culture. Smailes (1966) observes that it is the human or cultural factors which give the essential form, shape and sustenance to the town on a particular site according to the needs of age. Filling up vacant space in towns with multi-nuclear growth, and subsequent filling up space in post-independence period have resulted into the change in built-up area. Consequently, re-generation is taking place in the core area of larger towns, namely, Muzaffarpur, Darbhanga and Katihar. While examining the structure of Indian cities, Smailes (1968) notes that much of the massive extension and infilling of urban areas since 1947 is easily recognisable in its forms as pertaining to a new morphological period. It is observed that recently some towns of North Bihar have grown from centrally located villages that have easy accessibility, imparted either by roads or railways or both. Enormous developments in trade and commerce with the provision of better transport facilities have led to human agglomeration at these sites.

The above analysis reveals that the earliest towns of North Bihar grew to meet the needs of defence, administrative expediency and political strategy. These towns were generally located on the banks of rivers which were then the main arteries of trade and commerce. Performance of religious and cultural rites also favoured the growth of a few towns on the numerous *ghats* along the Ganga and the Gandak rivers (Plate 3).

Plate 3: Konhara Ghat Nepali temple at Hajipur, sited at the left bank of the Gandak River.

In the Muslim periods the needs of administration for the development of trade and commerce led to the growth of a number of towns purely as trade and distributing and collecting centres. During the British rule, although the administrative and political strategy was responsible for the development of many towns, the development of commerce and trade led to the growth of a number of towns purely as trade centre. The growth of railway also led to the growth of a number of towns. It is, however, an obvious fact that the railways, by bringing in their wake facilities for commerce and industries, have remarkably fostered the growth of the town along their routes (Ahmad, 1979, p. 162). The growth of market town as a consequence of overgrown villages is the product of recent time.

REFERENCES

Ahmad, E. (1956): "Origin and Evolution of Towns in U.P." *Geographical Outlook*, 1, pp. 38-58.

Ahmad, E. (1979): *Social and Geographical Aspects of Human Settlements*. Classical Publications, New Delhi.

Chaudhury, P.C.R. (1958): *Bihar District Gazetteers. Muzaffarpur*, Secretariat Press, Bihar, Patna.

Chaudhury, P.C.R. (1960): *Bihar District Gazetteers. Champaran*, Secretariat Press, Bihar, Patna.

Chaudhury, P.C.R. (1963): *Bihar District Gazetteers.*, Purnea, Secretariat Press, Bihar, Patna.

Chaudhury, P.C.R. (1964): *Bihar District Gazetteers. Darbhanga*, Secretariat Press, Bihar, Patna.

Dickinson, R.E. (1948): "The Scope and Status of Urban Geography", in H.M. Mayer and C.F. Kohn, (Eds.) (1967): *Readings in Urban Geography*, Allahabad, pp. 10-26.

Diwakar, R.R. (Ed.) (1957): *Bihar Through the Ages*, Orient Longmans, Bombay.

Pandey, M.S. (1964): *Historical Geography and Topography of Bihar*, Motilal Banarasidas, Varanasi.

Prasad, K. (1975): Was Cherund a Kusan Town. *Proceedings* of 36th Session of Indian History Congress, Aligarh, pp. 43-49.

Singh, S.C. (1973): "Changes in the Courses of Rivers and their Effects on Urban Settlement in the Middle Ganga plain", N.G.S.I., Varanasi.

Smailes, A.E. (1966): *Geography of Towns*, London.

Smailes, A.E. (1973): "Indian City Structure". In R.L. Singh (Ed.), *Urban Geography in Developing Countries*. N.G.S.I., Varanasi, pp. 50-59.

Taneja, K.L. (1971): *Morphology of Indian Cities*. N.G.S.I. Research Publication No. 7, Varanasi.

4

GENERAL MORPHOLOGICAL CHARACTERISTICS OF TOWNS

THE MORPHOLOGICAL aspects of a town are highly important and diagnostic (Ahmad, 1976, p.295). Both the processes of town formation and development of an organic form are quite similar to the concept of landform evolution. In other words, as the geomorphic landscape is a function of structure, process and stage, the morphology of a town is largely the function of site factors, historical vicissitudes, impact of successive cultures and economic setting and development (Ahmad, 1976, p.295). Three stages in the developmental biology of an embryo have been recognised, i.e.

(i) histogenesis,
(ii) pattern formation, and
(iii) morphogenesis (Wolpert, 1967, p.85).

Histogenesis is the process of transformation occurring with time in a cell or group of cells in the biological realm' whereas pattern formation describes mainly the differences in space rather than in time. The pattern is defined as an arrangement of parts that suggests a design or orderly distribution. In developmental biology, the term pattern denotes the non-random occurrence of given cell types, or their products, in the organism (Ursprung, 1966, p.177). The morphogenesis is the successive growth like development of flesh on the skeleton of body (Taneja, 1973, p.37).

The present structure and characteristics of a town cannot be comprehended without an understanding of the historical background which led to its origin and subsequent growth. Thus, histogenesis attempts to describe the historical events that lead to town formation and later growth. Developments of roads and streets lead to pattern formation, resulting in the development of various nuclei of human agglomerations. In fact, they constitute the skeletal frame-work of town. Morphogenesis, however, relates to transformation which takes place after pattern formation, i.e., development of roads, streets and paths with lapse of time and multi-phased development in various spheres (social, cultural and economic) (Singh, 1971, p.8). In this context, a town is treated as a living organism, because the development of the built-up area along roads, streets and lanes occurs gradually as in any organic form.

Town Growth Model

The three well-known theoretical models of urban growth, namely, the concentric zone theory of Burgess (1925), the sector theory of Hoyt (1939) and multiple nuclei theory of Harris and Ullman (1945) are applicable only in limited degree to various towns of North Bihar.

Concentric Zone Theory

It is one of the early models of urban form arose from observation that towns developed outward from their central area more or less consistently in all directions (Thomas, 1975, p.89). Burgess recognised a concentric patterning to the land-use of city in terms of five concentric zones, namely, the central business area, wholesale light manufacturing, low-class residential, medium-class residential and high-class residential (Fig. 4.3A). Thus, land-use tended to sort themselves into reasonably consistent and regular concentric zones. This model, however, provides a successful description of urban growth.

Sector Theory

It provides that growth takes place along a particular axis of transportation usually consisting of similar types of land-use (Fig. 4.3B). The whole town is considered as a circle and the various areas as sectors radiating out from the centre of the town. Similar types of land-use tend to be arranged in sector radiating outward toward the periphery. This theory treats industry more realistically and accommodates the process of residential expansion.

Multiple Nuclei Theory

This model had a fundamentally cellular structure focused about growth points (Fig. 4.3C). They suggest that frequently the land-use pattern of a town is built around several nuclei rather than around a single centre. The number and position of the growth points depended upon the size of the town, the site condition and upon its historical development. Thus, this theory provides an indication of the way in which the urban area develops, of the precise nature of expected developments which might take place in association with existing nuclei.

These growth models seem to be woven into the fabric of any town in North Bihar which explain the development process in the growth of built-up areas.

Developmental Pattern

Colby (1933) observes that centripetal and centrifugal forces play dominant roles in town formation throughout the three stages of urban growth mentioned above. In the first stage, a set of centripetal forces originates with the formation of the main nucleus leading to concentric development of the built-up area. Religious nuclei, namely, temple, mosque and church, act as gravitational forces for the concentration of human agglomerations. The same is true of industrial establishments, administrative centres and educational institutions. In the second stage, institutions set up earlier operate as powerful magnets, attracting similar functional characteristics. This is known as 'functional magnetism' (Colby, 1933). In the third stage, centripetal forces lead to the concentration of rich business groups to sites in the central zone. Concentration of commercial and business activities in the central areas of the town activates centrifugal forces leading to the shifting of residential areas towards the outer margins of town. Thus, centripetal forces lead to concentric growth pattern in town development whereas centrifugal forces favour peripheral growth and expansion, including growth of residential areas on vacant and low-priced land in the outer margins, which is particularly favoured by people desirous of open-space and healthy living. Besides, existence of wide roads, suitable transportation facilities, good drainage and scope for better civic amenities promote outward growth.

It is evident that centrifugal forces are made up of a merging of impulses, namely a desire to leave one part of the urban area and an urge to go to another (Colby, 1933, p.292). Shifting of establishments from their original locations is mainly attributable to availability of better amenities in all respects, at alternative sites, particularly availability of large areas of cheap land and adequate transportation facilities. Traffic congestion and high cost of transportation in the central zone often forces various users to look for alternative sites on the outskirts of the town. Consequently an impulse towards shift is created and such force is termed as spatial force (Colby, 1933). The industrial establishments on the outskirts also become gravitational centres generating centrifugal forces from the inner zone of the town. Similarly, the educational and administrative set up also attract planned functional developments; this is known as situation force.

These forces are generally active in the outward expansion and growth of towns. Nevertheless, both physical and cultural factors play important roles in the concentric development around various nuclei as well as in the development of roads and streets. Thus, the town plan can be regarded, in some respects, as an embodiment of human relationship both in space and time; 'it is a mosaic whose different parts, growing in successive periods, show the varied interplay between geographical conditions and man's ever changing activities' (Davier, 1933, p.25).

General Pattern of Town Growth

Keeping in view the various processes and forces of town development, the growth characteristics of a few selected towns of North Bihar can be surveyed (Figs. 4.1 and 4.2).

Let us first take *Darbhanga* (pop. 1,32,059 in 1971). It is the largest town of North Bihar. It probably takes its name from one Darbhangi Khan, a Muslim free-booter of whom 'little is known' (Chaudhury, 1964, p.710). The city is situated on the eastern bank of the little Baghmati River, which flows N-S and is spanned by two large iron girder bridges. It first nucleated around Mirzapur which is an ideal site from the point of view of defence and is free from floods. This town grew prominently in the Mughal period when other nuclei, namely, Bakerganj, Rasulpur and Kadirabad, developed and subsequently engulfed each other by settling process. In the early British period, a

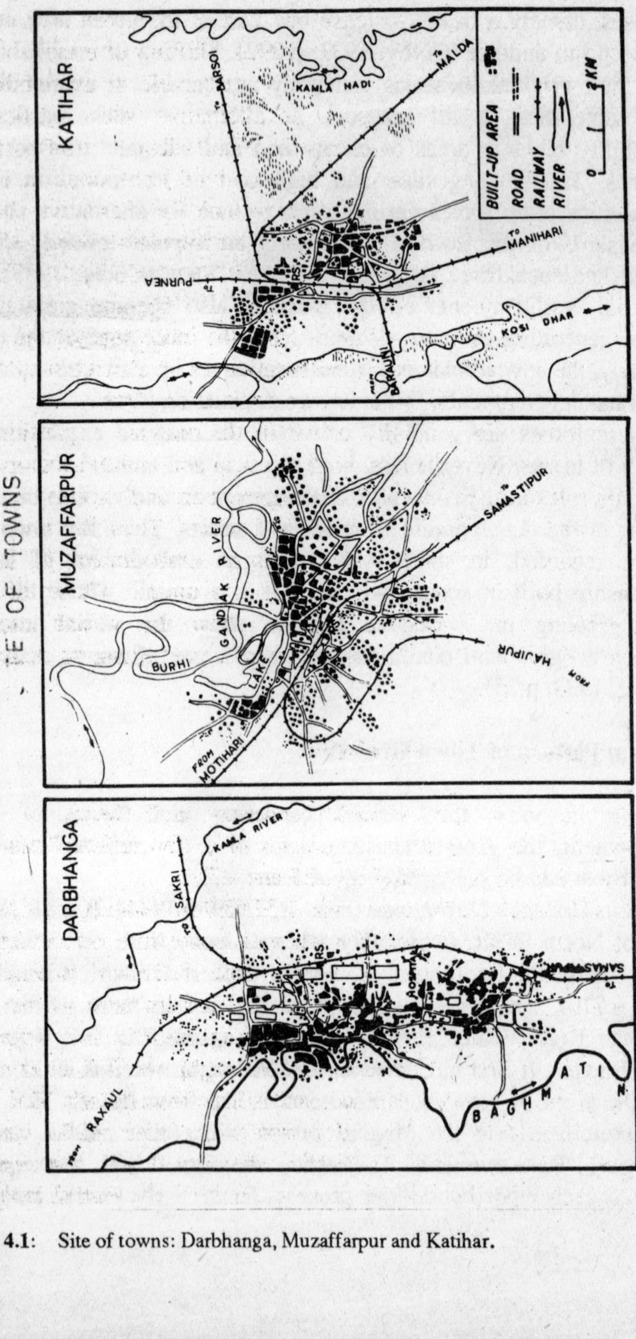

Fig. 4.1: Site of towns: Darbhanga, Muzaffarpur and Katihar.

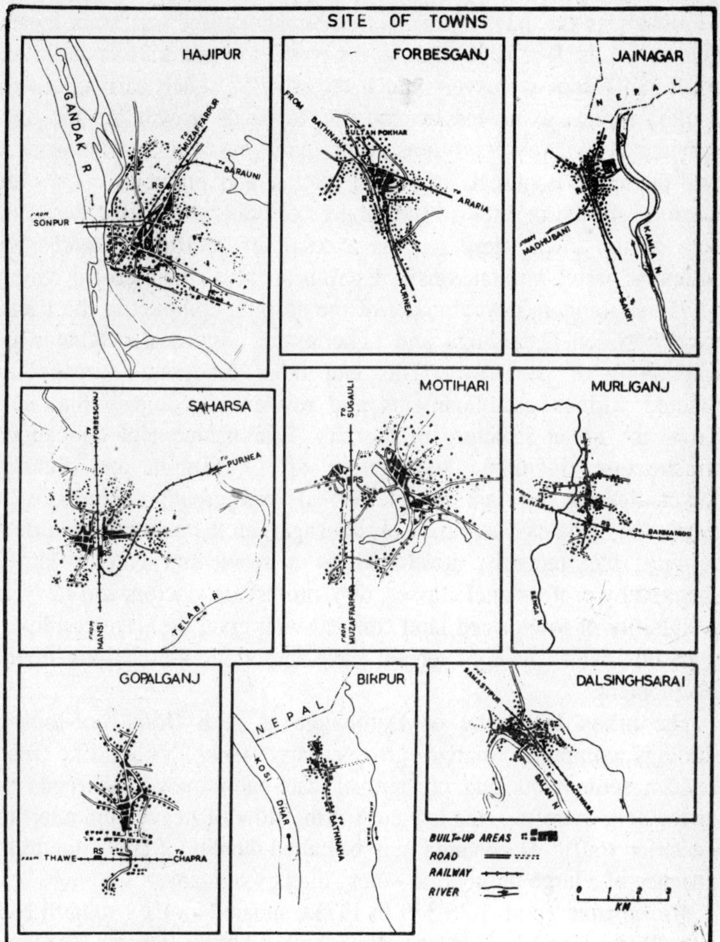

Fig. 4.2: Site of Towns: Hajipur, Forbesganj, Jainagar, Saharsa, Motihari, Murliganj, Gopalganj, Birpur, and Dalsinghsarai.

prominent nucleus developed at Subhankarpur under the patronage of the Maharaja of Darbhanga. This township was developed by the Maharaja as a separate entity from the main Muslim settlement. Still later, the administrative headquarters of the Darbhanga Raj was shifted to Lalbagh as the former nucleus of Subhankarpur was occasionally liable to floods. It is noted that, in the process of pattern formation, the centrifugal forces were very much effective as stated earlier, but the situation force was no less responsible for such growth. As the town experienced swampy conditions in the rainy season due to inundations from the little Baghmati, the civil station and public offices were, therefore, shifted in 1884 to the suburbs of Laheriasarai that lay to the south of the town. Here too, as a result of centrifugal forces, the settlement grew simultaneously. Establishment of the medical college in 1951 subsequent development of the hospital complex in the vacant space, between Darbhanga and Laheriasarai, vigorously changed the morphology of the town. This and other functional forces have attracted various establishments and residential colonies that have shaped the urban structure of the city. Establishment of educational infrastructure, including the setting up of Mithila and Sanskrit Universities in the last decade or so, has greatly influenced its morphology (Plates 4 and 5). Lakshmisagar, on the eastern outskirts of the city, has recently developed as a residential colony largely inhabited by professional classes, like, professors, doctors and lawyers. Availability of low-priced land coupled with good drainage conditions in an otherwise swampy terrain have important motivations in this development.

The urban landscape of Darbhanga as seen from roof-tops of buildings comprises mango groves, large tanks, ribbon-like roads between settlements and clusters of date-palm trees. The roads are narrow and, therefore, inadequate for the flow of heavy vehicular and pedestrian traffic. Darbhanga may be called the city of tanks due to the existence of a large number of watery ditches and tanks.

Muzaffarpur (pop. 1,26,379 in 1971), situated on the southern bank of the Burhi Gandak, is the headquarters of Tirhut division. The town was founded sometimes in the 18th century by Muzaffar Khan, a vassal owing allegiance to the Mughals of Delhi Durbar (Chaudhury, 1958, p.232). The earliest settlement grew here in concentric form at Sikandarpur, in the northern part of the town. Its second nucleus at Purani Bazar developed as the commercial hub of the town. A large number of people migrated to this area. Various centripetal and

Plate 4: A view of K.S.D. Sanskrit University housed in the Lakshmishwar Vilas Palace at Darbhanga.

Plate 5: A view L.N. Mithila University housed in the former Raj Palace at Darbhanga.

centrifugal forces of functional magnetism led to radial sectoral development of settlements in this part. Later, the town became the regional headquarters of various educational institutions; their gravitational attraction has led to further concentration of population. The establishment of Khadi industry at Kanhauli has further paved the way for filling up of the vacant space in the eastern part of the town. Subsequent to the shifting of functional areas due to operation of centrifugal forces also led to further expansion of the town. The earthquake of 1934 made a clean sweep of the congested localities of the town. It proved a blessing in disguise because not only new residential colonies, military cantonment and civil lines grew up at fresh sites but new constructions came up in the ruined areas. Availability of vacant space promoted the development of shopping area along the interconnecting roads in Purani Bazar, Kalyani and Saraiyaganj. This led to a complete transformation of the town morphology. In future, the town is likely to expand towards the south-east along the national highway. Though Muzaffarpur initially experienced multi-nuclear development, it has now assumed a compact form, which is largely because of its topographic characteristics.

Katihar (pop. 80,121 in 1971), formerly known as Saifganj, is said to have been established by Nawab Saif Khan (Chaudhury, 1963, p.720). This urban settlement frist grew in concentric form in and around the old site of Saifganj. Its outward growth has been somewhat restricted due to the presence of the Kali Kosi and the Kamla rivers on the west and east of the town, respectively. As it happened to be an important administrative centre during the Muslim period, many roads converged here from different parts of North Bihar. Consequently, a market developed along the main artery in a ribbon-like pattern. Mangal Bazar can be cited as an example of this type of growth. The town assumed a triangular shape with the coming up of the railways. Subsequently, numerous nuclei grew in haphazard manner on relatively higher grounds within the town; these include parts of Durgapur, Dalan, Mirchai and Baigana. Extension of built-up area towards the south and north later took place due to functional magnetism of the establishment of jute and flour mills and development of railway colonies, respectively. The expansion towards the east has been mainly under the impulse of outward growth from the congested core. Quite interesting is the growth of Civil Lines in the north-western part where the built-up area has developed in a linear fashion. Thus, Katihar exhibits multi-nuclear growth which has been largely ordained by the existence of low-lying tracts between various nuclei; these tracts get flooded during the rains. Recently, the town has been rapidly expanding west of the railway line where a planned residential colony is coming up. Though the multi-nuclear growth of the town has been initially determined by topographic variations, the subsequent development of functional magnetism, provided by industrial and administrative establishments, besides residential colonies, is expected to bring in important changes in its existing morphology.

Hajipur town, with a population of 41,890 in 1971, is situated on the eastern bank of the Gandak River, close to its confluence with the Ganga. It was founded by one Haji Illyas Samsuddin between 1345-1358 A.D. In the initial stage, its strategic location on the river bank, permitting navigation in three directions, gave the town considerable importance both for defence and commerce. Consequently, a large fort was built here whose ramparts are still evident. The town first grew in an elongated form on the high bank of the Gandak River. The Jama Masjid is supposed to be the focal point of this growth. Another nuclear growth took place in the neighbourhood of Konhara Ghat where Hindu pilgrims took sacred bath in the Gandak on religious occasions. Subsequently, Rambhadra and Ramchaura developed as Hindu nuclei and Dighi and Anwarpur as Muslim nuclei. It may be observed that these nuclei grew rather independently outwards from their core.

The assimilation process started in the British period, particularly after the construction of the railway lines which fostered town growth. Mention has to be made here of the shift in the site of the world-famous Harihar-Kshetra Mela (cattle-fair), which was formerly held at Hajipur, to Sonpur after the construction of the railway bridge over the Gandak. The old Mela site has now grown as a residential area. Thus, the present townscape is an amalgam of the abovementioned nuclei that developed during the medieval and modern times and subsequently submerging each other under the stress and strain of various centripetal and centrifugal forces of functional magnetism.

Motihari (pop. 40,352 in 1971) is situated on the banks of two ox-bow lakes which probably mark former course of the Dhanauti River, a tributary of the Gandak. Consequently its townscape has been largely affected by these water bodies. The earliest settlements started at Gudari Bazar which is now a trading centre of the town. It initially grew in concentric form but soon another nucleus grew at Meena Bazar which paved the way for town expansion towards the east. In the British period, various administrative offices were set up in the western part of the town, close to the railway lines that lie farther west. It is noted that the western lake divides Motihari into two distinct morphological units. East of the lake lie the older settlements of Gudari and Meena Bazars in the north and the residential-cum-industrial quarters of Bhawanipur Zerat in the south. But the area west of the lake, formerly occupied by European residences, has now developed into a compact and congested zone; it also has various administrative offices. The earthquake of 1934 destroyed more than 60 per cent of the residential houses and made inhabitable at least another 25 per cent (Chaudhury, 1960, p. 577). Consequently, a new urban profile came into existence as most of the buildings had to be re-built. The civil lines, then located in the western part, was subsequently shifted farther west to Luathaha. Later, an important industrial nucleus, comprising small rice and flour mills, developed in Chota Baniapur which now hums with commercial activity. The professional classes, formerly residing in the central zone, have now preferred to move out to the newly developed residential colony in Bhawanipur Zerat located on the southern periphery of the town, close to the eastern ox-bow lake. Thus, the urban fabric of Motihari, which initially developed in concentric form, now presents a somewhat spread-out demeanour.

Forbesganj (pop. 21,198 in 1971) town was founded by A.J. Forbes, the former proprietor of Sultanpur Estate. It is an important trading centre between India and Nepal, the earliest settlement grew here also in a nucleated form around Sultan Pokhar. Later, with the construction of the railways, the town expanded towards south along Sadar Bazar road and assumed an elongated shape. The subsequent establishment of administrative offices in Pokharbasti in the central part and development of 'Jute Mandi' in Hathikhola, west of the rail-track, led to its multi-nuclear growth. Still later, establishment of rice and oil mills, besides other industries, towards the south along the Purnea road has given it a triangular shape. It is expected that any further growth of settlements along the Purnea road will further aggravate the existing townscape.

Saharsa (pop. 23,217 in 1971) is a town of recent growth in the Kosi region. Its pre-urban landscape comprised villages with temporary hutments, muddy tracks and thick vegetation of *Kans* and *Pater*. The present townscape has developed in successive phases through multi-nuclear growth that generally took concentric form. The urban activity is concentrated in the vicinity of the railway junction that lies two km west of Saharsa village; it is the focal point of the town. The civil line-cum-administrative zone has developed in the north-western part of the town, about three km north of the railway station. Growth of settlements in these parts has led to a subtle transformation of the rural habitat. Thus, houses with thatched roofs have been replaced by *pucca* quarters and bungalows, particularly in the western part of the Civil Lines. Developed open spaces and agricultural land are found in the midst of built-up areas in Gangzala and Nariar. A recent expansion in the built-up area has taken place in Kayastha Tola towards the south. Another nucleus has developed in the north, lying to the east of the railway line; it is mostly residential in character. Thus, the built-up area of the town has multiplied four times in a small span of two decades. It is, however, noted that the commercial area has developed rather haphazardly around Chandni Chowk and Mahabir Chowk, close to the railway station and sandwiched between the rail-track on the east and Mir Tola on the west. Outward movement is expected to take place in future from this congested and compact zone. Thus, it is evident that the town of Saharsa, which has emerged from various nuclei exhibits a mixed urban-rural complexion with three storeyed *pucca* buildings occurring side by side with thatch-roofed houses.

Murliganj (pop. 12,688 in 1971) is also a newly emerged town of the Kosi region. It is situated on the banks of the Benga River, a former channel of the Kosi River that has migrated westwards. The town initially grew at Gol Bazar, which now represents its commercial as well as residential kernel. Its subsequent expansion has taken place towards the north and the east. In the wake of this expansion a few villages adjoining the commercial zone, namely, Panchgachhia in the south, Jairampur and Tapra Tola in the west (across the river) and Ghachha Tola in the north, have been overwhelmed and incorporated in the town area. As a result of this process of urban growth, a few residential hutments have been converted into shopping centres. The town is still experiencing multi-nuclear growth as large tracts of agricultural land are found between the various nuclei. Filling up of these open spaces may take place in future with the establishment of industries and construction of public offices and residential quarters.

Birpur (pop. 10,103 in 1971) has grown into a town subsequent to the construction of the Kosi Barrage. It is located in Saharsa district, only a few kilometres to the south of the Indo-Nepal international boundary. Originally Birpur consisted of a cluster of hamlets that were generally isolated and cut-off in the rainy season due to the flood ravages of the Kosi. The development of this township began from early 1955 with the construction of the main Kosi barrage whose site lay a few kilometres to the west in Nepal.

As the process of colonisation grew in intensity with the increasing pace of construction of the Kosi barrage, the small number of merchants and shop-keepers of Birpur village were literally overwhelmed by the large influx of population from outside. With the selection of Birpur as the sub-district headquarters in 1975, an all round development in built-up area is inevitable which ultimately may give it a concentric form.

Gopalganj (pop. 17,253 in 1971) town has grown out of the tiny hamlet of the same name. Initially, its pace of urbanisation has been very slow. But it has developed considerably since 1957, subsequent to the construction of the railway lines (Siwan-Chapra loop) and establishment of a sugar refinery in the southern part of the town at Harakhuwa; the latter, in particular, brought commercial prosperity to this township. Its elevation as the district headquarters of the newly formed district of Gopalganj, in 1975, paved the way for its further growth which ultimately resulted in the inclusion of a number of neighbouring villages within the town limits. The town has enough scope for development with the expansion of road and rail facilities in the area. It has just started growing outwards in a haphazard manner, largely due to availability of low cost vacant land.

Jainagar (pop. 9,917 in 1971) town is situated on the western bank of the Kamla-Balan River. It is the northernmost terminus of rail and road transports in North Bihar and, in fact, is the gateway to Nepal. Its location on the Indo-Nepal border makes it important both commercially and strategically. The town has experienced successive periods of growth and decline during the medieval times. The earliest settlement grew in the 16th century around a mud fort, now in ruins (Chaudhury, 1964, p.118). Later, the town was abandoned by its rulers, which led to its subsequent decay and decline. However, it again started growing up during the British period because of its strategic location in controlling the movement of trade and commerce to and from Nepal. The present expansion of town has taken place in a ribbon-like pattern, along the main N-S road running parallel to the railway line. Its linear growth has been also favoured by the location of a rice mill on the northern outskirts of the town.

After a discussion of the various developmental processes active in the formation of the town pattern in North Bihar, it is pertinent to analyse this pattern under two aspects, namely (i) The Internal Plan, and (ii) The External Form.

The Internal Plan

Road Pattern

Roads and streets act as arteries and veins of a town; they greatly affect its internal morphology and external form. Formation of roads and streets generally takes place to meet the needs of interaction between various nodes, clots, nuclei or continuum of human agglomerations. The road pattern of a town is largely influenced by its site conditions, historical and cultural background and functional characteristics. Transportation is an integral thread of urban fabric, which in turn is affected by the road pattern. Topographic features, like, swamps, water bodies, steep slopes, cliffs and unstable terrains, greatly affect the development of roads; they act as physical constraints in transport and communication, and their imprint is often reflected in the road pattern.

The road patterns of Muzaffarpur, Katihar and Darbhanga are quite different from those of other towns of North Bihar due to topographical conditions (Figs. 4.3, 4.4, 4.5 and 4.6). Development of parallel roads along the river bank has taken place in case of towns sited along rivers. This is very much in evidence at Darbhanga where roads run N-S, parallel to the Baghmati River. Similar road patterns are also observed at Hajipur and Chapra where the main roads run parallel to the crest of the natural levees of the Gandak and Ghaghra rivers, respectively.

However, the towns of North Bihar do not exhibit any one type of road pattern. It is often a combination of several arrangements. Haphazard or irregular growth is characteristic of most of these towns; this is particularly true of towns with checkered historical antecedents (Ahmed, 1976, p.292). The roads and streets of these towns are mostly short, zig-zag, unplanned and irregular. Irregularity of roads is typical of the remain commercial areas which are also the most congested. Planned grid-iron or radial pattern of roads may be found in some parts of a few towns where re-generation or re-construction has taken place subsequent to their partial destruction. Examples of this pattern are

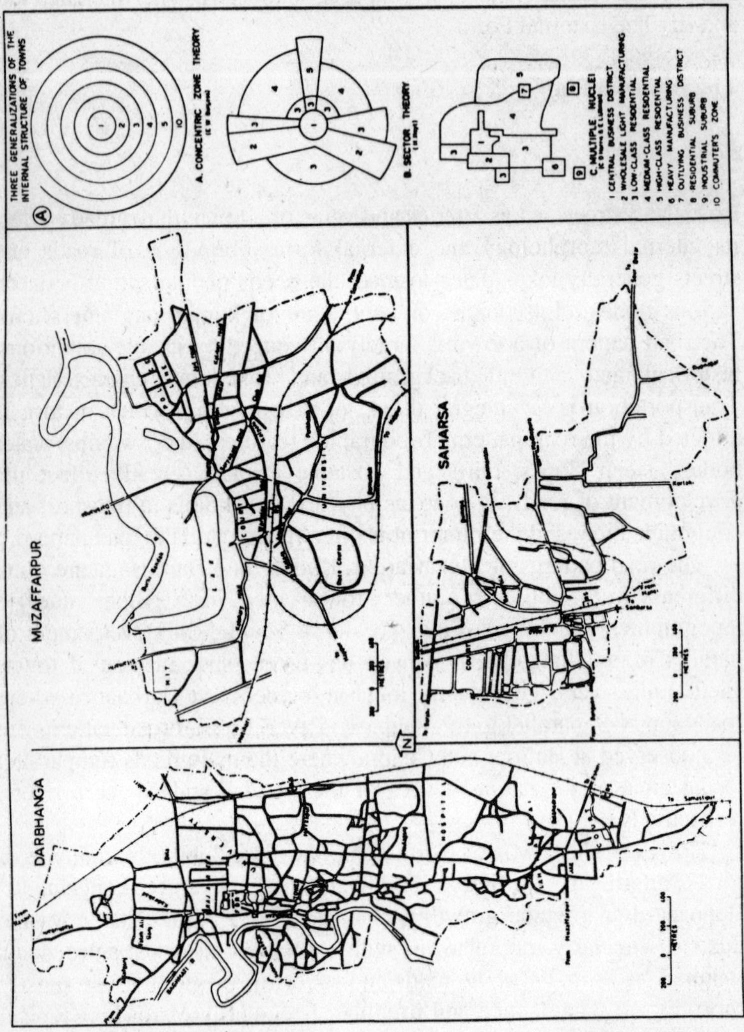

Fig. 4.3: Road pattern: Darbhanga, Muzaffarpur, Saharsa A. Three generalisation of the internal structure of towns.

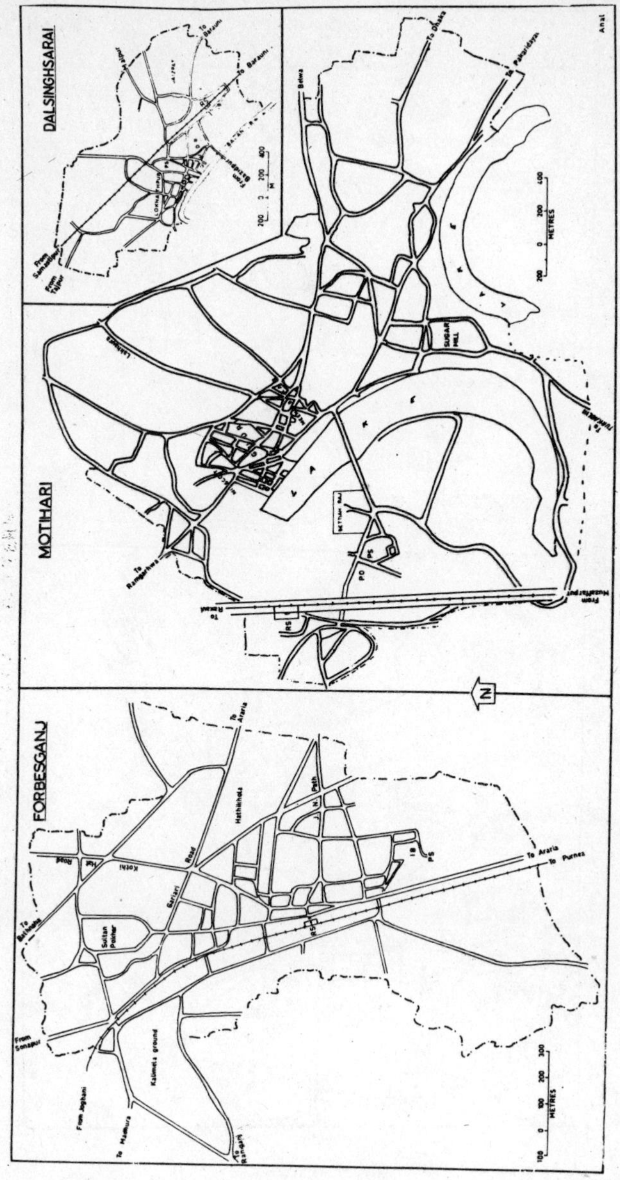

Fig. 4.4: Road pattern: Forbesganj, Motihari and Dalsinghsarai.

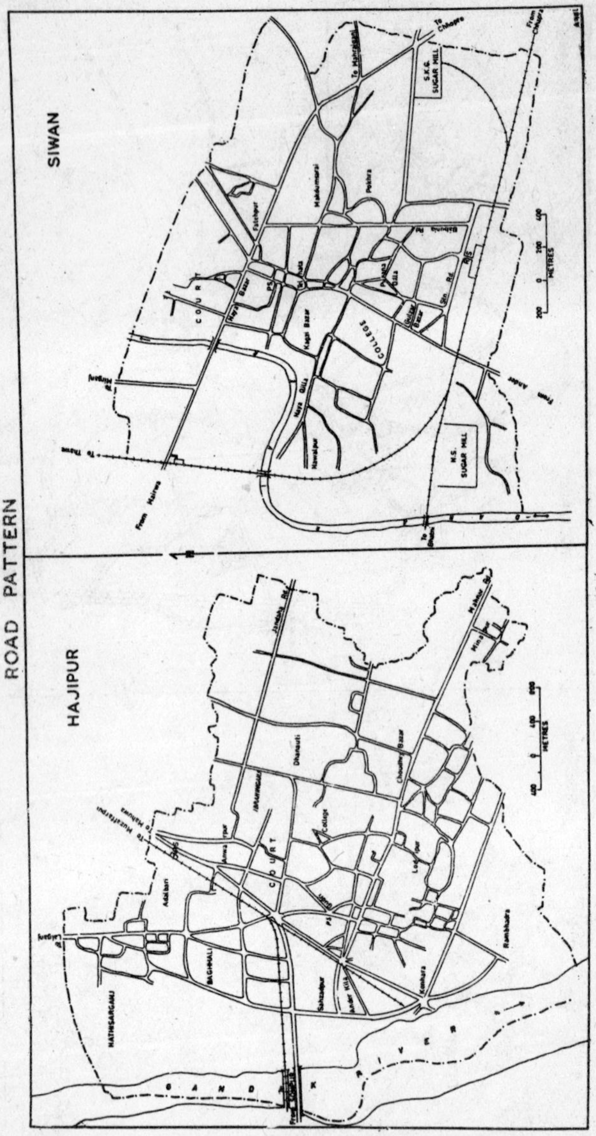

Fig. 4.5: Road pattern: Hajipur and Siwan.

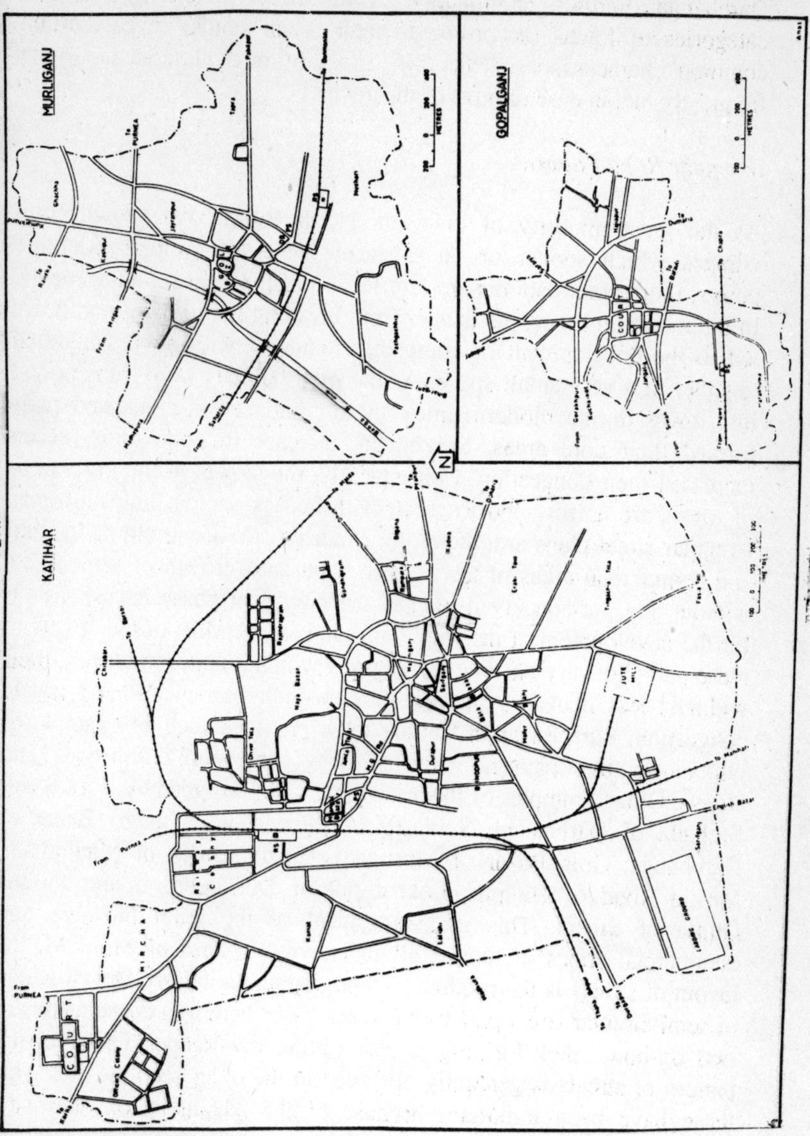

Fig. 4.6: Road pattern: Katihar, Murliganj and Gopalganj.

found in Ander Quila Mohalla of Hajipur and Saudagar Bazar of Darbhanga. Further, examination of the street patterns of various categories of towns (according to their urban status) reveal certain common characteristics. Thus, two types of road patterns are quite frequently met in case of most of the towns.

Irregular Road Pattern

As the great majority of towns in North Bihar have grown from villages which sooner or later became seats of politico-economic power, their street patterns are a reflection of their earlier antecedents. In the medieval times, the danger from invading hordes and marauders led to the development of compact settlements with houses huddled together in a very small space. As the rural habitats were transformed into towns during modern times, these compact and congested parts formed their core areas. Subsequent increase in population further increased their congestion. Consequently, the streets in the core areas of towns are narrow and irregular with houses encroaching on roads. Irregular street plans are, therefore, characteristic of the old residential and commercial areas of towns. The haphazard growth of settlements without any pre-conceived plan in the pre-urban phase is responsible for the development of the irregular road pattern. Most of the streets in these parts are very narrow, zig-zag and winding and, sometimes, their width is less than two metres, thus creating bottlenecks and traffic congestion. Bara Bazar in Katihar town provides such an example of unplanned street-pattern, with buildings encroaching on roads and streets. Other examples of this road pattern are provided by Bara Bazar Mohalla of Darbhanga, Sutapatti of Muzaffarpur, Gudari Bazar of Darbhanga, Gola Bazar of Murliganj, Gandhi Bazar of Madhubani, Masjid Road of Hajipur, Loknathpur of Dalsinghsarai and Purana Quilla of Siwan. This is also typical of the main business and commercial zones of almost all the towns. In case of Motihari, the layout of streets is the product of topographic variations. Development of semi-circular street pattern has taken place here as a consequence of two ox-bow lakes forming a part of the townscape. The irregular pattern of streets is generally observed in the older sections of towns; these have been important because of the advantage of their site. Several old streets in these parts, however, have been reconstructed with the re-generation and re-growth of towns.

Regular Road Pattern

Regular street pattern is the product of deliberate planning. Consequently, regular street pattern is observed in the areas of recent growth as also in older sections which have experienced re-construction or re-generation. Streets in the administrative zone (*Katchhary*), railway colony and planned residential areas are generally broad, metalled and lined with trees, providing shady arcade. This has given rise to grid-iron or rectangular-grid pattern in which the streets are laid at right angles to one another. Rectangular-grid pattern is observed in the railway colonies of Katihar, Saharsa, Samastipur and Muzaffarpur; their locations on the outskirts of the town, close to railway station, have helped the development of this pattern. This road pattern is also characteristic of the I.O.C. township at Begusarai, thermal-power township at Barauni and Kosi project colony at Birpur. The rectangular-grid pattern of these townships and colonies is largely due to deliberate planning by the colonizers.

Linear streets pattern is quite common in the administrative zone and the civil lines of most of the towns. In these areas, construction of spacious building has taken place on both the sides of roads. The civil lines in the towns of Motihari, Sitamarhi, Saharsa and Katihar lie away from the main town; they exhibit either grid-iron or linear road pattern. In all other towns, the road pattern in the civil lines do not conform to any standard plan; instead the pattern development has been mostly guided by site considerations.

Radial street pattern is particularly observed in the core areas of towns. Streets radiate here in various directions from the central foci, for example, at Saraiyaganj in Muzaffarpur, Tower Chowk in Darbhanga and Gandhi Chowk in Laheriasarai. Numerous *Chowks* of other towns also exhibit the radial pattern. They are all important focal points where at least three or four roads meet. Convergence of three streets at a place often leads to the growth of a triangular or 'V'-shaped market place which greatly influences the town plan.

It may not be out of place here to mention that the road pattern is also influenced by the functional characteristics of various towns. These are discussed in detail in Chapters 5 to 8, dealing with urban morphology.

The External Form of the Towns

The external form of the town is of particular significance in urban morphology because it is a reflection of various physical and cultural factors associated with the site and situation of the town. Mention may be made here of river bank sites which are especially important for religious and navigational purposes.

Figure 4.7 shows the general configuration of towns, including their outer forms and morphological characteristics. These are classified as elongated, rectangular, circular, triangular, crescentic and amorphous. Various physical and cultural factors activating town growth at various sites are responsible for the development of these forms which are described as under (Figs. 4.1, 4.2).

Elongated and Elliptical Shape

The elongated shape of a town is generally due to restrictive forces operative at the site, namely, a river or waterway or road. This is often due to linear growth of settlements along a single road as in case of Jogbani and Jainagar, located close to the Indo-Nepal international boundary. Here the road, besides being the main artery of transport, also serves as the main market place of the town, thus favouring linear town growth. The elongated shape of Madhubani is due to its location on the former high bank of the Kamla River which is generally free from floods. It also aided bylinear growth of settlements along the main road that follows the crest of the bluff. Development of side lanes, joining the main road at right angles, have given rise to ribbon-like street pattern.

Transformation of elongated to elliptical form, sometimes, takes place as the rib-patterned streets meet the main or central road that follows the curvature of a river or railway track. The town of Darbhanga exhibits the elliptical form which has developed due to existence of low-lying flood-affected areas east of the railway embankment and the Baghmati River in the west, thus restricting town growth in these directions.

Triangular Shape

A few towns show triangular form as a consequence of restrictive forces like river, railway track or road-crossings hindering town-growth from three directions. Sometimes, the initial growth of settlements along a river or road is followed by subsequent growth along the railway track or another road running at right angles to the

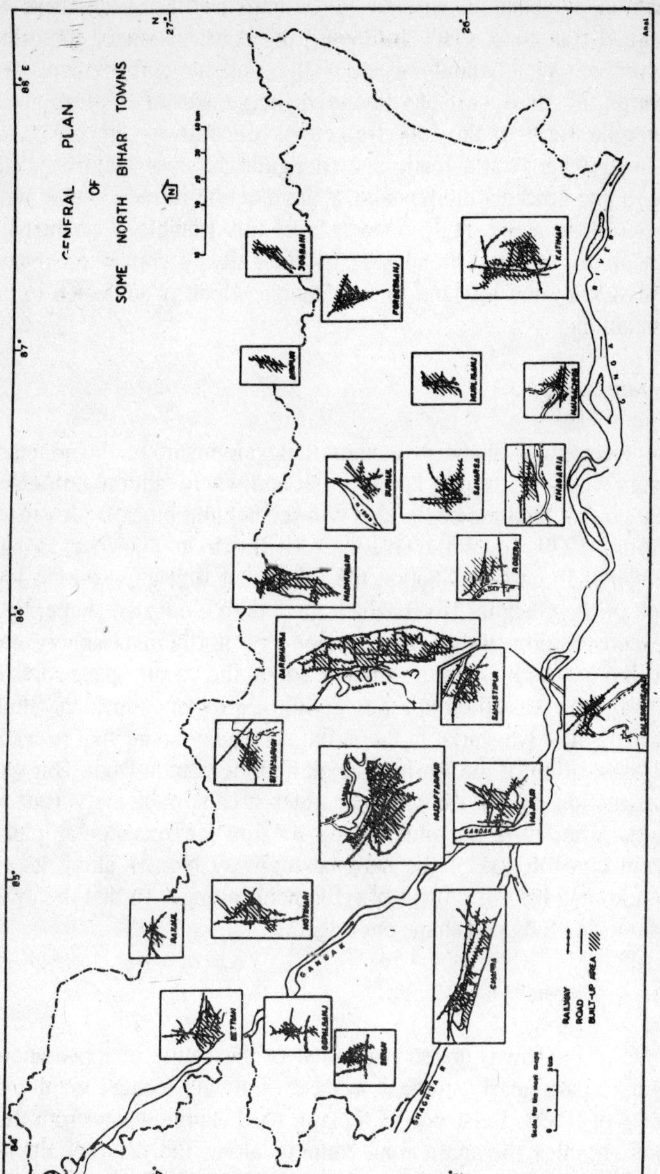

Fig. 4.7: General plan of some North Bihar towns.

previous growth-area. This produces triangular form which is very much in evidence in case of Forbesganj and Katihar. These towns assumed triangular shape following the construction of the railways. Occurrence of lowlands west of the railway embankment as also towards the south-east has favoured the growth of built-up area in a triangular form in the fork formed by the railway embankment and Sultan Pokhar-Araria road. The triangular form of Hajipur is largely due to site considerations, namely the meeting of the Gandak with the Ganga at an acute angle. One side of this triangle is formed by the Gandak River, the second side by the railway embankment and the third side by the lowland of the Ganga, which is subjected to annual inundation.

Rectangular Shape

The rectangular shape is a natural development in the plains. This occurs where the terrain is rather flat and where cultural attitudes have decreed that the land be divided into rectangular blocks (Alexander and Gibson, 1979, p. 386). This is very much in evidence in case of Khagaria. In case of Chapra, the settlement first grew on the levelled bank of the Ghaghra River which gave it an elongated shape, but after the construction of the railway along its northern periphery and the shifting of the Ghaghra towards the south, the vacant space south of the railway line was filled up, thus giving it a rectangular plan. Similarly, the growth of Khagaria, in the initial stage, was somewhat restricted by the disposition of the Burhi Gandak and the Kamla Dhar. But with the construction of the railways the inter-stream tract, only four km in width, was filled up, thus giving the town a rectangular plan. The recent construction of the national highway No. 31 along its eastern margin may lead to growth of settlements along it so that the town will assume an elongated shape once again.

Semi-Circular or Crescentic

Some of the towns are semi-circular or crescentic in appearance. This form is particularly marked in case of towns located on the curved banks of rivers. Existence of a major road leading away from the river bank, besides the main road running along the crest of the natural levee, helps this growth. It is noted that Samastipur, Rosera, Dalsinghsarai and Muzaffarpur exhibit the semi-circular form. The growth of Samastipur has taken place as a bridge-head town on the curved bank of the Burhi Gandak, where convergence of communication lines has resulted in a very compact development of the built-up area. Similarly, existence of physical obstructions, like Sikandarpur lake and the curved bank of the Burhi Gandak in the north and elevated land in the south, have conspired to give Muzaffarpur a semi-circular shape. Similarly, Dalsinghsarai is crescentic in appearance as it has developed on the curved bank of the Balan River.

Circular Shape

Circular towns generally had fortifying walls in the initial stage, and though the walls, except a few gates, have disappeared by now, their influence on the town plan is quite apparent (Ahmad, 1976, p. 294). These towns may or may not have a fort, but they certainly have a central market. The street pattern of these towns is generally radial, converging on the central market place. Sitamarhi is an example of such circular town in this region. It has grown from village, exhibits radial street pattern. Existence of a central market place in this town has contributed, in varying degrees, to the development of the circular form.

Amorphous Shape

There are some towns which do not conform to any of the foregoing shapes, with the result that they exhibit certain degrees of irregularities. Most of these towns are small in size. Their irregular shape is often the product of either physical obstructions, provided by a river or lowland or swamp or lake on the one hand and the attractions provided by cultural elements, like, the railway, court, hospital, market place or industry on the other.

It is, therefore, obvious that the shape of the towns of North Bihar has been the product of various physical factors that have inhibited or favoured certain growth patterns. These shapes have been later modified with the construction of the railways and the road network.

Morphological Zone

Analysis of the plans of the towns of North Bihar reveals their increasing functional complexity with the increase in pace of economic development and commercial activity. This has often resulted in linkage of various land-uses which, in the past, occurred as discrete units. The size of various functional zones varies from town to town, depending on size-class and special characteristics of the town concerned. Thus, four morphological zones are identified in almost all the towns of North Bihar on the basis of the ground plan (arrangement of roads and streets) and the intensity of the usage of the built-up land; these are described as follows:

The Inner Zone

This is generally the oldest settlement of the town and now forms its commercial hub. The buildings in this zone look aged and are used both for commercial and residential purposes. There is concentration of both retail and wholesale business, together with hotels and eating places, in this area. For example, Bara Bazar and Saraiyaganj are the commercial hubs of Darbhanga and Muzaffarpur, respectively. Lack of open space and few possibilities for building construction account for very high land rent in this part of the town. Trading, commerce, banking and shopping facilities, all requiring central locations, compete for accommodation. Radiating street pattern, leading to other parts or sections of the town, are typical of this zone. The streets are generally narrow and quite inadequate to cater to the present traffic needs. Thus, traffic congestion often results at peak hours, particularly in larger town. Shopping establishments are mostly located along the main roads. These establishments are found on the ground floor of buildings while their upper floor and their back portions are used for residential purposes.

The Middle Zone

This zone is primarily used for residential purposes. But, sometimes, business and administrative uses also occur, including public and semi-public buildings and some residential units. It is characterised by compactly built middle-class residential dwellings whose density is very high. The streets linking this zone with the central and other parts of the town are comparatively wider.

The Outer Zone

The outer zone comprises high-class as well as low-class planned residences and slums, often occurring in a scattered fashion, almost next to agricultural fields (Plate 6). Isolated shopping nucleations, transport nodes and a few administrative buildings also occur in this zone. It also houses big educational institution and some industrial units. Consequently, this zone is still in the process of transformation. Its layout and growth vary widely according to physical built and the mode of its expansion.

Plate 6: High-class residential buildings occurring adjacent to Paddy fields on the newly developed area of Lakshmisagar at Darbhanga.

The Suburban Zone

This zone generally lies beyond the municipal limits, and constitutes the 'rural-urban fringe'. Projections of built-up area from the outer urban zone, sometimes also having industrial units, occur along the highways that pass through rural areas. It is quite evident in case of Begusarai and Barauni towns. This zone has developed in ribbon-like manner along the highways where industrial sites and urban amenities are being developed. Villages, located close to this suburban zone, are also experiencing some change in their basic functions.

Sky-Line

The sky-line forms an important aspect of the urban morphology. It represents the third dimension of the town plan. The sky-line of the built-up area, viewed from a vintage point, reveals different aspects. It is generally observed that the old commercial areas of the town usually have multi-storeyed buildings, indicating thereby a high density of population. Sometimes a clock tower, located in the central part of the town, forms the highest object in this sky-line. Generally, the sky-line becomes irregular and undulating towards the outskirts of the town. Their vertical dimension also decreases as the density of houses in these parts is low. An abrupt break in the sky-line of Darbhanga and Laheriasarai is noted due to the presence of open spaces between various nuclei. In general, the residential areas are marked by uniform sky-line due to the occurrence of *pucca* flat-roofed buildings. It is noted that spires and domes of temples and mosques rather abruptly mould the rise and fall in the urban profile. Location of industries and factories on the outskirts of towns, like, Katihar and Forbesganj, is indicated by an abrupt rise of gas chimneys over workshops and godowns with roofs of corrugated tin sheets. This sky-line later merges into thatched or tile-roofed houses which are surrounded by cultivated fields.

REFERENCES

Ahmad, E. (1976): *Some Aspects of Indian Geography*, Allahabad.

Alexander, J.W. and L.J. Gibson (1979): *Economic Geography*, New Delhi.

Chaudhury, P.C.R. (1958): *District Gazetteers, Muzaffarpur*. Secretariat Press, Bihar, Patna.

Chaudhury, P.C.R. (1964): *District Gazetteers, Darbhanga*. Secretariat Press, Bihar, Patna.

Colby, C.C. (1933): Centrifugal and Centripetal Forces in Urban Geography. *Annals of the Association of American Geographers*, XXIII, pp.1-20.

Davier, A., (1933): A Study in City Morphology and Historical Geography, *Geography*. 18, pp. 25-37.

Harris, C.D. and E.L. Ullman (1945): "The Nature of Cities", In P.K. Hatt and A.J. Reiss (Eds.) (1963), *Cities and Society*, New York, pp. 237-59.

Singh, R.L. (ed.) (1971): *Urban Geography in Developing Countries*, N.G.S.I., Varanasi.

Taneja, K.L. (1971): *Morphology of Indian Cities*, N.G.S.I., Varanasi.

Thomas, D. (1975): "Urban Land Evaluation", In J.A. Dawson and J.C. Doornkamp (Eds.): *Evaluating the Human Environment*, Edward Arnold, London, pp. 88-108.

Ursprung, H. (1966): "The Formation of Patterns in Development", In Michael Loche (Ed.): *Major Problems in Developmental Biology*, New York, pp.177-216.

Wolpert, L. *et al*. (1967): "Cell Movement and Cell Contact, in Sea Urchin Morphogenesis, *Endeavour*, XXVI, pp. 85-90.

5

FUNCTIONAL STRUCTURE OF SAMPLE TOWNS

THE IMPACT of urban functions is reflected in the morphological structure of towns. There are two aspects of urban functions, namely, the role of the city as the focus of its region and the inner diversity of functions within the city (Murphy, 1966, p. 5). It has been noted earlier that most of the towns of North Bihar exhibit marked differences in their internal and external plans. In fact, these differences have been caused by various geographical factors in which functions play no less important role. Hence, an attempt has been made here to provide the functional structures of some sample towns.

Sample Towns

Urban analysis of a large number of cities and towns, within a region, often present problems in investigation and representation owing to many diversities in their geographical conditions. Case studies, besides being unscientific and unreliable, can never be considered as true representations of the whole region. Hence, sample is generally preferred. Even though sample study has certain limitations (Hickoncen, 1950, p. 151) the errors inherent in a sampling process are less than the errors due to the inaccuracy and the incompleteness of the investigation. It is obvious that the most important aim of sampling studies is to obtain 'maximum information about the phenomena under study with the least sacrifice of money, time and energy' (Elhance, 1966, p. 663). The most important consideration in selecting a sample is to examine that it is a close representation of the region. As the towns of North Bihar belong to various size categories; stratified random sampling has been preferred in the selection of sample towns. The towns have been first grouped into five strata according to population size based on 1971 census data. Out of the total of 49 towns in North Bihar, thus, two lie in first, four in second, 15 in third, 22 in fourth and only six in fifth and sixth categories taken together (see Appendix). Selection of sample towns has been made from each group or strata which has been considered as homogeneous case. Considering various factors, like, location, site and origin, a total of 11 sample towns have been selected which gives a sampling fraction of 1-5 or 20 per cent (Table 5.1).

The town thus selected have been analysed with reference to their setting, spatial shape, population growth, functional character and functional structure. The analysis of functional structure is mainly related with the nature, extent, location and inter-relations of the various types of establishments which together form the physical functional morphology of the towns.

Table 5.1: Size class of sample towns (1971)

Size class with population range	*Total No. of towns*	*No. of samples required*	*Selected sample (with serial No.)*
I. 1,00,000 and above	2	1	1. Darbhanga
II. 50,000-99,999	4	1	2. Katihar
III. 20,000-49,999	15	3	3. Hajipur
			4. Saharsa
			5. Forbesganj
IV. 10,000-19,999	22	4	6. Gopalganj
			7. Murliganj
			8. Dalsinghsarai
			9. Birpur
V&VI. 9,999 and below	6	2	10. Jainagar
			11. Mairwa

Setting of Sample Towns

The site being the actual ground, upon which a town stands, is responsible for the origin of the urban nucleus at a particular spot. Situation on the land relates to the relative position of a town with respect to its surroundings and, therefore, it controls both expansion and function of a town (Smailes, 1966, p.40). It is rather difficult to find any two identical or exactly similar geographical situations for town growth. Though all the sample towns do not have similar sites, but it is noted that quite a few sample towns, namely, Darbhanga, Hajipur, Dalsinghsarai and Jainagar, have river-side locations (Figs. 4.1 and 4.2). Consideration of defence, during earlier days, was an important factor in the location of these towns. The river bluff provided commanding sites both for the fort and the town, and the protection afforded by the stream at least on one side was considered an important advantage. Both Darbhanga and Hajipur have been located in this manner. Hajipur, located at the confluence of the River Gandak and the Ganga, has then added advantages of river navigation in three directions and the sacredness of these streams attract pilgrims from far and near. Such a favourable situation necessarily stimulates the urban growth (Ramesh, 1973, p. 225). The towns of Jainagar and Dalsinghsarai exhibit more favourable situation as these centres, initially located on navigational rivers, later grew into focal points of road and rail transports in the region. Consequently, these urban nuclei have experienced considerable expansion during recent times.

Nodal points make the second most important urban nuclei in the region. Katihar and Forbesganj are examples of nodal points' towns. It is noted that rail routes converge from different directions at Katihar, making it possible to handle transit trade on a large scale. Forbesganj, which originated as a local commercial town, has developed marked nodality during recent times as road and rail transports converge at this point to cater to the growing trade with Nepal.

The towns of Gopalganj, Saharsa, Murliganj and Mairwa have grown subsequent to the development of the rail and road networks. These sites, prior to the development of the railways, were used for periodical markets, locally known as *Hat* (weekly market). Local road junctions often formed sites for the *Hat*, a retail trade which provided outlet for its tributary areas. In Dickinson's (1932, p.10) terminology, these 'urban villages' acted as nuclei for later development of towns.

Birpur has grown as a consequence of Kosi project. Situated at cross-roads and endowed with an enterprising population, the township with official quarters is transformed into a little town with brilliant future. Its elevation as sub-divisional headquarters of the same name has given it added importance.

The above analysis reveals that the growth and expansion of a good number of sample towns have been factors of the change in situation in which development of road and railway transports accelerated their growth. Constructions of lateral roads and National Highways which came to join these towns have further helped to extend services and facilities in their urban field.

It is noted that the expansion of the built-up area of all sample towns is taking place along the axial roads, spreading out from the main market, with the establishment of industrial units, educational institutions and administrative centres. Consequently, the surrounding villages are steadily being engulfed by the urban land-use. Further, with the inclusion of a large number of villages within the municipal area is also responsible for the expansion of built-up area.

Spatial Shape

The study of spatial shape of urban areas is important in urban geography and ecology, as well as for planning purposes (Gibbs, 1961, p.105). It is largely guided by topographical attributes of the site, nature and type of municipal transportation system and traffic management, besides the relative position of the sub-urban centres in the neighbourhood, etc. The urban planner is often required to find solutions to various problems associated with the spatial shape of towns. Gibbs observes that, in general, the urban centres are either circular or rectangular or star-shaped or elongated in design. Sometimes, variations of these forms are also noted.

The spatial form of the towns of North Bihar has been analysed on the basis of their municipal limits. It may be mentioned here that the urban built-up areas, in several cases, do not coincide with the town boundary. Hartman (1954, p. 244), however, contends that in spite of the great complexity and irregularity of shapes . . ., a definite geometrical pattern can still be discernible. Boyce and Clark (1964) have introduced the technique of radial distance to measure the shape of urban areas. But, in the present analysis, Gibbs' method of calculating circularity index has been applied to obtain the spatial shape of sample towns. This method is based on the assumption that the boundaries of a town generally tend to resemble a circle. His formula for calculating the circularity index is given as under:

$$\text{Measure of circularity or } Mc = \frac{100\,Aa}{(3.1416)(Dp/2)^2},$$

Where *Aa* is the actual area contained in the urban unit, and
Dp the distance between two most distant points on the boundary of the unit.

Table 5.2 gives the circularity indices of the municipal limits of the sample towns of North Bihar. The *Mc* values not only express the degree of circularity of these towns but also indicate the type of geometrical figure to which the town shape can be compared. The absolute maximum value of *Mc* can be 100, which will represent a circle, as the value decreases the town tends to resemble first a square or star, then a thin winding or elongated strip, and at the lowest values, a narrow rectangle (Gibbs, 1961, p. 103).

Table 5.2: Circularity Indices of the sample towns in North Bihar

Towns	*Area of town in Sq. km*	*Distance in km between two most distant points on town's periphery (Dp)*	*Circularity Index (Mc)*
1. Darbhanga	19.2	9.0	25.95
2. Katihar	16.5	6.8	45.59
3. Hajipur	19.6	7.8	41.10
4. Saharsa	14.0	7.1	35.58
5. Forbesganj	10.4	3.8	92.14
6. Gopalganj	9.2	4.6	55.74
7. Murliganj	14.2	4.6	84.65
8. Dalsinghsarai	2.9	2.6	55.37
9. Birpur	13.4	5.6	54.56
10. Jainagar	1.5	2.8	25.16
11. Mairwa	4.3	3.2	54.35

Source: Data computed by the author based on Census of India, Series 4, Bihar, 1971.

Thus, out of 11 sample towns, Forbesganj and Murliganj with their circularity indices of 92.14 and 84.65, respectively, are circular in design. Gopalganj, Dalsinghsarai, Birpur and Mairwa seem to resemble a square; their Mc values are only 55.74, 55.37, 54.56 and 54.35, respectively. Similarly, Katihar, Hajipur and Saharsa with their Mc values as 45.59, 41.10 and 35.51, respectively, are star-oriented. However, their built-up areas are triangular in design. Lower Mc values of Darbhanga (25.95) and Jainagar (25.16) are indicative of their narrow and elongated rectangular shape (Fig. 5.1C).

Growth of Population in Sample Towns

The rate of population growth has to be considered in relation to urban area and occupational structure of sample towns. At the beginning of the 20th century, sample towns, like, Darbhanga, Katihar and Hajipur, were of small sizes. A nominal decrease in their population (except Katihar) in the first two decades (1901-11 and 1911-21) was followed by a slight increase in the third decade (1921-31) (Table 5.3). Subsequently, there has been steady and fairly rapid growth not only in the population of these towns but also in that of the region as a whole. The last two decades (1951-61 and 1961-71) have witnessed a phenomenal increase in urban population. Consequently, a large number of new towns, particularly Saharsa, Dalsinghsarai, Gopalganj, Murliganj, Birpur and Mairwa, emerged. These towns have also expanded enormously in the last decade (Fig. 5.1A).

It is noted that there is no uniform rate of growth in the population of the sample towns. A few towns, Jainagar in particular, have remained stagnant while Katihar has expanded enormously.

Table 5.3: Annual rate of population growth in sample towns (1901-1971)

Sample towns	*Decades*						
	1901-1911	*1911-1921*	*1921-1931*	*1931-1941*	*1941-1951*	*1951-1961*	*1961-1971*
Darbhanga	–0.54	1.42	1.29	1.40	2.25	2.14	2.81
Katihar	0.46	4.22	0.91	6.59	6.09	4.00	3.50
Hajipur	–0.101	–1.28	1.51	1.38	1.45	3.53	2.30
Saharsa	—	—	—	—	—	—	5.60
Forbesganj	—	—	1.95	4.79	3.14	3.71	3.37
Gopalganj	—	—	—	—	—	–0.08	2.24
Murliganj	—	—	—	—	—	—	2.88
Dalsinghsarai	—	—	—	—	—	5.96	–1.42
Birpur	—	—	—	—	—	—	2.53
Jainagar	—	—	0.79	–3.42	6.16	1.27	2.54

Source: Census of India, 1971, Series 4, Bihar, Part 11-A General Population Tables.

Darbhanga, the largest town of the region, had a population of 66,244 persons in 1901 as against 1,32,059 in 1971. Its population declined by as much as 5.46 per cent and 14.26 per cent during the first two decades of the century. This loss was, however, partly made up by a gain in population by 12.99 per cent during 1921-31. After 1941, its population has increased steadily more than 2.1 per cent per annum. But its growth rate has been considerably lower than that of Muzaffarpur whose population has increased at an annual rate of 3.17 per cent. In fact, Muzaffarpur, the largest town in the region prior to 1961, now ranks next to Darbhanga in population.

Katihar attained urban status in 1901 when it had a population of 9,761 persons. It is the only town in the region which has shown progressive growth in the last seven decades with the result that it had a population of 80,121 persons in 1971. The area of this town has also expanded from 4.6 sq. km in 1941 to 16.54 sq. km in 1971. Its population is expected to increase at a fast rate even in future as well, because of its importance as a centre of trade and transport.

The population of Hajipur, a class III town at present, has not increased as fast. In 1901, it had more population than that of Katihar. But its population decreased considerably during 1901-11 and 1911-21 when the losses were 10.16 per cent and 12.18 per cent respectively. It experienced a moderate increase of 14.51 per cent during 1941-51. In the later decades, the pace of population rise greatly increased with the result that during 1951-61 and 1961-71, the additional accrual in population was by 35.37 per cent and 23.05 per cent respectively. Recently the town has been selected as the headquarters of the newly formed district of Vaishali; which will lead to further increase in its population.

Forbesganj had a population of 4,968 persons in 1921, which has shown a progressive growth in the last five decades. Consequently, a population of 21,198 persons was recorded in 1971 with an annual rate of 3.3 per cent.

Saharsa, now a Class III town attained urban status in 1961 when it had a population of 14,803 persons. Its population in 1971 increased to 23,217 persons which gave it a very fast growth rate of (5.6 per cent) per annum. The town was selected as the headquarters of the Kosi Division, which has greatly induced its urban growth recently.

Similarly, Gopalganj attained urban status in 1951 when it had a population of 12,213 persons. Its population remained almost stationary during 1951-61. In 1971, it recorded a population of 17,253 persons thus giving it an increase rate of 2.24 per cent per annum.

Murliganj obtained urban status in 1961 when it had a population of 9,484 persons. Its population increased to 12,688 in 1971 giving it an annual growth rate of 2.8 per cent. As it is growing trade centre, its population is also expected to increase considerably in future as well.

Dalsinghsarai, located between Samastipur and Barauni, assumed town status in 1951 when it had a population of 7,853 persons. Its population increased to 12,538 persons in 1961, giving it an annual growth rate of 5.96 per cent. But during 1961-71 its population decreased by 14.28 per cent because of reduction in the town area by about two sq. km as a consequence of exclusion of a few villages from its town limits. The proposed establishment of a few industrial units at this place will lead to an increase in its population in the near future.

Birpur, a Class IV town, came into prominence as township of the Kosi Project in 1961 with a population of 8,061 persons. Its population has increased to 10,103 in 1971.

Jainagar attained its urban status in 1921 when it had a population of 6,113 persons. Its population declined during 1931-41 which is attributable to the uncertain conditions prevailing in its neighbourhood including floods and other natural calamities. Its subsequent growth has been also slow in 1971, its population was 9,917 persons which gave an annual growth rate of 2.5 per cent. Establishment of some industrial units and the growing trade with Nepal may lead to a further increase in the population of Jainagar.

Mairwa, a Class V town, obtained urban status in 1971 when it had a population of 6,766 persons. It is an important trade centre near U.P. border.

Occupational Structure

The growth of population is directly related to the character of the occupation or profession adopted by the city folk (Singh, 1955, p. 65). A discussion of the occupational structure of the working population of towns has to precede the analysis of their functional structure. Reddy (1973, p. 119) observed that the occupational structure reveals the broad economic facets of settlements because it is initially related to their functional structure. Figure 5.1B showing the occupational structure of sample towns reveals that not only the proportion of workers to non-workers varies from town to town, but the proportion of working population engaged in different professions is also variable.

Among the sample towns the proportion of working to total population ranges from 25 per cent to 33.4 per cent. Darbhanga has the lowest participation and Birpur the highest. It is somewhat intriguing that the working population in Murliganj, Gopalganj and Saharsa

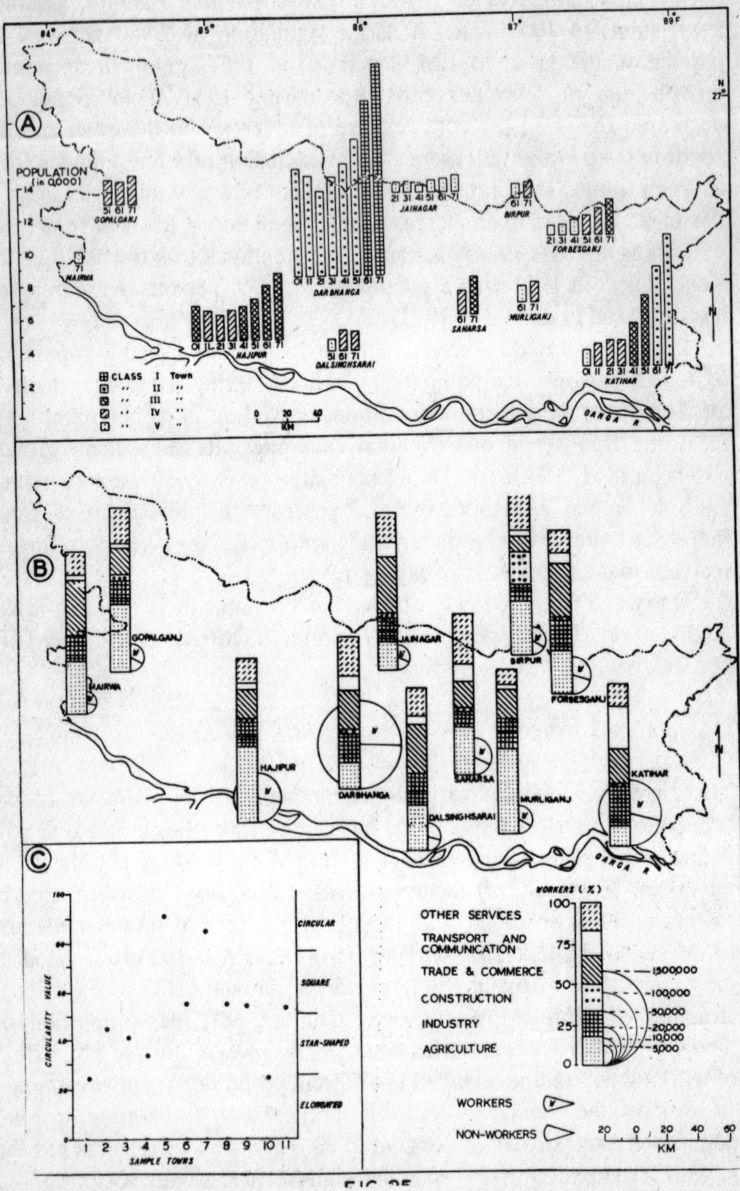

Fig. 5.1: Sample towns: (A) growth of population, 1901-71, (B) Occupational structure of population (1971), (C) Measurement of spatial shape.

account for 32, 32.1 and 31.1 per cent, respectively; these towns have comparatively high figures. It is noted that the high agricultural content of these towns' urban population — much of which is essentially rural in character — seems to be responsible for this position. The remaining sample towns, namely, Katihar, Hajipur, Forbesganj, Dalsinghsarai, Jainagar and Mairwa, account for 28.4, 26.8, 29.7, 29.8 and 26.5 per cent working population, respectively.

Analysis of working population indicates that secondary and tertiary activities generally occupy dominant positions particularly in larger towns but primary occupations become more important in smaller towns.

Darbhanga, the largest of the sample towns, has 29.3 per cent of its working force engaged in services or administration. The town is the administrative headquarters of the same name. It has several educational institutions, including two universities. Medical and other services are also well developed. About 23.7 per cent of its working population is engaged in trade and commerce as the town serves as the regional headquarters of the wholesale trade. Industries, particularly handloom and Khadi, account for 18 per cent of the working population. Other occupations are less important but agriculture claims 12 per cent of the work-force.

Major routes of transport and communication lines not only stimulate economic growth but also accelerate the process of urbanisation (Reddy, 1971, p. 136). Katihar, a Class II town, is richly endowed with communication facilities; it is an important rail junction and the divisional headquarters of N.F. Railway. Consequently, about 26 per cent of its working population is engaged in transport and communication. Its central location in the Kosi region has favoured its growth as an important centre of trade and commerce in which 21 per cent of its work-force is employed. Industries, chiefly jute, rice, flour, timber, etc., provide occupation to 19.8 per cent of its workers. Besides, this town has the privilege of having the highest percentage of working population engaged in construction (19.8%) in the whole North Bihar. Other activities are also well developed, with the result that administrative services, medical and professional workers taken together, account for 14.2 per cent; other occupations account for the rest of the work-force.

Mention has to be made of Hajipur, an old town of Class III category, which engages 44.1 per cent of its working force in primary occupation, namely, agriculture. This town is most famous for its horticultural produces, namely, banana, 'Lichhi', mango and seasonal vegetables. Consequently the town-dwellers have opted for fruit and vegetable gardening which is quite profitable. Availability of suitable land in and around the town has helped to promote this profession even by persons engaged in other activities. There is also a brisk trade in banana and vegetable seeds. Thus, trade and commerce account for 18.1 per cent of its working population. Employment in other services provides avenues for 15.1 per cent; other activities are less important.

Saharsa, another Class III town like Hajipur, has about 44 per cent of its working population engaged in primary occupation. It is a town of recent growth and large areas within town are still rural in character. In the absence of industrial opportunity, the town-dwellers have no option other than cultivation and vegetable gardening. Being a divisional headquarters, it provides avenues for employment in other services including educational and professional jobs, which account for 29.1 per cent of the working population. Trade and commerce come third, occupying 18.3 per cent. The town is a railway junction and roads radiate from this place to various destinations in its neighbourhood. Consequently, there has been some development in transport and communications which engage 9.8 per cent of the working population. Other categories of employment are less developed.

Forbesganj, though a Class III town, is leading centre of trade and commerce, particularly jute and foodgrains which claim 33 per cent of the working labour force. Rice and flour milling and small scale industries share 14 per cent and agriculture, particularly jute processing, accounts for 22 per cent. Administrative services, transport, storage and communication are other important avenues of employment for the town-dwellers.

The Class IV towns of Murliganj, Gopalganj and Birpur have very large proportions of gainful workers engaged in primary sector. Agriculture provides outlets for 51.1, 49.3 and 41.1 per cent of their working population, respectively. In fact, these towns are situated in the midst of intensively cultivated fertile tracts which give them a very strong rural setting. Also inclusion of a few villages in the town area gives them a rural overtone. Thus, in true sense, these towns are "urban villages" (Rao, 1962, p.11).

Both Gopalganj and Murliganj, with 15.6 and 17.9 per cent of the work-force, respectively, engaged in trade and commerce, show a certain degree of parity. In the case of Birpur, which grew into importance with the construction of the Kosi Barrage, other services and construction provide employment to 24.4 and 20.4 per cent of its working population, respectively. It is noted that at the time of 1971 census, the Kosi project and its eastern canals were still under construction. Thus, with the completion of the project, most of the workers then engaged in construction have moved to other primary activities.

Trade and commerce are the most important occupations in case of Dalsinghsarai (31%), Jainagar (35.3%) and Mairwa (34.5%). These towns have certain locational advantages which provide them with opportunities to carry brisk trade and commerce in their influence zone. They reveal almost similar occupational structures. Both Dalsinghsarai and Jainagar carry agriculture-based trade mostly paddy, tobacco, sugarcane and turmeric. Other activities, like services, household industries, transport, storage, etc., account for the rest of the working labour force.

Analysis of the occupational structure of the sample towns of North Bihar reveals that the most dominant occupations in these towns are primary activities, trade and commerce and professional services. Services followed by trade and commerce are the most important occupations in the city of Darbhanga. Towns, like, Forbesganj, Dalsinghsarai, Jainagar and Mairwa, which are not associated with the administrative hierarchy in any way, are important for trade and commerce and other services. Katihar is the only town in North Bihar which shows a much higher proportion of its working population engaged in industries, transport and trade and commerce. It is also noted that the percentage of working population engaged in primary activities decreases with the increase in the size-class of town. Development of trade and commerce and establishment of industries in larger towns often lead to spurt in secondary and tertiary activities.

Functional Structure and their Morphology

The internal structure of a town depends upon the nature of functions which it performs as also on the character of its functional areas. This is quite evident from a discussion of the occupational structure of the sample towns of North Bihar. Some of the functional characteristics may also be influenced by the cultural and historical background as also the physical conditions of site and the region in which this is located. The town, however, owes much of its character to the needs of its service area and the functions it performs to meet such needs (Dickinson, 1948, p. 20). Planning of a new urban communities has to be necessarily made after a thorough analysis of the functional structure of the existing towns. Hence, any effective planning for the improvement or re-arrangement of the future city must take account of the present pattern of land-use within the city, "of the factors which have produced this pattern and of the facilities required by activities localised within particular districts" (Harris and Ullman, 1945, p. 282). The internal land-use pattern produces an imbroglio picture which is the result of the interaction of one part of the town with the other. "These interactions are reflected in the amount, direction, time and character of movement of persons and goods between the various functional areas" (Mayer and Kohn, 1967, p. 5). Thus, keeping in view the future planning needs of the towns in North Bihar, a general picture of the functional structure of the sample towns is presented here. An attempt has been also made to find out the spatial interactions of various functional areas and their impact on the existing urban land-use.

Figures 5.2 to 5.9 show various functional areas of sample towns, based on detailed fieldwork. These functional areas have been identified as commercial (wholesale and retail taken together), residential, administrative, industrial, recreational (cinema, club, etc.), religious (temple, church and mosque), orchards, open spaces and other areas, including railways and hospital.

Commercial Areas

The morphology of commercial areas in the sample towns is like a mosaic. In most of the towns, there is hardly a compact business zone. But the principle shopping areas are generally located in the heart of the towns. They often occupy focal points of the internal route system. Thus, they may develop, sometimes, outside the central zone of the town. The arrangements of shops in the shopping areas generally follow the pattern of roads and streets. Next to commercial areas lie the residential areas which engulf the former. In some towns shopping places lie close to the administrative areas. These are flanked by open spaces in case of smaller towns.

The shape and size of commercial areas are subject to continuous change following the expansion in size and functions of the town. This is quite evident in case of Darbhanga. The old shopping areas of the

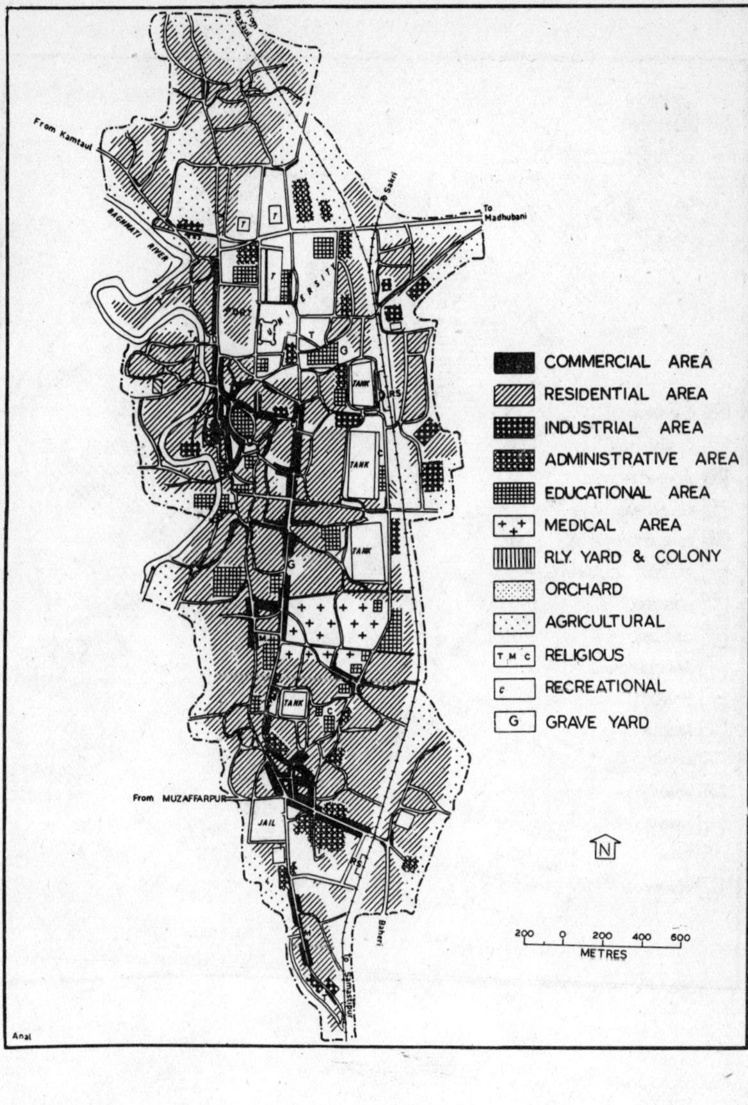

Fig. 5.2: Darbhanga: functional structure.

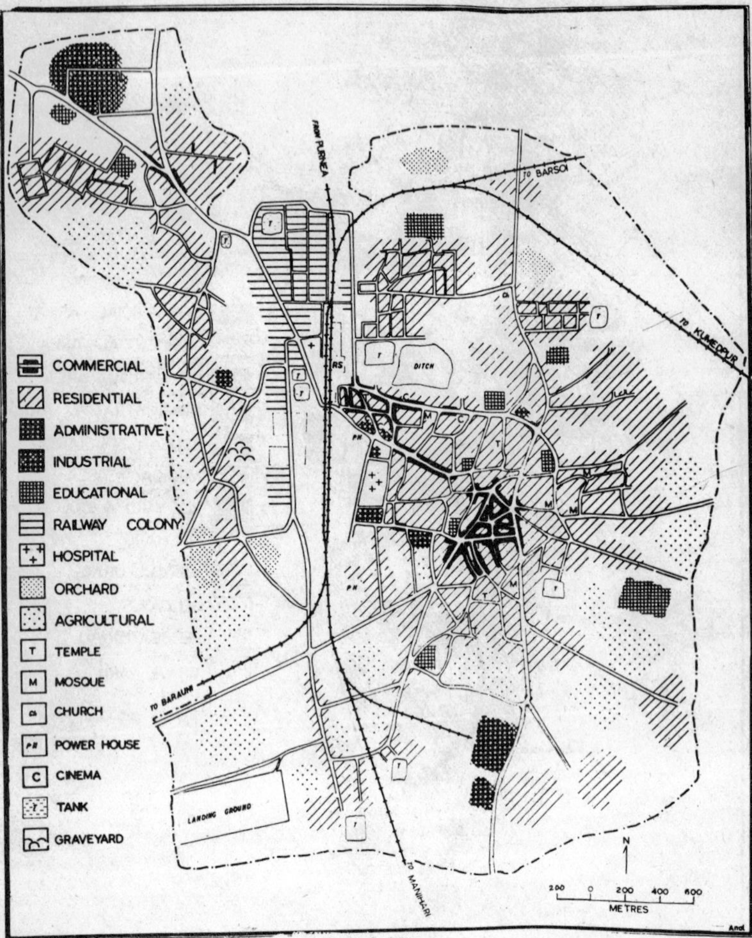

Fig. 5.3: Katihar: functional structure.

town lie at two distant places, one at Darbhanga proper, the other at Laheriasarai. Both are known as Gudari Bazar. Initially these two nuclei served as the hub of commercial activity. But later, as the town expanded, its business kernel also shifted to Bari Bazar and Lalbagh in the north and east, respectively, close to the clock Tower. Recently, another commercial area is growing near the bus station in Mirzapur. A similar expansion has taken place of Gudari Bazar at Laheriasarai following the development of metalled roads and establishment of administrative headquarters; this shopping area has expanded towards Bakerganj in the west and the railway station in the east, thereby giving it a rectangular shape.

The commercial area of Katihar, a Class II town, first grew at Saifganj in the heart of the town. This nucleus of commercial activity gradually expanded in a linear fashion along roads radiating in all directions. It is noted that shifting of business activity particularly took place with the construction of the railways. Consequently, growth of shopping centre took place at Mangal Bazar. Other shopping centres of lesser importance have sprouted at Driver Tola, Amla Tola, Binod Nagar and Mirchai. Retail pavement trading along the road-side is quite common in Katghara. Vegetable and fish market can be sighted along road-side in almost all the wards of Katihar. The business area of Bari Bazar has very disappointing sanitary conditions because of open drains and encroachments of godowns over the roads.

Hajipur, though a Class III town, exhibits specialised commercial activity like Darbhanga. Its commercial areas have developed along transportation lines (Fig. 5.4). Gudari Bazar, the business core of Hajipur, is situated in the older part of the town. The shops are arranged here in a linear pattern along the main road from Masjid Chowk to Rajendra Chowk, a distance of about two km. Similar growth of ribbon-like business areas is noted along the Station Road and Anwarpur Road, which run parallel to each other. These commercial areas specialise in machinery, engineering goods and agricultural raw inputs.

Besides, smaller shopping centres, comprising hotels, restaurants and sweet shops, have grown in front of the railway station and near Konhara Ghat and Gandak Bridge. At present the station road offers the best sites for commercial establishment. It is worth mentioning that the business areas and shopping centres of Hajipur generally have good drainage conditions.

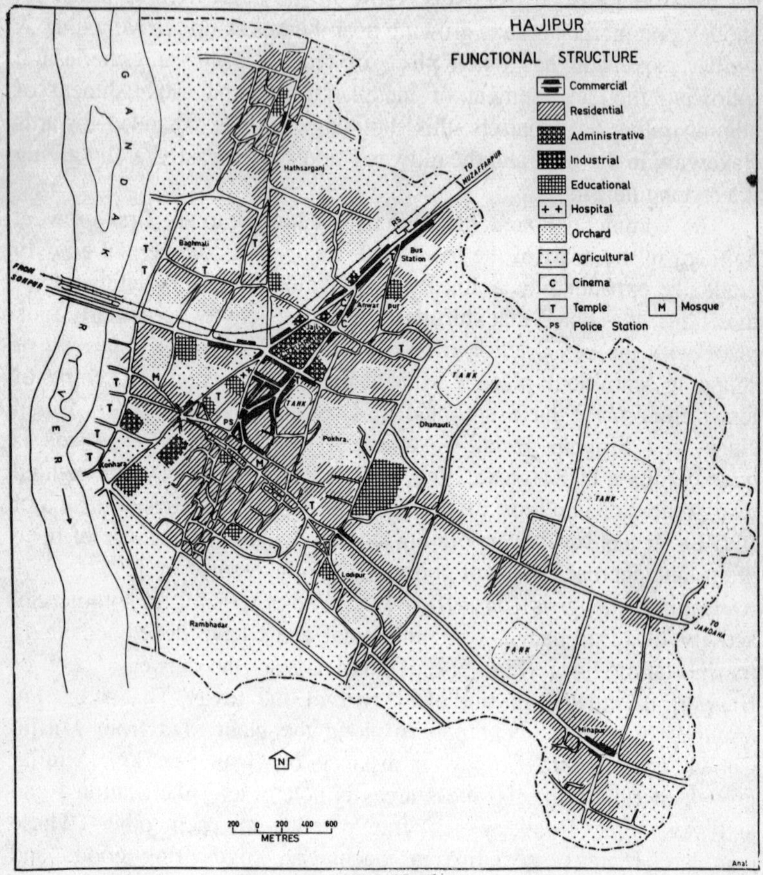

FIG. 28

Fig. 5.4: Hajipur: functional structure.

Saharsa and Forbesganj both Class III towns, differ in their commercial structure (Figs. 5.5 & 5.6). Saharsa is primarily an administrative centre whereas Forbesganj is a purely commercial and trading centre. The problem with Saharsa is that its trade influence area is quite small due to lack of transport facility; the region is also flood-affected. Consequently, it specialises in retail trade only. The main bazar of the town is located west of the railway station at Kaprapatti and Mahabir Chowk. They form the commercial hub of the town.

Trade and commerce are the most important functions at Forbesganj. Its main commercial areas are Hathikhola market, Sadar Bazar and the markets along S.K. Road, Manikchand Road and Ram Baran Lane. Hathikhola Bazar is a famous 'jute mandi' with a cluster of wholesale and retail *golas*. The market has expanded recently along the Sadar Bazar Road in a linear pattern. In recent years, a number of mixed shops have come up near jute and rice mills on the Purnea Road.

The commercial areas of Gopalganj, Murliganj, Dalsinghsarai and Birpur, all Class IV towns, differ greatly in content and pattern formation (Figs. 5.7 and 5.8).

In Gopalganj and Murliganj, the commercial core initially developed along the central route running through the heart of the town. Expansion of this commercial core has taken place recently along radial roads from the central route, leading to residential and commercial areas. The shopping areas of these towns are generally of the mixed type. New shopping centres, with scattered shops, have recently come up along the roads in the vicinity of railway and bus stations.

Dalsinghsarai has two well developed business nuclei. The main market clustered in the older settlement specialises in the wholesale trade of chillies, turmeric and tobacco whereas the retail and other shopping centres are concentrated along the Station Road.

There has not been sufficient growth of trade and commerce in the new town of Birpur. However, a small shopping centre has emerged here in linear pattern along the Bathnaha Road.

There is little difference in the business of Class V and VI towns; they present almost the same characteristics. The business cores of Jainagar and Mairwa, two important Class V towns, have developed in the central parts of the town. Footpath vendors carry on general business along the Station Road; they install their shops in the day time and wind them up in the night. This development is largely due to the rural characteristics of both the sellers and purchasers where bargaining is a common practice.

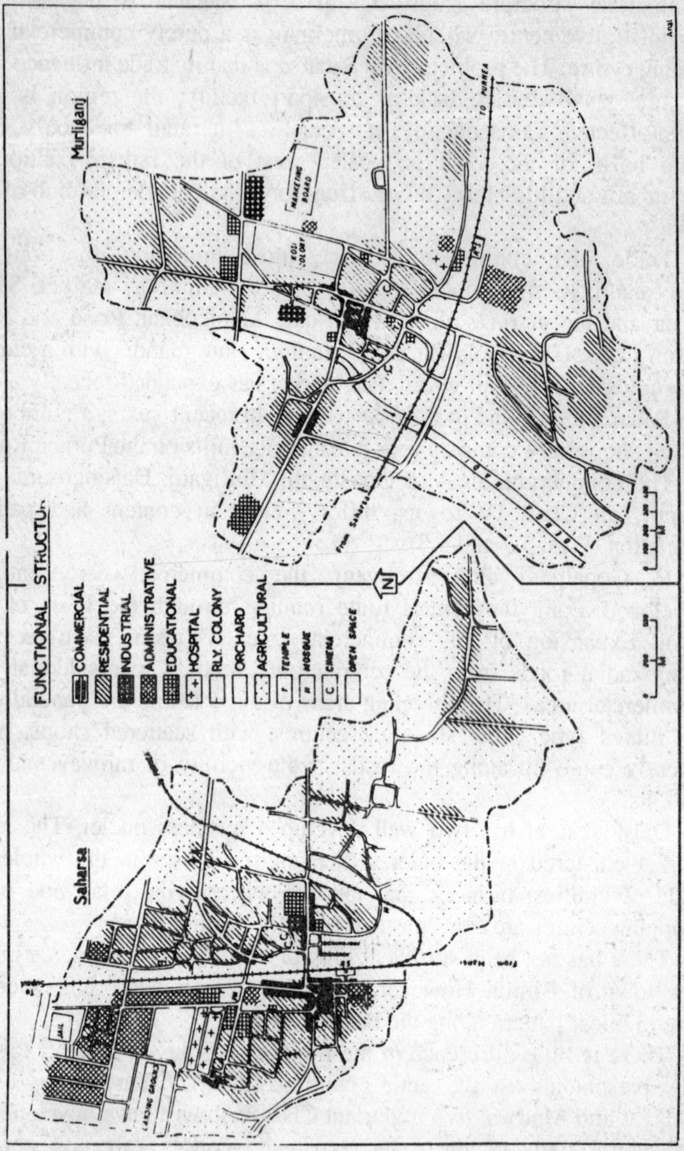

Fig. 5.5: Functional structure: Saharsa and Murliganj.

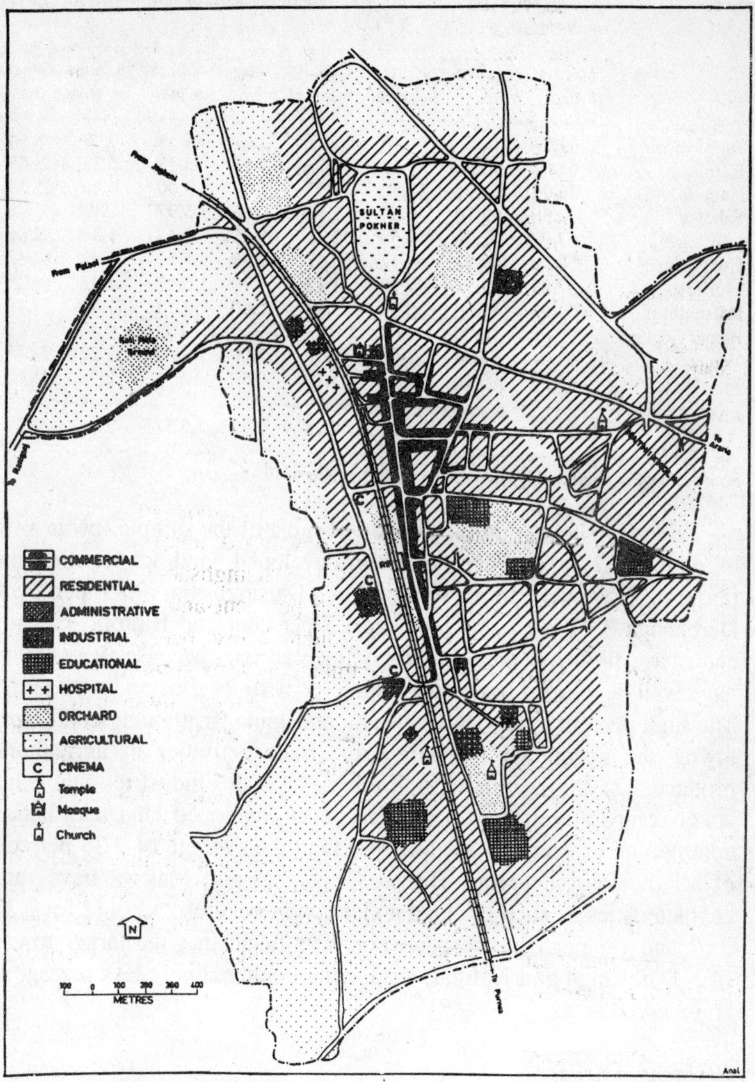

Fig. 5.6: Functional structure: Forbesganj.

Table 5.4: Proportion of area in different types of land-uses in sample towns of North Bihar

Sample total	*Per cent to the total area*		*Per cent to the total developed area*					
	Developed	*Undeveloped*	*Residential*	*Commercial*	*Industrial*	*Educational*	*Administrative*	*Others*
Darbhanga	91.5	8.5	61.16	3.77	2.67	14.38	9.08	8.94
Katihar	63.62	36.38	58.14	2.17	4.48	6.48	5.38	23.68
Hajipur	38.09	61.91	52.50	3.35	1.00	3.00	4.40	35.75
Saharsa	50.30	49.70	50.66	2.14	0.28	3.97	11.92	31.03
Forbesganj	63.00	37.00	58.50	2.35	5.45	9.45	1.39	22.86
Gopalganj	50.50	49.50	54.77	0.67	2.38	5.94	1.92	34.32
Murliganj	57.83	42.17	49.97	1.15	1.70	6.12	1.83	40.23
Dalsinghsarai	53.50	46.50	50.98	3.85	2.80	3.73	1.49	37.15
Birpur	30.00	70.00	60.69	0.32	—	0.32	0.40	38.27
Jainagar	51.06	48.94	51.00	3.50	5.00	3.50	3.22	33.78
Mairwa	19.81	80.19	48.31	1.50	0.50	2.51	2.58	44.60
Average	51.75	48.25	54.23	2.25	2.37	5.37	3.94	31.87

Source: Data calculated by the author with the help of Planimeter.

Table 5.4 shows that on an average most of the sample towns have used about 2.25 per cent of their developed land for commercial purpose. However, some towns, like, Dalsinghsarai 3.85 per cent, Darbhanga 3.77 per cent, Jainagar 3.5 per cent and Hajipur 3.35 per cent, have higher percentage in commercial use, because these towns have well developed trade and commerce with its surrounding regions. The high percentage in Dalsinghsarai and Jainagar, though small-sized towns, are accounted for their large trade activities in agricultural produce. On the contrary, in Katihar, Railway, industries and other cover comparatively higher percentage of developed land and, hence, commercial use occupy slightly less than the average of 2.25 per cent of all the sample towns. Birpur, Gopalganj and Mairwa have rural characteristics as such the land under commercial use account for 0.32, 0.67 and 1.5 per cent, respectively. It is noted that the larger towns, like, Darbhanga and Katihar, are having comparatively less acreage in commercial areas.

Residential Areas

More land of the developed urban area, in general, is devoted to residential use than to any other use (Bartholomew, 1955, p. 26), and it is, in fact, the most important land-use in the sample towns. Analysis of land-uses in sample towns reveals that the percentage of the residential land to the total developed area of the town ranges from about 48.31 per cent in Mairwa to 61.46 per cent in Darbhanga. This indicates the predominance of residential uses in sample towns. Higher percentage in Darbhanga (61.16%), Birpur (60.69%), Katihar (58.14%), Forbesganj (58.50%) is mainly due to greater employment opportunities in trade and commerce, administrative offices as well as educational institutions. In other towns, namely, Gopalganj (54.77%), Hajipur (52.50%), Saharsa (50.66%), Dalsinghsarai (50.98%) and Jainagar (51%) residential land-use occupy less than average of 54.23 per cent of the developed area. These towns have vast agricultural land and the population density is also less which accounts for rural characteristics.

Nevertheless, urban dwellers use a large part of the townspace for residential purposes. Mayer (1967, p. 497) observes that 'residential space undergoes changes both in location and in character as a result of development in trade and commerce and technological advances'. It is noted that the residential zone, in the sample towns, is quite extensive and widely distributed so that it occupies a large part of the total settled space. In most cases it is rather inseparable from other land-uses. However, the residential area located in the inner zone of the town differs considerably with that located in the outer zone. It is evident that there is a lot of congestion in the older core of the town where the residential land-use often inter-mingles with commercial activity. Recent expansions in trade and commerce have led to encroachment upon the residential areas, in the inner part of town, by shops, godowns, etc. This is particularly in evidence at Saifganj in Katihar and Bari Bazar in Darbhanga. These older parts of the respective towns are characterised by congestion, poor drainage and unhygienic conditions. The multi-storeyed buildings both old and new, which are quite common in the inner zone, decrease in dimension and character towards the arterial roads that lead to the outer periphery of the town where the residential buildings are spacious, new and fitted with better civic amenities. Development of high, middle and lower class residential areas has often followed a distinct pattern in the wake of town expansion and laying of new transport network.

Administrative Zone

The administrative zone is distinct and well-developed in almost all the sample towns. According to administrative hierarchy, a town may have the block office and the police station at the lowest level to officers of the S.D.O., S.P., D.M., Commissioner and the judiciary at district and division. It is noted that the administrative area ranges from 0.40 per cent in Birpur to 11.92 per cent in Saharsa of the total developed area among the sample towns. The lower percentage in Darbhanga (9.08%), a divisional town, is due to compact housing and non-availability of suitable land in its vicinity. The other sample towns have somehow proportionately developed land under administrative use. The administrative zone in sample towns is still quite separate, but expansion in the area under other land-uses has obliterated its separate identity in larger towns. For example, administrative building in Darbhanga, once located separately on the southern fringe of the town in Laheriasarai, had now been engulfed by expansion in residential areas from all sides.

Special mention has to be made of the district headquarters of Gopalganj and Hajipur, where administrative zones occupy the core of the towns and are surrounded by residential and commercial areas. However, in Katihar and Saharsa, the administrative zone occurs separately from other functional areas. In other sample towns, this zone is located along the arterial road adjoining the residential area.

Industrial Zone

There is general lack of large-scale industrial establishments in the sample towns of North Bihar, mainly because they have grown in a predominantly agrarian set up. Hence, it is difficult to identify the industrial zone in these towns. The land devoted to industries is higher in Forbesganj (5.45%), Jainagar (5.0%) and Katihar (4.48%). In these towns about 19 per cent of working population depend on industries. Darbhanga, the larger town, has only 2.67 per cent of the developed land under industrial landscape.

Birpur (nil), Saharsa (0.28%), Hajipur (1.0%) and Mairwa (0.5%) towns are industrially less developed and they do not exhibit distinct industrial landschape. However, a small industrial zone especialising in jute processing and flour milling is identified in the southern part of Katihar. This zone occurs separately from other urban land-use, somewhat close to the paddy fields. Development of similar industrial zone has also taken place at Forbesganj. It is worth noting that in the sample towns most of the household industrial establishments generally run inside the residential houses as a traditional profession and cottage industries. Consequently, they do not form a separate industrial landscape.

Educational Zone

The educational institutions, ranging from primary school to university colleges, also do not form a distinct zone in most of the sample towns. The land devoted to educational use ranges from 0.32 per cent in Birpur to 14.38 per cent in Darbhanga, of the total developed area. Higher percentage of developed area under educational use is the reflection of town economy and prosperity. Towns having percentage less than Darbhanga are Forbesganj (9.45%), Katihar (6.15%), Murliganj (6.12%), Gopalganj (5.94%), Jainagar (3.5%), Saharsa (3.97%), Dalsinghsarai (3.73%), Hajipur (3.0%) and Mairwa (2.51%). There is a general tendency to establish educational institutions particularly colleges in the outer parts of towns mainly because of the availability of cheap land. This is very much in evidence at Katihar, Murliganj, Forbesganj, Gopalganj and Mairwa. The primary and secondary schools, however, are located in the developed and settled parts of the towns.

Agricultural Area

Agricultural land in urban study is treated as undeveloped land. The area devoted to agriculture or horticulture is quite large in some sample towns where it forms the most dominant occupation. On an average about 48.25 per cent of urban area is devoted to agricultural use in sample towns. Agricultural area ranges from 8.5 per cent in Darbhanga to 80.19 per cent in Mairwa. Birpur (70.0%), Hajipur (61.91%), have higher percentage whereas Saharsa (49.7%), Gopalganj (49.5%), Jainagar (48.9%), Dalsinghsarai (46.5%), Murliganj (42.1%), Forbesganj (37.0%) and Katihar (36.3%) have more or less than the average of sample towns. It is noted that the agricultural area, within the town and in its neighbourhood, is usually devoted to horticulture and vegetable production. But in some sample towns, namely, Mairwa, Birpur and Hajipur, production of cereals, like, wheat and maize, also takes place. These lands are in the process of being developed as residential area or for other urban uses.

Other Functional Zones

Among other functional zones, the transport zone is well developed and easily identifiable at various railway stations and their adjacent quarters. For example, Katihar, Saharsa and Darbhanga have well distinct railway zones where these account for 12.21, 4.65 and 5.35 per cent of the total developed land, respectively. This zone is also found in all the sample towns, except Birpur. It is noted that a large urban space is occupied by railway quarters and establishments at Katihar. The layout plans of railway quarters are so identical that they present a monotonous picture both architecturally and otherwise. Though this zone is provided with civic amenities, like, running water, electricity and toilets with flushing system, it suffers from coal dust pollution.

A number of religious institutions, namely, temples, mosques and churches occur in a scattered manner in almost all the sample towns. Consequently, they do not form a zone. It may be, however, true that in some towns these religious centres formed the nuclei of town growth. The area lying between Konhara Ghat to Gandak bridge in Hajipur can be cited for such dominant religious nucleus.

Civic amenities like a club or park or play-ground is still a taboo in most of the sample towns. However, commercial recreation is available in the form of a cinema-house in almost all the towns. This is located either in commercial zone or residential area. Large towns, like, Darbhanga, Katihar, Hajipur and Saharsa, have more than two cinema-houses. These towns also have football grounds which are sometimes used for occasional open air theatres and public gatherings. These open spaces are generally located on the outer periphery of the town.

Hospitals and dispensaries, forming the medical zone, are generally located near the administrative area. This is particularly in evidence a Darbhanga where the medical college and attached hospital form a compact medical zone, which accounts for 4.34 per cent of the developed land of the town, surrounded by residential area on all sides. However, the primary health centres at smaller towns, like, Murliganj and Dalsinghsarai, are located in an isolated manner which do not form a zone.

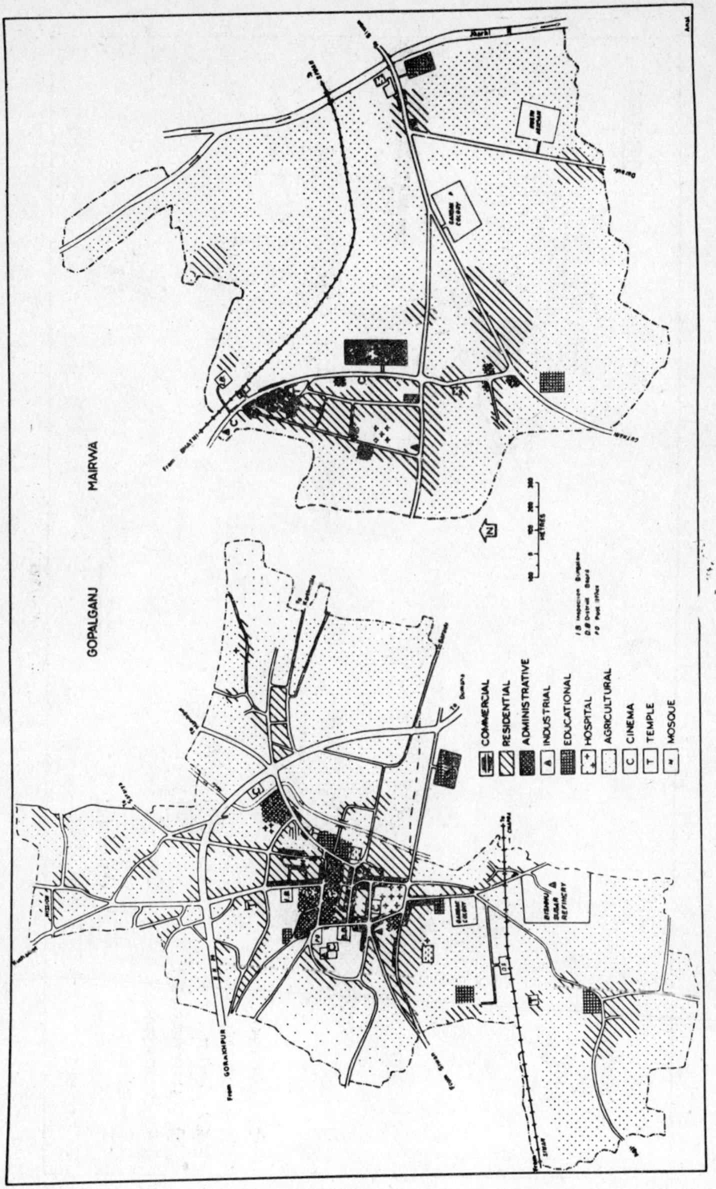

Fig. 5.7: Functional structure: Gopalganj and Mairwa.

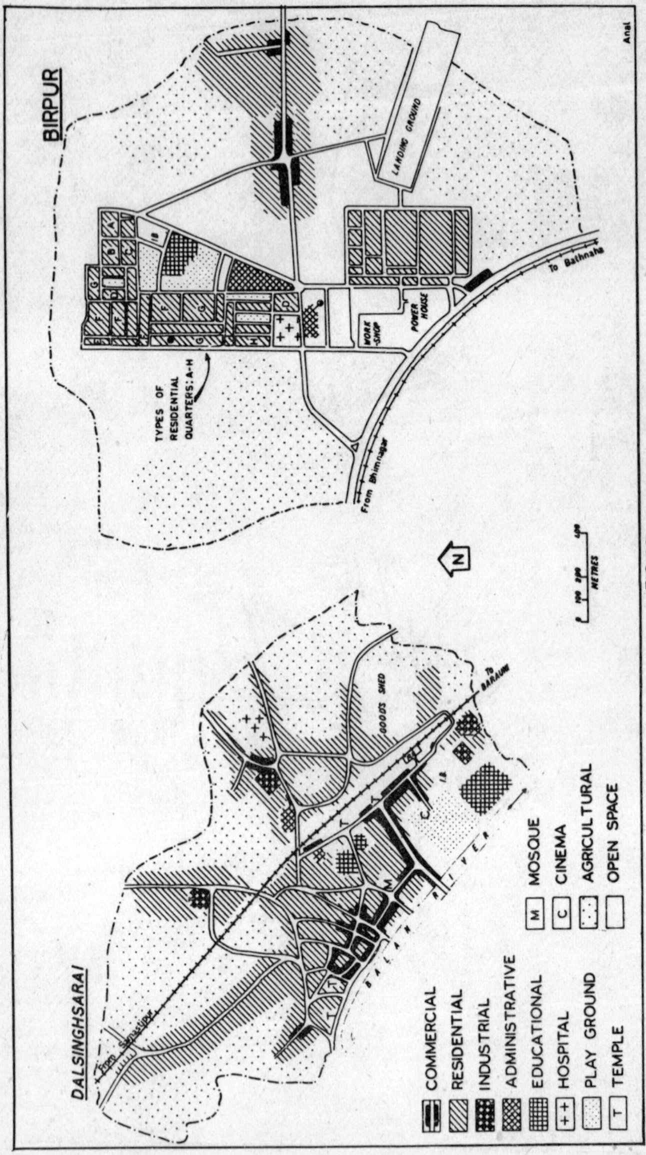

Fig. 5.8: Functional structure: Dalsinghsarai and Birpur,

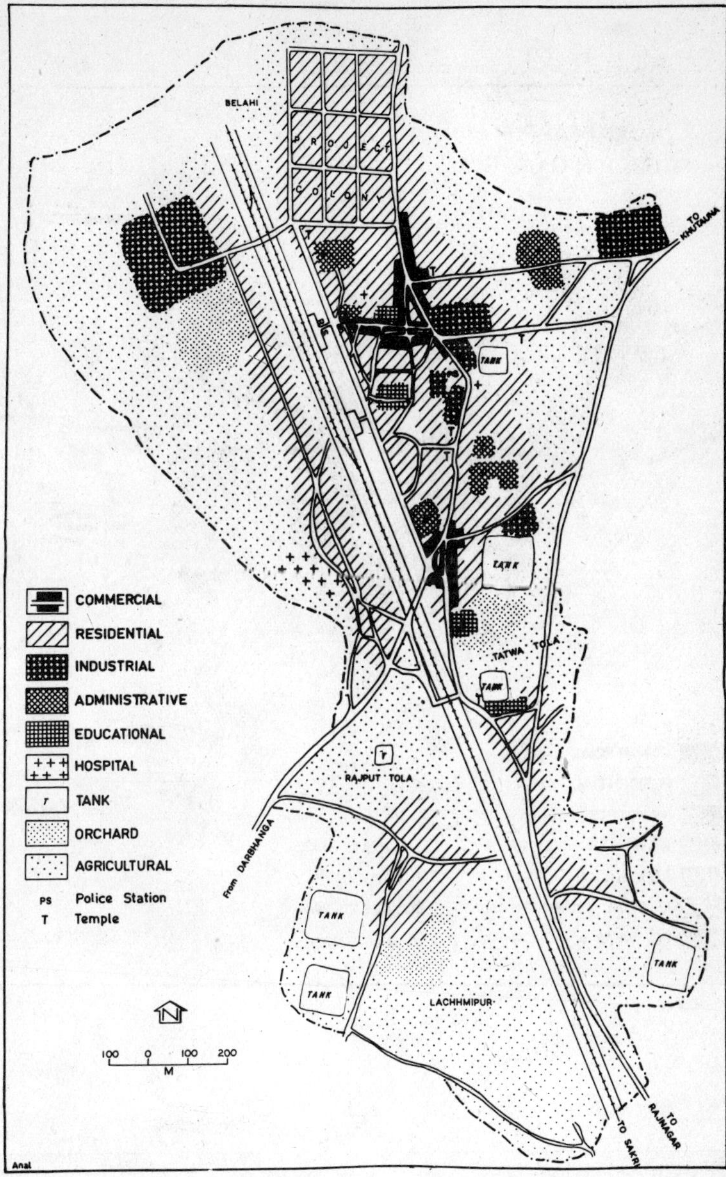

Fig. 5.9: Jainagar: functional structure.

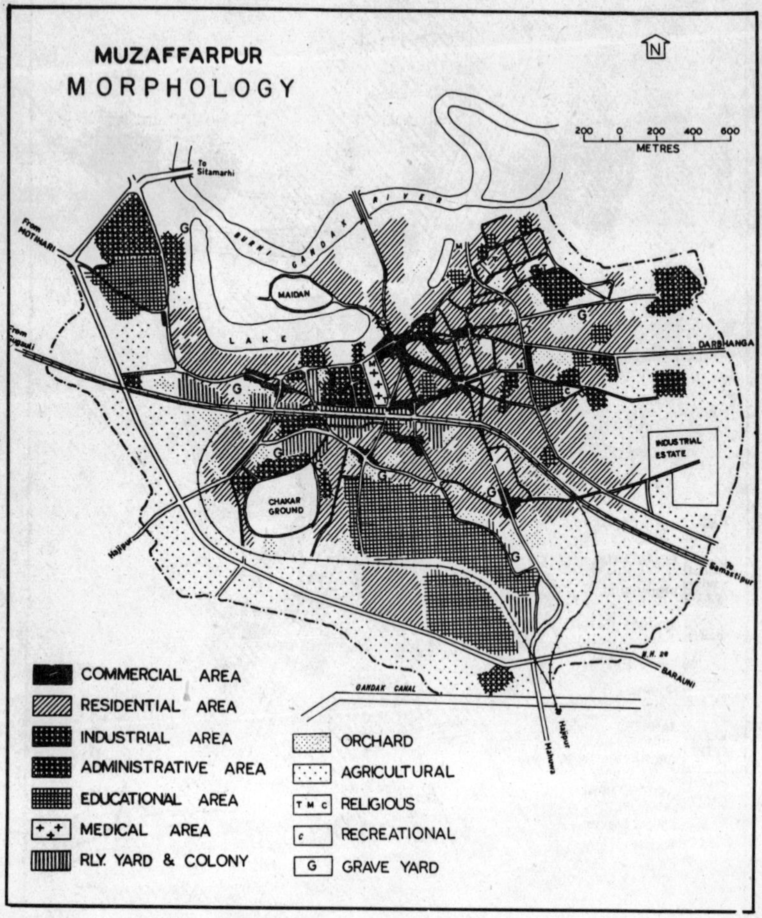

Fig. 5.9A: Muzaffarpur: morphology.

REFERENCES

Bartholomew, Harland and Jack Wood (1955): *Land Uses in American Cities*, Cambridge.

Boyce, Ronald R. and W.A.V. Clark (1964): The Concept of Shape in Geography, *Geographical Review*, LIV, 4, pp. 561-72.

Dickinson, R.E. (1932): The Distribution and Function of the Small Urban Settlement of East Anglia, *Geography*, 17, pp. 19-31.

Dickinson, R.E. (1948): "The Scope and Status of Urban Geography. An Assessment", In (Mayer, H.M. *et al.* (Ed.) 1967. *Readings in Urban Geography*), pp. 10-26.

Elhance, D.N. (1966): *Fundamental of Statistics*, Allahabad.

Gibbs, Jack, P. (Ed.) (1961): *Urban Research Method*. D.Van Nostrand Company, Inc. Affiliated East-West Press Pvt. Ltd., New Delhi.

Harris, C.D. and E.L. Ullman (1945): "The Nature of Cities", In H.M. Mayer and C.F. Kohn (Ed.): *Readings in Urban Geography*, Allahabad, pp. 277-86.

Hartman, George, W. (1950): The Central Business District—A Study in Urban Geography, *Economic Geography*, 26, pp. 237-44.

Hickoncen, G.M. (1950): The Sample Study — a Method of its Limitations, *Journal of Geography*, LIX, pp. 151-59.

Mayer, Harold M. and C.F. Kohn, (Ed.) (1967): *Readings in Urban Geography*, Central Book Depot, Allahabad.

Murphy, Raymond E. (1966): *The American City: An Urban Geography*, McGraw-Hill Book Company, New York.

Ramesh, A. (1973): "Some Aspects of the Functional Morphology of the Towns of the Tamil Nadu, Deccan", In R.L. Singh (Ed.): *Urban Geography in Developing Countries*, N.G.S.I., Varanasi, pp. 224-33.

Rao, V.L.S.P. (1962): Macro Urban Analysis Geographer's Contribution, *Bombay Geographical Magazine*, 2, pp. 5-11.

Reddy, N.B.K. (1973): "Occupational Structure of the Urban Settlements in the Krishna and Godavari Deltas", in R.L. Singh (Ed.) 1973. *Urban Geography in Developing Countries*, N.G.S.I., Varanasi, pp. 119-36.

Singh, R.L. (1955): *Banaras: A study in Urban Geography*, N.K. and Bros, Varanasi.

Smailesr, A.E. (1953): *The Geography of Towns*, London.

6

MORPHOLOGY OF RESIDENTIAL AREAS

THE ARCHITECTURAL pattern of buildings and their layout plans not only vary from one town to the other but also within the same town, depending upon the period of town development. A large proportion of the land in our urban centres is used for residential purposes. Consequently, the residential area is the largest component of the urban space (Taneja, 1973, p. 70). Its impact on the urban structure is manifold, because it provides accommodation to the urban-dwellers as well as the commuters. Any increase in city population leads to a corresponding increase in demand for land for housing purposes and for structures which yield housing services (Hirsch, 1973, p. 59).

Residential Location

The urban space in the towns of North Bihar is largely used for residential purposes; this is equally true of large and small towns. In the last three decades, there has been not only a phenomenal increase in town population but also in the percentage of urban-dwellers owning their residential quarters or residential land. This trend is likely to further intensify in the coming decades. The mosaic of residential area in general is an out-growth of socio-economic factors operating through time. It is noted that the wealthy urban-dwellers owning large residential quarters generally live in the central part whereas the poorer classes live on the outer fringes. Social factors, such as tendency of people to live in groups based on income or profession or caste or region or language, also determine the nature and character of residential areas. Thus, residential colonies of doctors, advocates and professors, having more or less similar tastes, are commonly met with in these towns. Nearness to the place of work is also a factor influencing location of residential quarters. However, residential location is dynamic; it undergoes changes through time with the development of the urban transport network.

As noted earlier, a majority of the towns of North Bihar still reflects their rural or urban antecedents as expressed by the architectural character of buildings and the nature of their functions. Though some of these towns, exhibiting exotic impulses, have grown into huge complexes they have not yet been able to discard some of their former rural characteristics. It is noted that the residential quarters occur, in large or small measure, in almost all the parts of the town. Even the interstices between the main shopping streets are used for residential use. Quite often, there is a haphazard mixture of styles and classes of dwellings, from *Pucca* to thatched ones, interspersed among market lots or vacant land. Thus, Smailes (1953, p. 90) rightly notes that residential segmentation is a familiar feature and soon makes its appearance as a town grows.

The cumulative effect of certain centrifugal and centripetal tendencies can be clearly discerned, in determining both the original layout and the later expansion of the residential area (Smailes, 1953, p. 89). Taylor observes that in the initial stage of town growth there is perhaps no control over the inter-mingling of various town functions. Consequently, even today in almost all the towns of North Bihar, the area immediately surrounding the business section presents a different picture, as regards its physical structure as well as its social control (Nigam, 1964, p. 48). The ground-floor on the front side of buildings along the main arterial roads in the business area is used for commercial purposes but their upper floors and back-portions are often utilised for residential purposes. However, the most attractive residential sections of towns have developed only recently; they occur where natural and cultural conditions have combined to facilitate the development of exceptionally beautiful and dignified houses, owned by traders, doctors and other affluent communities.

Distributional Pattern of Residential Areas

Cities differ from one another in residential characteristics (Murphy, 1966, p. 373). But a large part of the town is occupied by residential land-use of different kinds. Most of the towns, with medieval antecedents, are characterised by both old and modern designs of architecture. However, a few towns with modern architectural designs have emerged only recently as a consequence of deliberate planning. The residential areas of older towns are characterised by compactness and congestion while those of newer towns, developed particularly after the introduction of the railways and improvements in road transport, have wider roads and palatial buildings with all sorts of modern amenities. Thus, the residential characteristics of towns or their segments, developed in the medieval, British and post-independence periods, are discussed separately.

Medieval Period

A large number of towns were founded, in North Bihar, by Muslim rulers during the medieval times. Considerations of defence led them to build towns, like, Darbhanga, Hajipur and Samastipur, at commanding sites on river banks. Consequently, the houses in general were constructed huddled together in a compact manner (Karan, 1957, p. 70), on the small stretch of the natural levee that remained unaffected by floods. Muslim culture and their social taboos are usually reflected in the style of architecture and the pattern and design of these buildings. Segregation of settlements from other communities happened to be an important consideration, resulting in the growth of separate Muslim enclaves and *Mohallas*, which can even now be identified. Examples of such Muslim enclaves or *Mohallas* are Mirzapur and Maulaganj in Darbhanga, Anwarpur and Ismailpur in Hajipur and Saifganj in Katihar. Quite often, the whim of the ruler counted a lot in the expansion of residential areas in a number of towns. Conversion of temples into mosques and some of the Hindu population into Muslims resulted in the development of a mixed, often complex, design of architecture. The compact residential pattern, developed in the Muslim period on defence considerations, is characterised by narrow, zig-zag and winding lanes, along which generally occur single-storeyed houses made up of lime and brick powder, with pigeon-hole type windows and small entrance gates. Prevalence of the *Purdah* system, among the Muslim women and among the women of the conservative caste Hindus, during former times, has been responsible for the development of this type of residential design. Examples of this design are found in the predominantly Muslim *Mohallas* of Darbhanga, Hajipur and Siwan.

British Period

A rapid expansion in the residential areas of towns of North Bihar took place during the British period. Elevation of some towns or urban centres into district and sub-divisional headquarters either contributed to congestion in the existing residential areas or led to town expansion under the impact of various centripetal and centrifugal forces. Consequently, Civil Lines, railway colonies and cantonments were developed distinctly apart from the pre-existing residential areas. Thus, bungalow-type residential areas with lawns attached to residences, besides parks, play-grounds, open spaces and roads lined with trees, developed in the Civil Lines. The old residential areas, however, continued to grow in congestion and unhygienic conditions. It is noted that distance from the work-place or the central business area and the time taken to cover that distance are important considerations influencing residential growth. Consequently, development of roads not only led to expansion in the residential built-up towards the outer margins of towns but also brought radical changes in their former character, which has been mostly rural or urban.

The structure and design of buildings in the civil line, railway colony and cantonment are quite different than those in other residential areas. The civil line is mainly administrative in function, and contains various government offices and spacious bungalows for officers. Its size varies from town to town, depending upon the importance of the administrative function. Buildings in the civil line are invariably made of bricks with either sloping tiled or flat-cemented roofs, and have large windows, wide verandahs, a courtyard and spacious lawns. Consequently, the density of dwellings here is much lower as compared to the older residential sections of towns. The residential quarters in the railway colony, though made of brick and cement, are often less accommodious and, with lower heights of ceilings, present a monotonous sight.

Post-Independence Period

Regeneration of residential areas in the commercial core and their outward expansion, leading to the growth of suburbs, have taken place particularly in the post-independence period. Adoption of the European building style by well-to-do elites and traders has resulted in recent construction of spacious bungalows on the outskirts of towns where ample open space is available. A few planned residential colonies with modern sanitary facilities have also been developed by various public and semi-public organisations, whose employees prefer to stay near the places of their work. Construction of these residential colonies, generally on the periphery of the town, has also generated an impulse for the shift in population from the congested and over-crowded central zone of the town towards its periphery. Development of the road transport and commuter services have also led to the construction of detached and semi-detached residential buildings along the road-side in a 'ribbon-like fashion'.

The phenomenal increase in population in the post-independence period has not only put a great strain on the existing residential space but has also led to development of new residential areas, both planned and unplanned. Thus, on the one hand we find Western-style modern bungalows in localities which have been developed in a planned manner whereas *Jhuggis* and *Jhumpris*, with mud-walls and roofs of tin-sheets or straw and tile, constitute an eye-sore in the unplanned localities where most of the constructions are unauthorised. Not only new multi-storeyed and multi-family dwellings of the well-to-do families have come up on the outskirts of towns but most of the old residential houses in the central zone have been either renovated or completely re-built with additions in floor space. Government-owned residential buildings, both bungalows and flat-types, can be seen in the civil lines, railway colonies and the new townships at Begusarai, Barauni and Birpur.

Morphological Characteristics of Existing Residential Areas

The prosperity of urban-dwellers is often reflected in the architectural design and the morphological pattern of residential buildings. Economic and social factors set in certain aggregational and segregational trends, resulting in the growth and evolution of different types of residential areas. The towns of North Bihar still reflect, in some measure, their former rural antecedents, including areal differentiation based on caste, religion and feudalistic approach. In general, people tend to reside in areas inhabited by their own caste-men or religious group. Thus, residential areas also exhibit both cultural and occupational segregations. This is also true of West European countries where, according to Carter (1976, p. 264), individuals tend to gravitate not only to areas in which they can compete for livelihood more effectively but also areas populated by others of similar race, interests, culture or economic status. A similar trend has been identified, to some extent, in the towns of North Bihar. For example, sweepers or *Bhangis* who have been until recently considered as social out-castes and are employed in menial and low-paying occupations, tend to live in a segregated manner. But occurrence of residential segregation is far greater in occupational groups with clearly defined status rather than in case of groups whose status is ambiguous (Carter, 1976, p. 264).

Though no two towns of North Bihar have experienced identical growth conditions, there is, however, some similarity in their land-use patterns. For example, let us examine the residential land-use pattern of Saharsa, a town which has emerged only recently (Fig. 6.1A). Segregation of various residential areas in this town is largely based on considerations of language, caste and religion. The business core of the town has been acquired by the *Marwaris* whereas the Muslims have settled in its south-eastern portion where, in course of time, all the Urdu-speaking persons have congregated. Among the Maithili-speaking groups, the Rajputs, Kayasthas and Brahmins have developed their separate residential enclaves at Gangzala, Kayasthtola and Chanakyapuri, respectively. The *Goalas* also maintain their separate identity in Gangzala ward. The *Bengalis*, who are less numerous, have settled near the railway station; their dwellings are mostly compact and congested. Other residential areas have a mixed population of various castes, sects and linguistic groups.

Sometimes, segregation of residential areas has taken place on the basis of occupations. This is particularly in evidence at Katihar where industrial workers engaged in jute, rice and flour mills have their residences in close proximity to these mills located on the southern extremity of the town while the railway officials and engine drivers live in graded Railway quarters in Amla Toli and Driver's Toli, respectively. The civil line is still in the process of development in Mirchai *mohalla* towards the north-west and the traders have their residential colony in Saifganj. Landless sweepers have constructed their hutments on Government land, between the two rail tracks in the neighbourhood of Tatma Tola on the northern extremity of the town (Fig. 6.1B). A similar segregation of residential areas on the basis of occupational specialisation is also seen in Forbesganj and other towns of North Bihar.

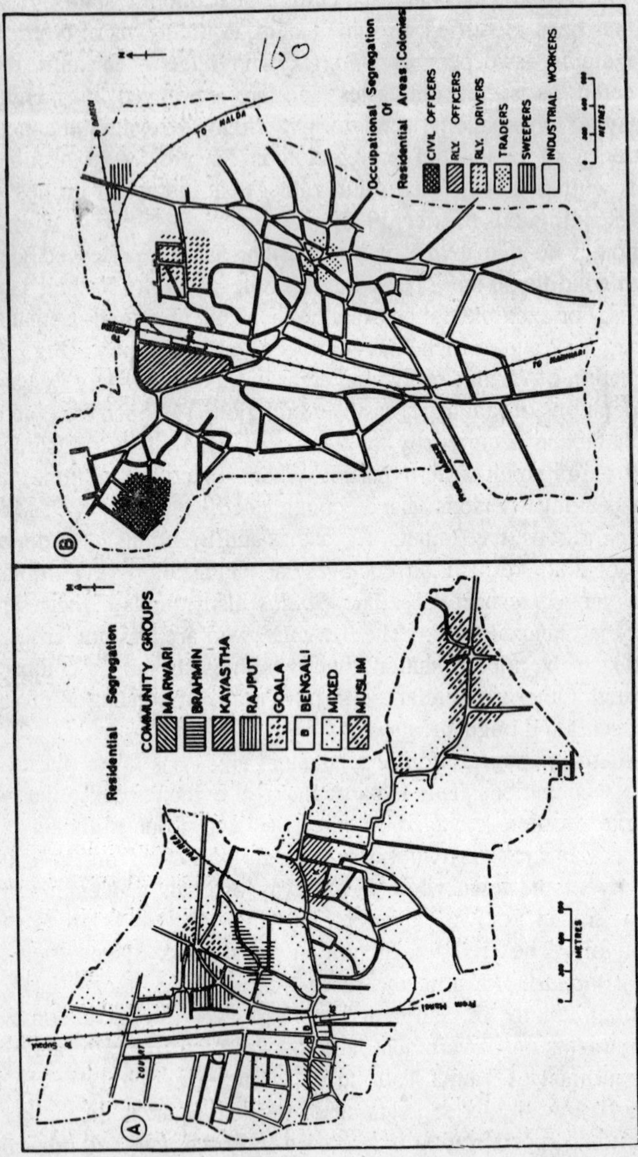

Fig. 6.1: (A) Saharsa: residential segregation, (B) Katihar: occupational segregation of residential areas: colonies.

Residential Zones

Economic and social forces have distinct bearings on the physical fabric of residential areas. The aesthetic sense of the town-dwellers and their income status are often indicated by the type of residential accommodation they occupy. Each building, whether palatial or wattle-walled or thatch-roofed, not only reflects the economic status of its owner but also his cultural background. Thus, three classes of residences or residential areas – higher, middle and lower – can be identified on the basis of the type and style of building structures and the amount of civic amenities available therein. Recent expansion of urban centres has set in a distinct trend that indicates some shifting in these classes of residential areas. Figures 6.2-6.4, showing the spatial distribution of the above-mentioned types of residential areas, in some towns of North Bihar, also reveal inter-fusions and inter-minglings of various types. Thus, high class residences, sometimes, occur side by side with the other type as a result of unplanned constructions. Though the residential pattern, suggested by Burgess and others (Murphy, 1966, p. 207) for the towns of Western countries, does not apply to the towns of North Bihar, still there is some similarity in the growth pattern of residential areas in both the Western and North Bihar towns.

In general, high class residences occupy only about five per cent of the total residential space in the towns of North Bihar. But in larger towns, like, Darbhanga, Muzaffarpur and Katihar, the proportion of high class residences is slightly higher because of their importance as administrative, commercial, industrial and transport centres. The high class residential area in Darbhanga lies towards the north and is synonymous with the 'Raj area' of former times. It is a well-planned locality having avenues lined with ornamental and shady trees which have now grown quite old. Imposing mansions, like the 'Raj Palace' and Anandbagh buildings, are located here in a garden-cum-orchard complex with large ponds and play-grounds (Plate 7). A large number of modern, Western-style bungalows have recently come up around 'the Raj area' compound and beyond the municipal limits in the north-east. High class residences are also found in close proximity to the Civil Lines and the Medical College complex in Laheriasarai (Figs. 4.3 and 6.2).

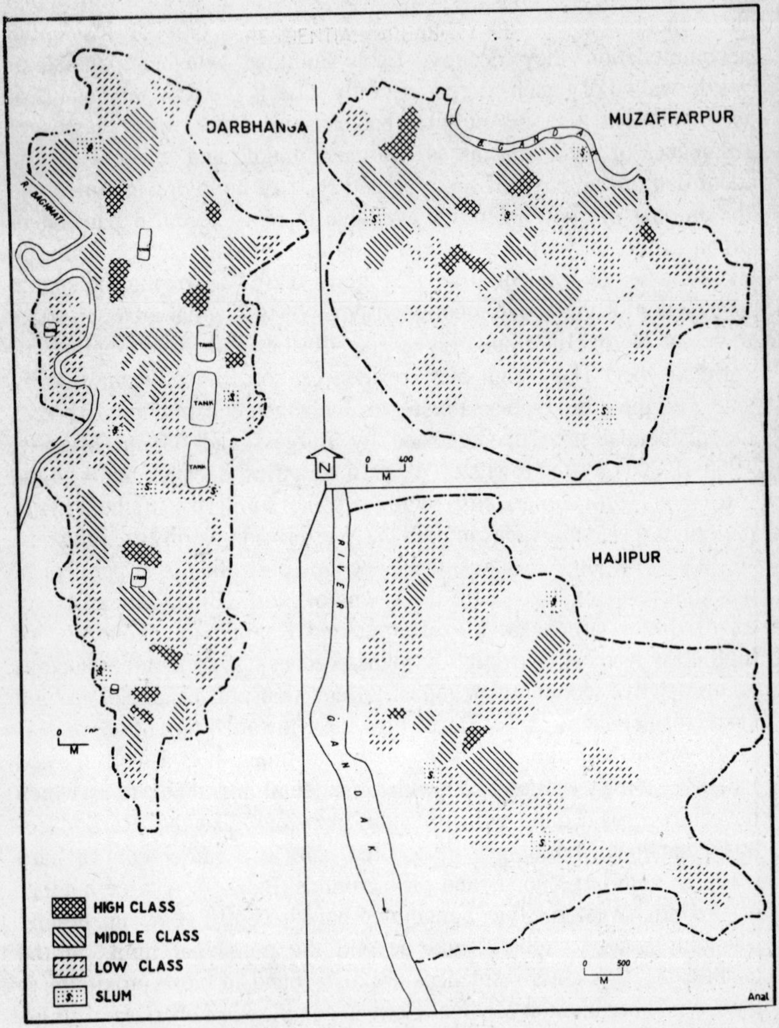

Fig. 6.2: Residential area: Types; Darbhanga, Muzaffarpur and Hajipur.

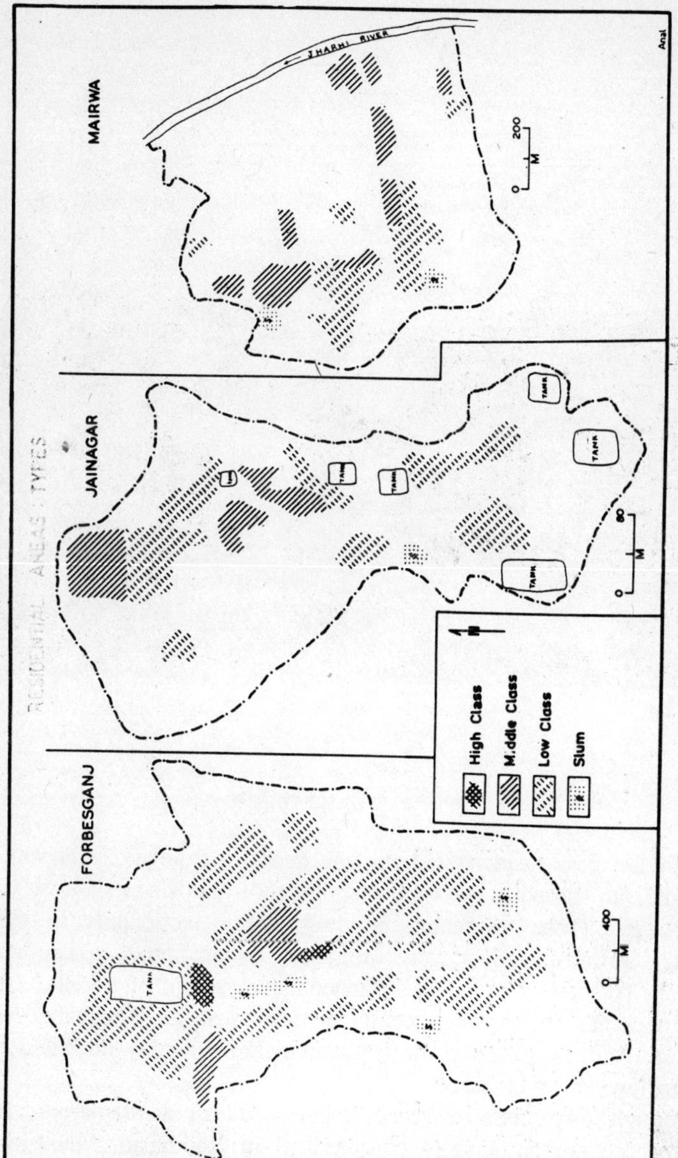

Fig. 6.3: Residential areas: Types; Forbesganj, Jainagar and Mairwa.

Plate 7: The Raj Palace at Anandbagh in the city of Darbhanga.

Middle class residences, both one and two-storeyed, comprise a considerable proportion of the residential area in the town of Darbhanga. These residential buildings occur particularly in Bari Bazar, Gullubara, Saudagar Mohalla, Balbhadrapur, Bakerganj, Bengali Tola and Misir Tola. Planned development of middle class residences has taken place recently in Lakshmisagar, Bibipakhar and near the Railway Colony. The latter areas are generally inhabited by traders, lawyers and teachers.

Though lower class residences occur in almost all the parts of the town, these are particularly concentrated in Kadirabad, Maulaganj, Mirzapur, Pandasarai, parts of Misir Tola, Bengali Tola and eastern Balbhadrapur. High density of houses and population, besides lack of civic amenities, are characteristics of these areas. Sometimes, the houses are so compact and close to one another that these have contributed to the development of slum conditions as in Kathalbari, Mullaganj, Saifullaganj and Saidpur. These areas are mostly inhabited by street hawkers, vegetable sellers and poor people doing menial jobs. Lower class residences are also found as pockets in Kilaghat, Subhankarpur and near the railway station.

The residential fabric of Muzaffarpur has been largely affected by its importance as an administrative, commercial and transport centre. Consequently, high class residences developed in close proximity to the administrative, railway and industrial establishments. However, isolated clusters of high class residences of civil officials and other elites of the town, namely, traders, doctors, lawyers and professors, can be observed in various parts of the city. Middle class residences occupy a comparatively much larger area than the lower class residences. These include spacious houses, both single and double storeyed, made of concrete and cement, particularly in Damuchak, Tinkothia Colony, Police Line, Suttapatti, Saraiyaganj, Motijheel, Kalyani, Kalambagh and Pankhatoli wards of the city.

Lower class residences have come up on land initially available on cheaper rates. They, however, occur side by side with the middle class residences. The areas of lower class residences are Kabari Tola, Gudari Bazar, Chhota Bazar, Kachisarai, Pakkisarai and Purani Bazar. These *Mohallas*, with the exception of Pakkisarai and Kachisarai, form parts of the commercial zone of the town; the latter, located on the eastern margin of the town, exhibits rural characteristics. Brick-built single-storey houses, occurring close together along narrow roads and streets that are often without footpaths, and a high density of population are characteristics of these areas which are inhabited by traders, shopkeepers and rikshaw-pullers. Also, existence of low-level industrial activity and employment opportunity have adversely affected the building pattern in the residential area. Consequently, poor people have developed their *Jhugi-Jhumpris*, which are very much identified as slums, in Kasai Tola, Nonia Tola and Amgola in the north and Chatrabhuj *mohalla* in the east. Slums have also come up near the Railway Colony.

Katihar also reflects the same pattern of residential growth as Muzaffarpur. Here high class residences occur in a scattered manner in Mirchai and Amla Tola (Figs. 4.6, 5.3 and 6.4). The middle class residences are found in close proximity to the business areas of the town, located in Mangal Bazar, Saifganj, Baigana, Binodpur and Dalan *mohallas*. The Railway Colony and the workers' quarters of the industrial establishments in the south are also identified as middle class residential areas. Lower class residences comparatively occupy a much larger area. Though these are distributed throughout the town, their predominance is noted in Dighi-Katihar, Gauri Tola, Eraki Tola, Durgapur and Harigram *mohallas*. In addition, numerous slums, inhabited by labourers and displaced persons, have developed as pockets in the lower and middle class residential areas.

Development of high class residential area is yet to take place in Hajipur and Saharsa. A few high class buildings have been, however, erected recently in these towns, in the midst of middle and lower class residences (Fig. 4.5, 5.4 and 6.2). The central part of Hajipur (Plate 8), characterised by double-storeyed buildings and having a large number of commercial establishments, can be classed as middle class residential area. Lower class residences are particularly noted in Anwarpur and Hathisarganj Tola in the eastern and northern parts of the town respectively. A few high class residences are also observed in Anwarpur and near the railway bridge.

The residential pattern of Saharsa is more rural than urban. It is characterised by a preponderance of lower class residences which are found throughout the town. Middle class residences occur only as pockets in the lower class residential area. Other sample towns exhibit similar residential characteristics as noted in the case of Hajipur and Saharsa (Fig. 6.3). The preponderance of lower class residences in these towns is so great that it is rather difficult to differentiate the various residential types. The larger towns, in general, show a greater degree of segregation. Consequently, cities, like, Darbhanga and Muzaffarpur, exhibit not only segregation of various residential types but also functional changes with the passage of time.

Analysis of the residential fabric of sample towns reveals that high class residences occur discretely both in the intermediate zone and towards the outer margins of towns. These are generally found in close proximity to the Civil Line or the administrative zone or as isolated clusters along the main roads. Construction of high class spacious buildings on the periphery of towns has been particularly made possible because of the availability of ample open space at reasonable rates. These are mostly of recent origin, and their separation from other residential types is quite difficult.

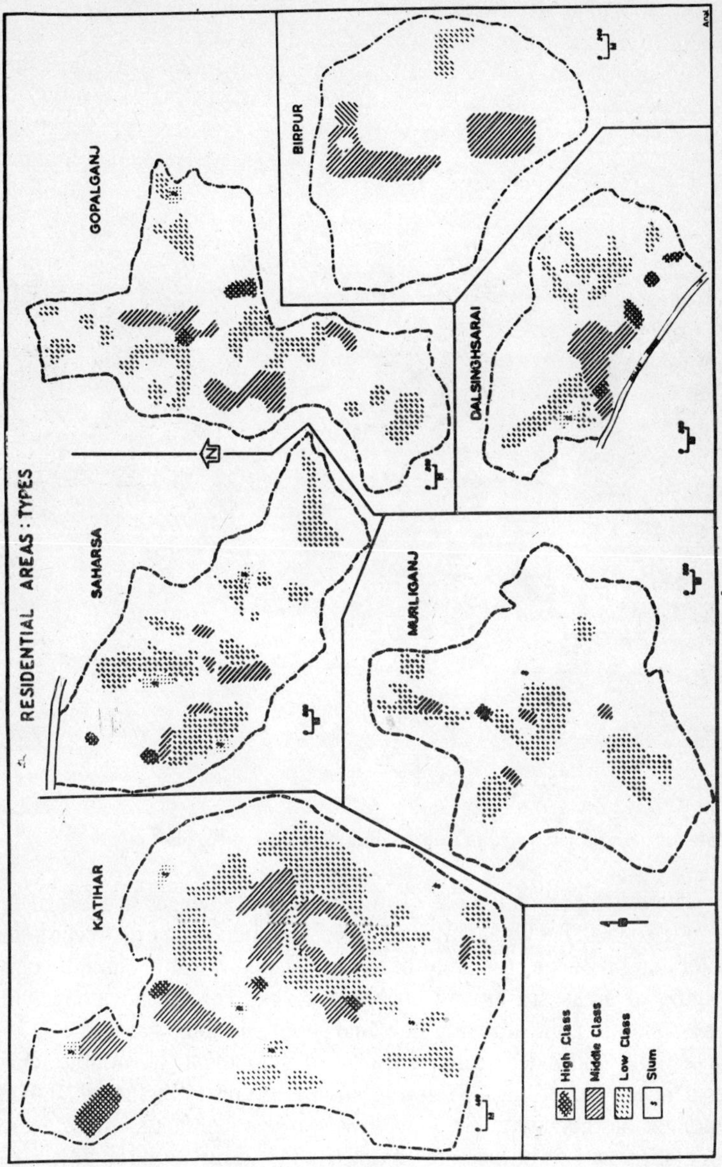

Fig. 6.4: Residential areas: Types; Katihar, Saharsa, Gopalganj, Murliganj, Dalsinghsarai and Birpur.

Plate 8: A terrace-top view of the Administrative block at Hajipur.

There is a preponderance of middle class residences in most of the sample towns. They generally occur in the middle ring or towards the outer margin of the core areas of towns. The houses in the middle class residential areas are mostly double-storeyed. They stand along wide roads and are comparatively new and more spacious than those in the older and congested core. Sectoral development of middle class residences, according to professional groups, including labour colonies, has been noted in some towns. It is noted that the densities of population and dwellings are comparatively lower in the middle class residential areas than those in the lower class residential areas.

Development of lower class residences has taken place generally in the older parts or the core areas of towns. Sometimes, they occur as isolated nuclei in other parts also. This area is marked by congestion and poor sanitation. People tend to reside here for no other reason than the nearness to the places of their work.

Though lower class residences cover large areas in almost all the towns of North Bihar, their proportion is much greater in lower status towns. It has been noted that lower class residential areas have high densities of both population and dwellings. They also exhibit wide variations in their internal structure, either due to admixture of other functions or expansions resulting from natural increase in population and immigration from rural areas. Buildings vacated by earlier occupants are often occupied for use by other occupants. Sometimes, a few of these may be demolished and replaced by better structures. Thus, changes from lower to middle class residences are not infrequent in these towns.

Slums

Urban slum means poor quality, sub-standard housing (Hirsch, 1973, p. 61). It can be also defined as an area of extremely deteriorated dwelling units occupied by low-income families, particularly the very poor wage earners. A high degree of congestion and overcrowding characterises this area. In America, the slum has been, sometimes, identified with *ghettos*, which are characterised by myriad of images – rotting tenements, garbage-strewn vacant lots, teeming population, congestion, pollution, poverty, crime and generally middle class environment (Ford and Griffin, 1979, p. 140). Over-crowding, fifth and insanitation often make it a breeding ground of diseases. Thus, it is a terrible place where people have been forced to live.

The slums of North Bihar towns usually consist of wattle-walled and thatch-roofed huts or mud-walled *Kachha* houses without any sanitary amenities. These are generally inhabited by people with poor economic status. In the last 30-40 years, there has been a big spurt in the migration of job-seekers from rural areas to the neighbouring towns in North Bihar which has necessarily aggravated the housing problem in urban areas. Thus, the less fortunate ones, with meagre income, have been left with no other option but to live in the blighted areas with other households, which has created further congestion and insanitation. Also, persons engaged in menial jobs, who are unable to rent a house, have occupied vacant suburban land (both municipal and railway property) on which they have built thatch-roofed huts (Plate 9). Thus, a large number of tenements have sprung up in this manner, forming the nucleus of a slum. Once a slum is established in this manner, other slums also follow suit. Sometimes, overcrowding in older households and structures leads to their deterioration which produces slum conditions.

Plate 9: A slum close to the railway yard at Katihar.

Field observations reveal that the number of slums varies with the functional status of individual towns. Towns rendering industrial function usually have a larger number of slums. For example, establishments of the jute processing industry and the railway workshop have been responsible for the growth of slums at Katihar. Similarly, development of slum has taken place on the periphery of the older core of Muzaffarpur where low-paid people engaged in commercial activity at Saraiyaganj live. Another slum has developed near the railway station, following the establishment of industries.

Darbhanga, being non-industrial in character, has fewer slums. Some of the very poor residences in the northern part of Kadirabad, Maulaganj and Pashikhana (near Rahamganj) represent slum conditions in this town.

Untouchability has invariably led to the growth of the *Bhangi* colonies in almost all the sample towns of North Bihar. Influx of refugees from East Pakistan (now Bangladesh), following the vivisection of India, also led to the growth of a large number of slums in the towns of Purnea, Katihar, Forbesganj, Supaul and Saharsa.

The growth of slums in North Bihar towns is not only indicative of the shortage of residential accommodation but also of the poor economic conditions of its residents, who cannot find a better way of life. Most of the slum-dwellers are poor and illiterate and lack civic sense. They include petty shop-keepers, vendors in perishable items, like, vegetable, meat, fish and milk, besides washermen, hawkers, sweepers, rickshaw-pullers and squatters.

The slums seem to be growing and, at present, there seems to be no effort towards slum-improvement or resettlement of the slum-dwellers. These aspects need to be considered in detail in any plan for the improvement of towns.

Residential Use in Relation to Other Functional Uses

The residential use, in the towns of North Bihar, is often mixed with other uses because people prefer to live in close proximity to the places of their work. Consequently, it is difficult to separate other functional uses from the residential areas. The pattern and extent of mix-up of other functional uses with the residential function varies according to the nature, characteristics and age of the towns. It is noted that areas devoted to commercial and administrative uses also have residential facilities (Figs. 5.2 and 5.9A). For example, a large number of urban-dwellers resides in the commercial areas of Bara Bazar, Gullubara (from Clock Tower to Raj Fort) and Bakerganj (Laheriasarai) in Darbhanga, which is a town of medieval origin. In general, the ground floor of buildings with street frontage is utilised for commercial and business purposes, while their upper floors and back-portions are used as family residences. This is also illustrated by Saraiyaganj and Suttapatti, the main business area of Muzaffarpur where traders have set up their business establishments on the ground floor of buildings along the main roads while their upper floors and back-portions are used for residential purposes. An inter-mingling of commercial activity, administrative and residential land-uses is also noted in Kalyani and Motijheel, which are the main business thoroughfares of Muzaffarpur.

This inter-mingling of commercial and residential land-uses is also typical of Jainagar, Dalsinghsarai, Mairwa and other towns of North Bihar. Development of a few commercial pockets as distinct from the residential areas has, however, taken place in a planned manner in some towns, like, Barauni-Begusarai, Samastipur, Motihari and Chapra.

Growth of small-scale and cottage industries has been noted in the midst of residential areas. These industries include handicrafts and household industries, particularly handloom weaving, printing and brass-work, besides small engineering units. The owners of these units and the artisans working therein prefer to live either under the same roof or in close proximity to these units. New industrial estates have come up only where large-scale industries have been set up, like the petro-chemical complex at Barauni.

The growth of Civil Lines, as a residential unit in close proximity to the administrative zone, took place during the British period in order to keep the government officials aloof from the town-folk. Later, some affluent persons preferred to settle in close vicinity of the Civil Line as a matter of prestige. Thus, the residential pattern of this zone is quite distinct from other residential areas.

Figure 6.5, showing the residential structure of the south-eastern part of Saharsa, exhibits an inter-mingling of functions. It is noted that its residential growth has been hampered from three sides due to the occurrence of officers' colony in the north, the railway track and property in the west and the court-area in the south. Consequently, it has no other option but to expand towards the east, particularly along the road leading to Bangaon and Saur Bazar. Also much of the vacant land in the east is marshy and devoted to intensive cultivation. In the central part of Saharsa town, the roads from Gandhi Chowk to Mahabir Chowk and Kaprapatti, formerly used mostly for residential purposes, have been recently renovated for commercial use. The residential houses along D.B. Road are also undergoing transformation for commercial use. Establishment of engineering workshops, saw mills and other small units by artisans, in a scattered manner, in the residential area has further added to congestion in the town. Agricultural labourers and daily wage-earners live in Mirtola in the east which has mostly thatch-roofed houses. Naria Tola in the south, beyond the old court, is inhabited mostly by tile-makers. Absence of open land, parks and play-grounds is indicative of extreme congestion prevailing in the residential area.

Inter-mingling of other functional uses, namely, educational, medical and transport, with the residential use has been noted. Thus, emergence of Professors' Colony or Doctors' Colony has taken place as high class residential areas in close proximity to educational and medical institutions. Similarly, the railway and other transport agencies have set up residential colonies for their employees. Recently, a large number of semi-government and public offices have come up to cater to the needs of developmental planning and administration. This has given rise to residential-cum-office blocks in several towns. The township of Birpur, associated with the Kosi barrage, and the thermal power colony at Barauni, provide, examples of such growth. These functions have directly or indirectly promoted planned development of residential neighbourhood (Plate 10).

Residential Building

Structure

A correct appraisal of the quality of housing can be had only after obtaining information regarding the materials used in the construction of the wall and the roof of dwellings. In general, burnt-brick-built walls predominate in almost all the towns of North Bihar. Their proportion, however, decreases in the towns of the districts of Purnea and Saharsa and to some extent in Champaran. Walls made of reeds, grasses, etc., are found in good proportion in the towns of Katihar, Purnea, Forbesganj, Saharsa, Murliganj, Madhepura, Narkatiaganj and Raxaul. Similarly, roofs of bricks and lime or cement are common in most of the towns, except Saharsa, Supaul and Naugachhia. Tiled roofs predominate in Chapra, Gopalganj, Hajipur, Dalsinghsarai and Mairwa. Low quality roofs made of grass are quite common in the towns of the Kosi region. The residences in the suburbs and shanty areas of cities, like, Muzaffarpur and Darbhanga, have walls and roofs largely made of grass, reeds and bamboo.

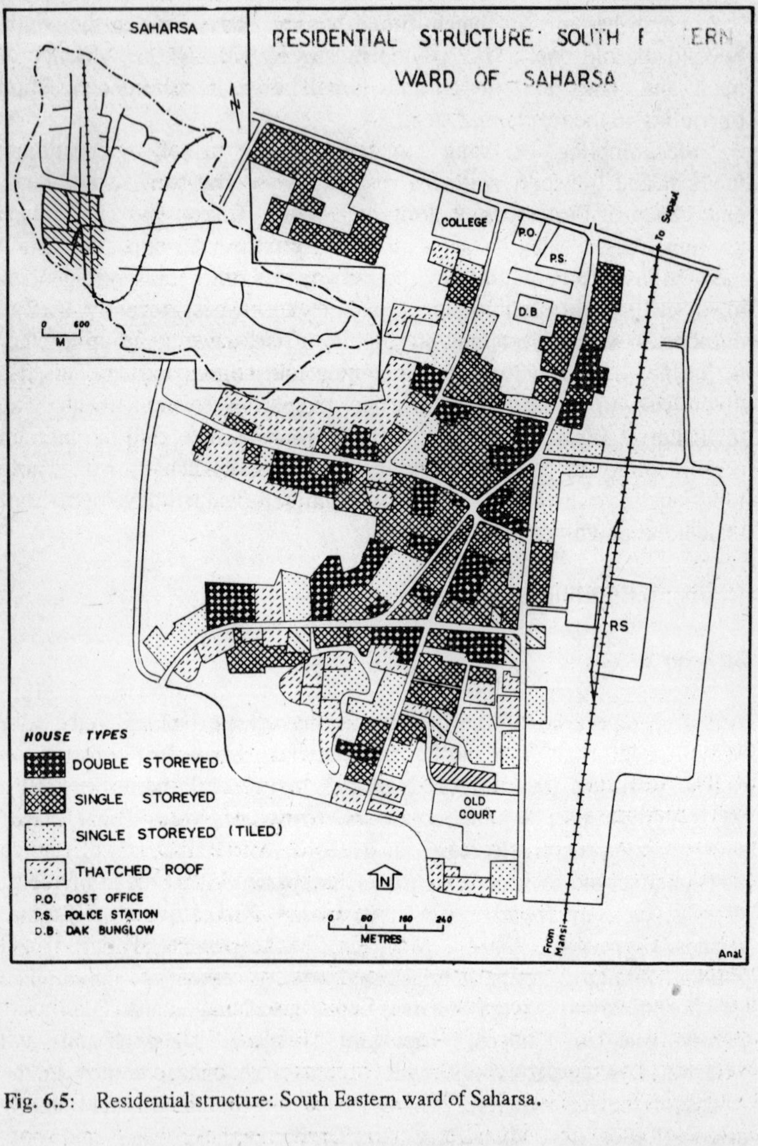

Fig. 6.5: Residential structure: South Eastern ward of Saharsa.

Plate 10: A view of planned residential colony at Birpur.

The materials used for building non-residential houses also vary. For example, buildings meant for commercial use are generally brick-built *pucca* structures, having roofs or corrugated iron sheets. The public and semi-public buildings have roofs of corrugated asbestos sheets.

In general, the towns of North Bihar have a large proportion of houses with poor quality walls and roofs. Yet, the trend in the last decade has been towards the construction of good quality buildings. Predominance of poor quality buildings is largely due to poor economic conditions prevailing in the region, besides non-availability of building materials, poor transport facilities and frequent flood hazards. Consequently, the town-dwellers prefer to use locally available raw materials.

Recent improvements in road and rail transports have been of considerable help in bringing in cement, mortar, steel girders, stone chips, lime, etc., which are now being increasingly used in the construction of dwellings. Thus, constructions made in the last two decades generally have superior quality walls. The progress towards having better roofs has been rather slow. Recently, however, there has been a marked trend towards having better roofs, particularly in larger towns, like, Katihar, Darbhanga, Muzaffarpur, Dalsinghsarai and Mairwa. Poor dwellings characterise most of the smaller towns of the region. This is more true in case of towns in the districts of Champaran, Saharsa and Purnea.

Residential Accommodation

There has been a tremendous rise in urban population in the post-independence period, both through natural growth and continuous migration of rural folk to urban areas in search for employment. The latter has, in particular, created an acute problem of housing in urban areas, because new constructions have not been able to keep pace with the increase in urban population. Moreover, there has been a tendency towards a break-up of the joint family household so that, under conditions of independent living, the sub-units of the same household now require more residential space. In the last two decades, creation of infrastructure for development and more effective administration, establishment of schools, colleges and industrial units and phenomenal growth in trade, transport and commercial activities, that are mostly located in towns, have further aggravated the problem of urban housing. Growth of slums, including *Jhuggis* and *Jhumpris*, and one-room tenements, where privacy is guarded by mutilated tin sheets, rags, reeds, grasses or card-boards, is a manifestation of this problem. Thus, the problem of urban housing has both quantitative and qualitative dimensions.

Analysis of housing census reveals a shortage of adequate residential accommodation in almost all the towns of North Bihar. In 1971, the total number of occupied residential houses in the towns of North Bihar was 2,09,965 which, in all, accommodated 2,29,589 households. Thus, on an average, 109 households occupied 100 residential houses.

Table 6.1 shows the density of urban population and houses,

besides the number of households per 100 occupied residential houses in various districts/sub-division of North Bihar.

Table 6.1: Number of urban households per 100 occupied residential houses (1971)

Districts/ Sub-division	*No. of towns*	*Population density (Persons/sq. km)*	*Housing density (Houses/sq. km)*	*Number of households per 100 occupied residential houses*
Saran	7	3,028	439	108
Champaran	9	1,964	317	106
Muzaffarpur	7	3,453	510	112
Darbhanga	6	7,564	1,132	115
Saharsa	7	1,648	270	105
Purnea	7	1,511	267	105
North Monghyr	5	2,876	427	115
Naugachhia (Sub-division)	1	2,159	281	105

Source: Census of India (1971), Series 4, Bihar, Part II-A. General Population Tables.

It is noted that the densely populated districts of Darbhanga, Muzaffarpur and North Monghyr have the largest number of urban householders occupying every 100 residential houses. In contrast, the districts of Saharsa, Purnea and Champaran and Naugachhia sub-division, with lower densities of population, have comparatively lesser number of urban households occupying every 100 residential houses. Thus, the problem of urban housing is more acute in the towns of the districts of Darbhanga, Muzaffarpur and North Monghyr.

The extent of residential congestion in urban areas can be measured in terms of housing density. In 1961, the average housing density in urban areas was 406′ sq. km, which increased to 633′ sq. km in 1971. Some of the highest housing densities are noted in the towns of the districts of Darbhanga (1,132′ sq. km) and Muzaffarpur (510′ sq. km). In contrast, the lowest housing densities are recorded in the towns of Purnea (267′ sq. km) and Saharsa (270′ sq. km). The town of Darbhanga (1,132′ sq. km) is the most congested in the whole region.

A more reasonable indicator of urban congestion is the average number of persons residing per room. There is no standard fixed in this regard, but the desirable optimum can be taken as two persons per room. Any larger number of persons residing in a room would indicate congestion. The average number of persons residing per room in the towns of North Bihar comes to 2.6, which is indicative of all-round congestion.

The extent of congestion can also be gauged by obtaining the percentage distribution of households according to the size of dwellings.

Table 6.2 reveals that (68.7%) or nearly two-third of the urban households, in North Bihar, live in dwellings having one or two rooms. The proportion of such households is very high in the towns of Purnea (78.4 per cent), Darbhanga (71.4%) and Saharsa (69.6%) districts and Naugachhia (72.8%) sub-division.

Table 6.2: Percentage distribution of urban households according to the size of dwellings (1971)

	Dwellings				
Districts/ Sub-division	*One room*	*Two rooms*	*Three rooms*	*Four rooms*	*Five rooms or more*
Saran	29.3	29.8	17.2	10.3	13.4
Champaran	32.7	31.7	17.6	8.5	9.4
Muzaffarpur	38.9	28.5	15.0	7.9	9.7
Darbhanga	40.1	31.3	13.0	7.6	8.0
Saharsa	36.8	32.8	16.8	6.9	6.7
Purnea	49.7	28.7	11.0	5.4	5.2
North Monghyr	37.4	29.3	15.5	8.8	8.9
Naugachhia (Sub-division)	42.4	30.4	15.2	6.2	5.8
Average	38.4	30.3	15.1	7.7	8.3

Source: Census of India, 1971. Series 4, Bihar Part-IV. Housing Report and Tables.

Though, the towns of Saran district have comparatively lower percentages of householders residing in one and two-room dwellings, their proportions are still very high in the total residential fabric of these towns. Thus, householders living in one-room dwellings comprise, by far, the largest single group in almost all the larger towns of North Bihar. For example, one-room dwelling accounts for about 50 per cent, 40 per cent, 35 per cent and 34 per cent of the total number of households in the towns of Katihar, Darbhanga, Muzaffarpur and

Chapra, respectively. The proportions of medium and large dwellings are generally low. It is noted that about 23 per cent of the householders live in medium-size dwellings having three to four rooms, and only 9.9 per cent live in large sized some dwellings having five rooms or more. The towns of Muzaffarpur and Chapra have the largest proportions of medium-size dwellings. Large-size dwellings are met commonly in the urban areas of Saran district.

A more realistic picture of congestion can be obtained by analysing the percentage of urban population living in dwellings having either one, two, three, four, five or more rooms (Table 6.3). The proportion of urban population living in one-room dwellings is as high as 37.8 per cent in the district of Purnea and as low as 18.8 per cent in the district of Saran.

Table 6.3: Percentage of urban population living in various sizes of Dwellings (1971)

	Dwellings				
Districts/ Sub-division	*One rooms*	*Two rooms*	*Three rooms*	*Four rooms*	*Five rooms or more*
Saran	18.83	26.42	18.91	13.63	12.21
Champaran	21.87	30.17	20.45	18.35	9.61
Muzaffarpur	27.01	28.28	17.62	17.85	9.44
Darbhanga	28.62	31.19	15.91	13.64	10.64
Saharsa	27.37	33.32	19.24	13.74	6.33
Purnea	37.88	30.40	14.07	12.08	5.57
North Monghyr	26.28	28.97	17.59	15.75	11.41
Naugachhia (Sub-division)	34.15	32.38	12.28	15.11	6.08
Average	27.75	30.14	17.00	15.00	8.85

Source: Census of India 1971, Series 4, Bihar Part-IV, Housing Report and Tables.

A large proportion of the urban population resides in two to three room dwellings. The proportion of population living in two-room dwellings is the highest in the urban areas of Saharsa (33.3%) and Darbhanga (31.2%). This analysis also reveals that most of the urban population (45% to 68%) of the region lives in one or two-room dwellings, which are mostly concentrated in larger towns.

Tenure Status of Urban-Dwellers

The tenure status of urban-dwellers provides information if the dwellings occupied by the householders are actually owned by them or taken on rent or lease. In 1971, about 71.5 per cent of the householders living in the towns of North Bihar owned their dwellings, while the remaining 28.5 per cent lived in rented houses. It has been noted that the percentage of householders living in rented houses was comparatively higher in the city of Muzaffarpur (45.6%) because of continuous migration of the rural folk seeking employment in this town. The city of Darbhanga, in contrast, has a very high percentage of householders (76.2%) living in dwelling owned by them. This is

Plate 11: A view of one-storey concrete building occurring in the midst of thatched huts of Murliganj.

because of the fact that in the period of 'the Raj', most of the important buildings of this town were owned either by the Maharaja or people associated with him. There has been little change in this condition during recent times, except that the buildings formerly owned by the Maharaja are now under the control of the Government or the university. Also mention has to be made of the fact that the possibility of dwellings occupied by their owners increases with the increase in the size of dwellings.

Social structure and economic status are important factors in determining the size, type and quality of dwellings. The great majority of dwellings in the towns of North Bihar is generally poor to very poor in quality. Nevertheless, it is not uncommon to find a few high class residences existing in close proximity to mud-wall houses or unauthorised *Jhuggis* and *Jhumpris* (Plate 11). This indicates rather haphazard and unplanned development of residential areas. Recently, some attention has been paid, by municipal and other authorities, towards a rational and planned development of residential facilities, but the private householders often try to bypass housing regulations, either with a view to earning more rent or gaining some advantage. Thus compromises have been made at the cost of sanitary, living conditions and, sometimes, even with the quality of housing.

REFERENCES

Carter, H. (1976): *The Study of Urban Geography*, New Delhi.

Ford, L. and E. Griffin (1979): Ghettoisation Paradise, *Geographical Review*, 69, pp. 140-58.

Hirsch, W.Z. (1973): *Urban Economic Analysis*, New Delhi.

Karan, P.P. (1957): The Pattern of Indian Towns, *Journal of American Institute of Planners*, 23, pp. 70-74.

Murphy, R.E. (1966): *The American City: An Urban Geography*, McGraw Hill, New York.

Nigam, M.N. (1964): Functional Regions of Lucknow, *National Geographical Journal of India*, X-I, pp. 38-52.

Smailes, A.E. (1953): *Geography of Towns*, London.

Taneja, K.L. (1971): *Morphology of Indian Cities, N.G.S.I.*, Research Publication No. 7, Varanasi.

7

MORPHOLOGY OF COMMERCIAL AREAS

THE TOWN exists because it renders various services. The chief reason people live in cities is to carry on commercial or business activities (Murphy, 1966, p. 254). Mark Jefferson (1931, p. 446) observes that cities do not grow up of themselves, it is the countryside that sets them up to do tasks which must be performed in central places. No town lives to itself. It serves as area which may be termed as its hinterland or market region. In the words of Webb (1959, p. 55) a town acts as a funnel, through which passes the products of many other urban places to increasingly indeterminate tributary areas. Thus, it also acts as a centre of exchange where specialised products, brought in from its hinterland, are passed on to other towns for utilisation and distribution in their hinterland and *vice versa*. Commercial activities are generally associated with the core areas of towns. In fact, in every town, old or new, large or small, the centre has its own particular appearance (Beaujeu-Garnier and Chabot, 1971, p. 297). This is known as the nucleus or the commercial hub which generally lies at cross-roads, locally known *Chauraha* or *Chowk*.

Commercial activities engaged about 10 per cent of the working population in the towns of North Bihar as a whole. These activities are generally associated with the older core of the town but, sometimes, also occur in a ribbon-like fashion along the main arterial roads of the residential and administrative areas. The nature and pattern of commercial land-uses vary from town to town, depending upon its 'economic foundation' and its ties with the region (Alexander, 1954, p. 246).

'Commercial activities can be broadly classed into basic and non-basic activities. The basic activities account for the very existence of the town since they bring income from outside; the non-basic activities service the essential workers and their dependents' (Dickinson, 1964, p. 68). These factors determine the value of trade carried by each town. The commercial land-use, however, occupies only a small segment of the urban space. It presents a myriad appearance, depending upon the size of the town.

Evolution of Commercial Areas

The location of commercial activity varies with the functional nature of individual towns in North Bihar. Its growth pattern is often a reflection of the origin and development of the town. It is noted that the irregular character of shopping streets is generally the result of the physical dominance of the site attributes. In older towns, the growth of commercial areas initially took place close to the residential zone, along the river front, as identified in Dalsinghsarai, Darbhanga, Khagaria, Samastipur, Jainagar and Purnea. The then dominance of the river-bound trade made these sites most advantageous for commercial activity. Expansion of these commercial nodes later took place with the construction of roads and linkages that provided connections with other towns and the surrounding town region. This often resulted in the expansion of shopping activity along the connecting roads. However, the most important commercial activities remained confined to the central part or parts of the town which provided relative protection from marauders and external attacks. Later, development of rail transport led to de-centralisation in commercial activity due to nucleation of new commercial areas close to railway junctions. But the newly emerged commercial nucleations, located either in the Civil Lines or the residential colony near the railway junctions, have functioned as subsidiaries to the main commercial areas which are still located on the river fronts.

In the post-independence period, growth of planned and modern style commercial areas has taken place in a number of newly grown townships, particularly to cater to the needs of the neighbourhood community. Nevertheless, it is noted that the old commercial areas still control a large share of commercial activity in almost all the towns of North Bihar.

There is a general lack of planned shopping areas in the towns of North Bihar. The main commercial centre has often developed in the midst of residential areas due to historic considerations. Recently, there has been a locational shift in some commercial activities, particularly automobile parts and agricultural goods and implements, as a consequence of the development of private transport. Thus, in Purnea, Katihar, Jainagar and Forbesganj, the wholesale and retail trades in bulky goods have shifted either closer to the railway station or along the main highways. The retail shopping, however, has developed on the link roads, adjoining the residential colonies.

Commercial Structure

The pattern of commercial activity in the towns of North Bihar is both intricate and unschematic. There is an inter-mingling of commercial activity with other morphological functions, largely due to physical considerations of site and historic growth factors.Though the nature of business activity differs from town to town, it usually has a tendency to cluster at particular locations within the urban area. Hence, the origin, evolution and pattern of commercial structure have to be considered in relation to urban morphology. Attention has to be also given to the nature of urban retail structure which forms an important aspect of the commercial pattern. In this context, it is pertinent to mention here the following five types of retail structures identified in the principal cities of U.S.A. (Proudfoot, 1939, p. 425):

- (i) The central business district or C.B.D.,
- (ii) The outlying business centres,
- (iii) The principal business thoroughfare,
- (iv) The neighbourhood business street, and
- (v) The isolated store cluster.

Later studies, notably by Ratcliff (1949), Murphy and Vance (1954) and Hoyt (1958), have confirmed the presence of the above-mentioned retail structure in many other cities of the Western countries. Though the retail structure in towns of North Bihar does not exactly conform to Proudfoot's retail classification, his nomenclature has been freely used, sometimes with modification, whenever a similarity has been noted.

A general decrease in commercial activity takes place as one moves from the central part of the town to its periphery. The central part, a fully built-up area, is given to commercial activity in almost all the towns. Both the land value and shop rentals are among the highest in this part. The shops here are generally congested; the degree of congestion depends on local conditions. In contrast, the land values and shop rentals in isolated shopping nucleations, located in other parts of the town, are comparatively lower. In Saharsa, for instance, the main commercial area, located in the midst of a residential locality deals in consumer goods like foodgrains, general merchandise and groceries. The Station Road Bazar specialises in groceries, fresh and dry fruits, vegetables, fish, meat and other consumable goods. Nayabazar, located near the hospital, has small shops clustered along the road-side. These shops cater to the needs of persons visiting the hospital and the residential colony (of Govt. officials) in the neighbourhood. A similar distributional pattern of commercial activity is also observed in other towns of North Bihar. It is evident that the type and nature of business carried by each commercial locality largely depends on variations in shop rental values and consumer accessibility.

The price range of consumer goods varies from one commercial locality to the other. It is generally lower in isolated and localised commercial establishments, occurring on the outskirts of the town. The neighbourhood commercial area occurs in a nucleated fashion, adjoining the commercial core of the towns. A moderate to moderately high intensity of commercial activity is noted in this area.

'A hierarchy of shopping centres exists within a city inasmuch the same way that a hierarchy of cities, characterised by a range of commodities produced, may be said to exist' (Muth, 1975, p. 58). It is noted that in the towns of North Bihar, the intensity of shopping nucleations varies from larger to small towns almost in hierarchical order. Thus, the following hierarchy of commercial areas can be identified for the towns of North Bihar:

(i) The Central Business Area; with high to very high intensity of commercial activity,
(ii) The Neighbourhood Shopping Centre; with moderate to moderately high commercial activity, and
(iii) The Isolated Shopping Nucleation, with low to moderately low commercial activity.

Recognition of the above-mentioned hierarchy of commercial areas is based on the intensity of commercial activity, which is dependent on the size of the shopping catchment area and the purchasing power of its inhabitants. But this hierarchy of commercial areas has not developed in smaller towns. The larger towns, with more functions, usually have a especialised retail structure, including the C.B.A. which is the highest order commercial zone. This zone is characterised by clustering of different types of commercial establishments where the intensity of commercial activity is at a maximum. The neighbourhood shopping centre caters to the shopping requirements of the surrounding residential zone and has relatively restricted consumer accessibility. It is an area of moderate to moderately high commercial activity. The isolated shopping nucleation, usually a cluster of a few shops is found in various out-lying parts of the town. The most apparent change, taking place today, is the growth of ribbon-type commercial areas providing service facilities along the main road passing through the town (Vaughan, 1960, p. 130). Sometimes, the neighbourhood shopping centre also has a core, which is linked by roads to the C.B.A. on the one hand and the isolated shopping nucleations on the other.

It will not be out of place to mention here the notable characteristics of the above-mentioned types of commercial areas.

The Central Business Area (C.B.A.)

All the towns, whether large or small, have a central or major commercial area which forms a distinct region. The range of functions and facilities contained in a limited area provide both variety and conflict (Maher, 1979, p. 112). The variety supplies both interest and attraction, the conflict brings change. In fact, it is an area of shops or stores of wholesale and retail trades, generally located at the convergence of chief local and regional transportation routes. This area has tremendous advantages for carrying on business, including maximum accessibility from all parts of the town. It is the place where a maximum number of persons are accustomed to transact business on a large scale. Thus, it dominates the local wholesale and retail trades. Such an urban area, in the towns of North Bihar, may be called as the central business area or the C.B.A. It is an area of great intensity of commercial land-use, which may be regarded as the commercial core and the prime nucleus of the town.

Identification of C.B.D., the business nucleus of American cities, has been made by geographers, like Murphy and Vance (1954), on the basis of land values, building height, central business index, land tenure status and movement of day and night time population. Though the C.B.A. in the towns of North Bihar does not exactly conform to the C.B.D. of the American city, still it has some aspects in common such as high rental values and parity in day and night population movements. In contrast to the C.B.D., C.B.A. is densely populated where the residential function is as important as the commercial function. Also, it does not contain administrative and recreational buildings.

The C.B.A. is generally associated with the oldest part of the town, which usually has a central location. It offers all sorts of goods and services not only to the town-dwellers but also to the inhabitants of the neighbouring rural area. As the town grows in size and importance, the central business area tends to assume more and more specialised commercial functions, including personnel and professional services. The location, form and size of the C.B.A are sometimes, guided by site attributes, which also lead to convergence of regional and local transportation routes at that place. Concentration of a wide range of functions has produced an intense competition for space, which accounts for its exorbitant land values.

Morphogenesis of C.B.A.

The C.B.A. of North Bihar towns is found either at the convergence of roads or at road crossings or around some important cultural nucleus. It derives its unique character because of concentration of economic, social and cultural activities in a limited space. In the early period of town growth, the commercial establishments were put up at accessible points in close proximity to the residential areas, so that these could be conveniently approached by a large number of local residents. However, with the development of transport facilities and expansion in town-size, the C.B.A. also grew in size, generally taking an elongated shape, along the important roads. The development of the C.B.A. has followed a set pattern in consonance with the growth in town size. In the beginning, the shops and service establishments had been guided by the initial street pattern. Commercial activity was later intensified by filling up of the gaps between the cross-roads and expansion along the main roads in the immediate neighbourhood of residential areas. With the passage of time, the older units disappeared and gave place to newer ones. A change in the relative position of various functional units also took place as a consequence of assimilation process. Thus, the C.B.A. is often characterised by traffic congestion and overcrowding. This problem is further aggravated by the existence of narrow shopping streets, often bifurcating from the main roads. It is obvious even to casual observers that the commercial intensity declines as one proceeds from the core to outer margins of the town.

The C.B.A. of Sample Towns

Field observation reveals that the C.B.A., in sample town, is generally located in the older parts of the town, mainly at cross-roads, locally known as *chowk* or *Gudari* (Fig. 7.1). *Gudari* Bazar is found in almost all the sample towns of North Bihar. The shape and size of the C.B.A. differs from town to town, depending upon their size, volume of trade and extent of business intensity. The retail structure, in these towns, is often a reflection of the nature and character of their urban fields.

The C.B.A. of Darbhanga is located in Bari Bazar which includes Tower Chowk, Gullubara, Gudari Bazar and Saudagar Mohalla. Obstructed by the Baghmati River in the west, it has been recently expanding along Mirzapur and Lalbagh roads in the east. In this process of expansion, it has engulfed C.M. Science College in the south. All sorts of commercial activities, including wholesale and retail are concentrated in this zone. The shopping streets are generally narrow and congested. The influx of pedestrian traffic is often so great that it retards the movement of vehicles and other carriers. Consequently, in Bari Bazar area, the movement of merchandise takes place with the help of porters, horses and push-carts. But, bullock-carts constitute the chief mode of transport in Gullubara.

In Muzaffarpur, the C.B.A. includes Saraiyaganj, Purani bazar and Suttapatti. The main wholesale and retail markets of this city are located along radial roads in Saraiyaganj. Recently, Motijheel has emerged as the most magnificent shopping parade. Muzaffarpur does not experience traffic congestion like Darbhanga because its streets, in the C.B.A., are fairly wide. The C.B.A. of Katihar lies in the heart of the town at Saifganj, which forms the focal point of several streets from various directions. It is characterised by narrow and congested streets which result in traffic hazards, during peak business hours, in the evening. Poor drainage conditions and lack of sewers often cause water-logging during the rainy season which adversely affects both the movement of merchandise and business transactions.

The C.B.A. of Hajipur is elongated in appearance. it extends from Masjid Chowk to Rajendra Chowk and includes Gudari Bazar as well. Nucleation of business activity has taken place here only along the main roads which are quite wide and straight. Both residential and commercial buildings occur side by side on these roads. The C.B.A. of

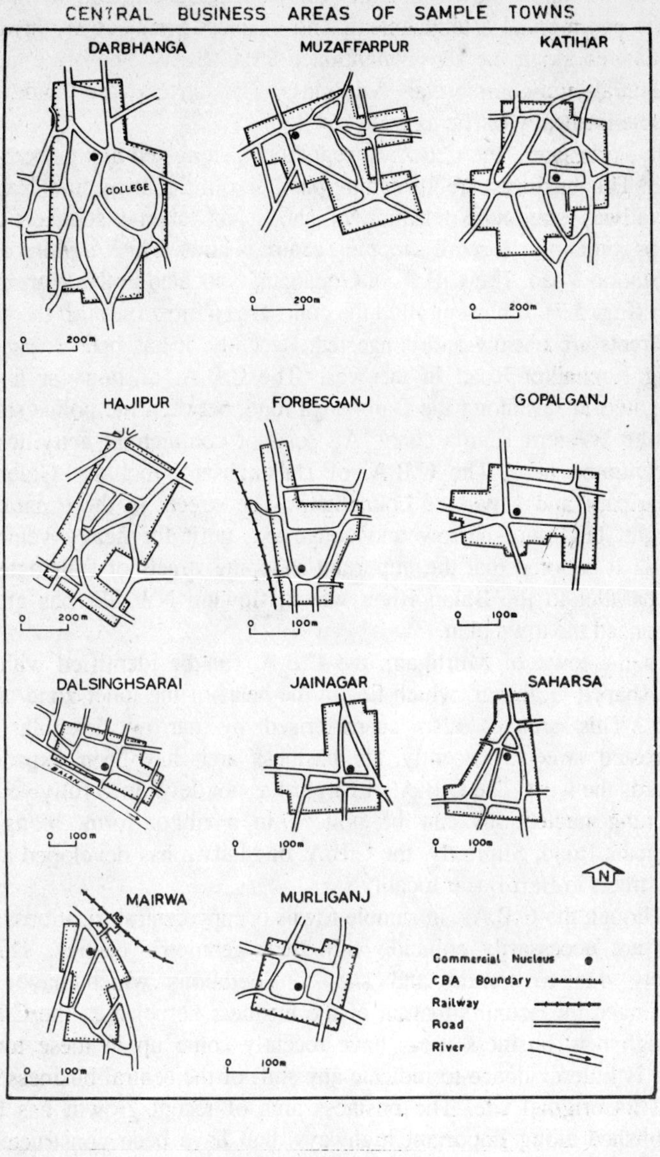

Fig. 7.1: Central business areas of sample towns.

Saharsa is ensconced in a triangle, formed by three cross-roads, namely, Mahabir Chowk, Chandni Chowk and Gandhi Chowk. Almost all the commercial establishments and business premises are hemmed in this area along the above-mentioned three streets. These are mostly residential-cum-commercial buildings. The streets are wide and suitable for heavy traffic as well.

In Forbesganj, the C.B.A. appears to be elongated along the Sadar Road. This business street, running parallel to the railway line, leads to the railway station. Nucleation of shops has taken place here in a compact manner. A retail shopping centre is housed in *Katghara* along the Station Road. The C.B.A. of Gopalganj is located in the heart of the town (Fig. 5.7). It has engulfed the court-area almost from all the sides. Its streets are narrow and congested. Recently, it has been expanding along Kuchaikot Road in the west. The C.B.A. of Jainagar is also elongated. It lies along the Darbhanga road, between the police station and the Western Kamla canal. All sorts of commercial activities are concentrated here. The C.B.A. of Dalsinghsarai includes Golepatti, Gudaripatti and a part of Loknathpur. The streets in these parts are straight, but quite narrow and congested, unfit for heavy vehicular traffic. It is noted that the important shopping streets of Dalsinghsarai run parallel to the Balan River which, flowing NW-SE, has greatly influenced the town plan.

In the town of Murliganj, the C.B.A. can be identified with the oval-shaped Golbazar, which lies in the heart of the inner zone of the town. This area is also characterised by narrow, irregular and congested streets. Recently, its business area has been expanding towards the west. The C.B.A. of Birpur has not developed fully yet, but shopping nucleations can be noticed in a ribbon-form, along the Bathnaha Road. Similarly, the C.B.A. of Mairwa has developed along two streets in Bari Bazar locality.

Though the C.B.As. in sample towns occupy central locations, they may not necessarily coincide with their geometric centres. This is largely due to terrain and site considerations which have also influenced the actual situation of the business kernel, i.e., the C.B.A. Though new business areas have recently come up in these towns, there is little evidence to indicate any shift of the central business area from its original site. The business area of recent growth has been established along important highways, that have been constructed in the post-independence period. For example, cities, like, Darbhanga, Muzaffarpur and Katihar, have persevered with their old commercial areas in spite of recent growth of commercial activities in other parts of these towns. The old C.B.A. has also expanded along radial roads which move outwards from the town kernel. With the outward expansion of the older commercial core, a continuum of business activity is noted along thoroughfares which connect the C.B.A. with the newly developed commercial areas. Examples of this commercial continuum are provided by Bakerganj-Laheriasarai in Darbhanga, Motijheel-Kalyani in Muzaffarpur and Mangal Bazar of Katihar. Development of the transport network and assumption of new administrative functions by several towns have resulted in the siting of some specialised commercial functions in the recently developed commercial areas as distinct from the older C.B.A. which is already overcrowded and congested and not in a position to assume new functions or house new business establishments. The newly emerged shopping areas have advantages of wider roads and sufficient vacant land for future expansion. In smaller towns, the C.B.A. exists as a mono-unit. With the growth and expansion of these towns, the C.B.A. has also tended to grow in size. In the last decade, the C.B.As. in the towns of Begusarai, Samastipur, Madhubani, Hajipur and Sitamarhi, which have been upgraded from sub-divisional to district headquarters, have witnessed rapid expansion. Even then, the land-use under commercial activities accounts for only five per cent of the developed area; the residential function towers over all other functions in these towns.

Types of Commercial Activities

Commercial activities are generally located at points of convenience within a locality. Its actual location, however, depends upon site considerations. If the central business area is located at a true economic distance, its business turnover is much greater, as customers purchase goods from the shops in the C.B.A. fairly regularly. This also provides outward accessibility through radial roads, placed most conveniently for both the sellers and buyers. The wholesale and retail businesses occur side by side in the commercial areas of the towns in North Bihar. It is rather difficult to separate the two in smaller towns. Initially, the sample towns specialised in retail business only, but as the demands and sales grew, some of the business establishments took to wholesale trade. Still later, the establishments specialising in wholesale trade came to be located in specific parts of the C.B.A. of larger towns.

The wholesale business, in Darbhanga, is located in Baribazar, Gullubara and Saudagar *mohallas*, while the retail trade is concentrated in Tower Chowk area (Plate 12). The latter area is, somewhat, circular in form, as the shops have been put up along cross-roads. The *Chowk* is easily accessible from the surrounding areas. The wholesale trade in Baribazar specialises in cloth, hosiery and hardware, while the one at Gullubara is devoted to foodgrains and provisions. The Tower Chowk is particularly known for machinery, hardware, cycles, electric appliances and general merchandise (Fig. 7.2).

Muzaffarpur has a larger C.B.A. than Darbhanga. The wholesale business, in Muzaffarpur, is located at Suttapatti, Saraiyaganj and Purani Bazar (Plate 13). Suttapatti and Saraiyaganj deal in cloth and foodgrains, while Purani Bazar specialises in hardware and general merchandise. The retail shops, concentrated in Kalyani and Motijheel, are devoted mostly to the sale of cloth, cycles, auto-spares, electrical and luxury goods and to tailoring and hotels.

Bara Bazar, also known as Saifganj, is the commercial hub of Katihar. The wholesale trade in foodgrains and provisions is located here along radial roads. It is also known for its jute *mandi* where jute is brought for sale from the surrounding rural areas. A part of this jute also enters the export business. The retail commercial activity is mostly concentrated along the M.G. Road, from the Water Tower crossing to Mangal Bazar. This market specialises in cloth, glass-wares, bangles (*Churi*), *bidi* leaves, utensils of aluminium and brass, furniture, idols and decoration pieces made of clay.

In Hajipur, the wholesale and principal retail markets, dealing mostly in foodgrains and general merchandise, occur along Gandhi Path of Gudari Bazar (Fig. 7.4). This market also specialises in agricultural inputs, like, vegetable seeds, pesticides, insecticides and fertilisers. There is a large turnover in these commodities which are also sent to other towns by trucks. Similarly, the wholesale business of Dalsinghsarai is located in Loknathpur and Gudari Bazar, which specialise in the trade of agricultural produce, particularly chillies, tobacco, sugar and turmeric widely grown in its umland. Forbesganj, an important trade centre in North Bihar, is particularly known for the wholesale trade of bulky and voluminous agricultural commodities, particularly jute, paddy, mustardseed and potato. Its chief jute and paddy *mandi* is located at Hathikhola, where the farmers from the far-flung interior bring in their products, on bullock-cart, for trade. The retail business, mostly comprising cloth and provisions, takes place in shops located in Ram Baran and Manickchand Lanes.

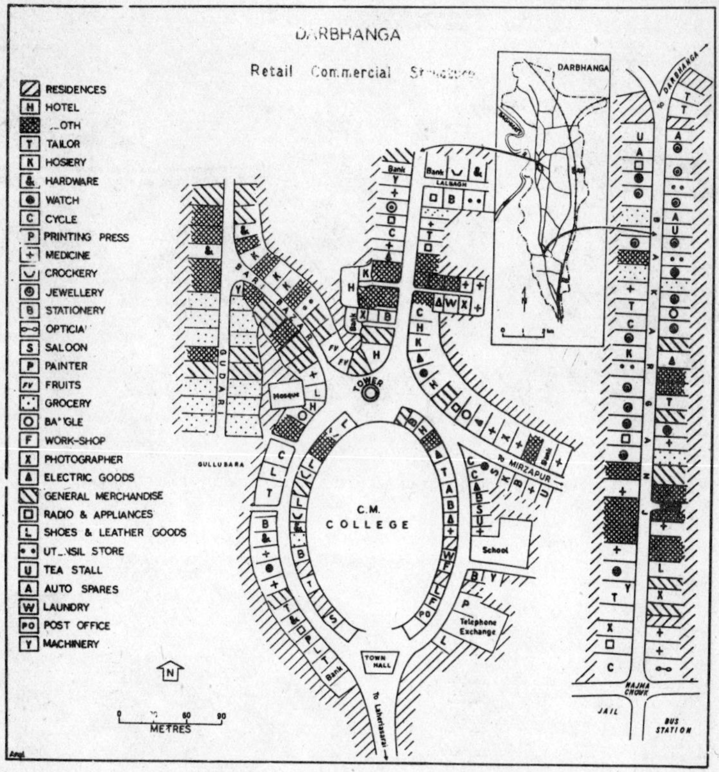

Fig. 7.2: Darbhanga: retail commercial structure.

Plate 12: A view of shopping area close to the Clock Tower at Darbhanga.

Plate 13: A view of Saraiyaganj, the oldest commercial core in the city of Muzaffarpur.

Plant 14: A view of the bazar along Station Road in Saharsa.

Saharsa is a trading centre of very little importance. Its market area is poorly developed (Plate 14). Nevertheless, shops located in Kaprapatti and Chandni Chowk carry on retail business in cloth, hardware and other essential commodities of daily use (Fig. 7.3). Murliganj, located in Saharsa district, is a place of great commercial importance. It carries brisk wholesale and retail trade in jute, paddy, linseed, oilseed and *ghee*. A large amount of raw jute, purchased at this place, is sent for processing either to Katihar or to Calcutta. Jainagar, located in close proximity to the Indo-Nepal International border in the district of Madhubani, also specialises in the wholesale trade of paddy, wheat and mustardseed. It carries voluminous import and export trade because of its frontier location. In the towns of Gopalganj and Mairwa, the business activity takes place in conjunction with the residential function. These towns carry on local trade in sugar, molasses and foodgrains.

In conclusion it can be said that the C.B.A. in the towns of North Bihar, like the C.B.D. of the Western countries, is in fact the pinnacle of major retail centre. Its chief function is to provide retails shopping to town-dwellers and other residents in its urban-field. The business establishments are generally located at important road junctions and along the main thoroughfares of the town. The wholesale business, in particular, is carried on in the core areas of the C.B.A., while the retail business takes place towards its outer margins. A good number of hotels, restaurants, roadside eating shops, tea-stalls, betel shops and barber's saloon occur within the C.B.A., which provide ready service to commuters and residents of the C.B.A.

The Shape and Size of the C.B.A.

The shape and size of the C.B.A. depend upon terrain conditions in the town-space and various historic or cultural factors responsible for its growth. Its size is almost proportionate to the volume of trade carried by individual towns. For example, the C.B.A. of Katihar is circular in form. Recently it is expanding westwards along a radial road due to coming up railway establishments. The C.B.As. of Forbesganj, Jainagar, Mairwa and Hajipur are elongated due to establishment of shops along single streets, while at Saharsa it is triangular due to occurrence of shops along three roads forming a triangle. In the cities of Darbhanga and Muzaffarpur, the C.B.As. are large, but irregular in appearance (see Fig. 7.1).

Land Values and Tenure Status in C.B.A.

The land value is the maximum in the C.B.A. of almost all the sample towns. In general, it decreases outwards from the core towards the periphery. Assessment of land value, according to the indexing method of Murphy and Vance (1954), could not be made because of the unreliability of the data available. Also, this method has its own limitations in the Indian context.

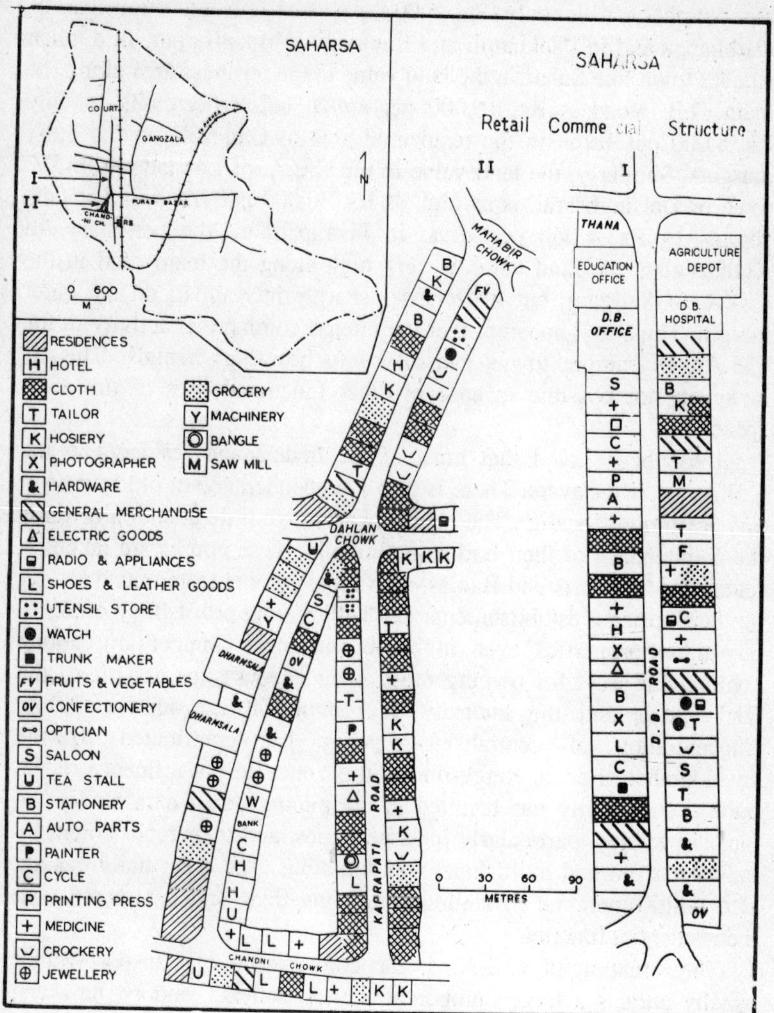

Fig. 7.3: Saharsa:retail commercial structure.

The land value in the C.B.A. of larger towns, particularly Bari Bazar in Darbhanga and Saraiyaganj in Muzaffarpur, is as high as Rs. 30,000 per *katha*; it progressively decreases outwards and towards the periphery it is only Rs. 5,000 per *katha* in Lakshmisagar of Darbhanga and in Pankhatoli and Kanhauli of Muzaffarpur. In a much smaller town like Saharsa, the land value in the business area along the main D.B. Road is Rs. 15,000 per *katha*, but it decreases to only Rs. 5,000 per *katha* in the residential area of Gangzala on the outer margins. Similarly, the land value in the C.B.A. of Loknathpur, in the town of Dalsinghsarai, is as high as Rs. 30,000 per *katha*, but it falls sharply to Rs. 4,000 per *katha* in Jayajipatti on the periphery. In Katihar also, the land value is very high along the main road in the C.B.A. of Saifganj, but it decreases sharply in Kalibari on the outer margin. Thus, it is apparent that the intense commercial activity in the C.B.As. of sample towns can afford to bear high rentals. This is, however, not possible in case of other functional uses of the town space.

It has been noted that most of the traders and residents in the C.B.A. are rent-payers. There is also a preponderance of old houses in this prestigious locality. The house-owners give little attention towards the maintenance of their buildings. Initially, these houses are taken on rentals by Marwaris and Banias, who usually come from outside to set up their business establishments, but with roaring profits they prefer to buy these properties even at exorbitant rates. Competition among commercial users for owning most advantageous sites has raised the land values and the intensity of commercial use in the C.B.A. Concentration of centralised services has contributed to the development of acute congestion in this zone. Recent affluence of the trading community has resulted in the pulling down of some of the older structures, particularly in larger cities, and their replacement by multi-storeyed and multi-functional buildings. The older buildings are also multi-functional in nature, combining trade and commerce with the residential function.

The situation of C.B.A. at the convergence of transport routes usually attracts a large number of buyers, sellers, vendors, hawkers, peddlers, dealers – both wholesalers and retailers – squatters, idlers, travellers, besides shop assistants and roundsmen. It is, therefore, marked by large concentrations of people during the day-light hours. The peak business hours are between 10.00 a.m. to 7.30 p.m., with a slight respite during 2.00 p.m. to 4.00 p.m. Usually overcrowding and traffic congestion take place in this area due to rush of pedestrian

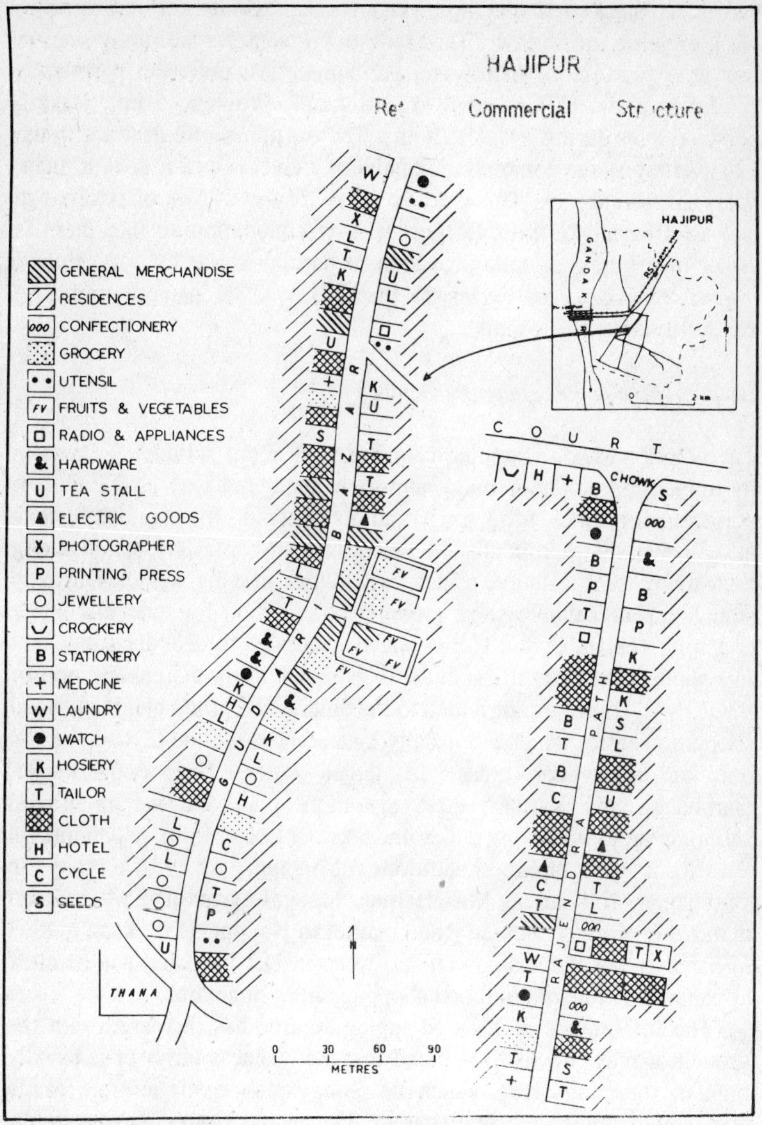

Fig. 7.4: Hajipur: retail commercial structure.

traffic and light and heavy motorised vehicles carrying passengers and marketable goods respectively. Besides, cycle-rickshaws, horse-driven carriages, hand-carts and bullock-carts also add to this congestion, often creating traffic jams. The fast-moving vehicles are rarely seen in this area because of narrow roads. Sometimes, even the permanent residents of the C.B.A. have to face traffic problems while making personal trips during business hours. The traffic usually declines in the late evening as the commuting population moves out of C.B.A. It, then, bears a deserted look. This is true even of Tower Chowk of Darbhanga and Saraiyaganj of Muzaffarpur. It is worthmentioning that there is either insufficient or little provision of parking space for cars, trucks, *tongas*, *rickshaws* or cycles in the C.B.A. This naturally adds to congestion and traffic jams.

The Neighbourhood Shopping Centres

The neighbourhood shopping centre renders retail services to areas in its immediate neighbourhood, almost in the same way as the C.B.A. performs. For the entire town and its umland. It, sometimes, may attract customers from distant places, because of its location along inter-town transportation routes, where fast-moving vehicles usually stop. Lack of suitable sites, growing competition for available space and high rentals in the C.B.A. have generally forced the small and independent retailers to establish their shops in the neighbourhood of the C.B.A. This has contributed to the emergence of the neighbourhood shopping centres which are usually located between the C.B.A. and the outlying residential areas. In larger cities, like, Muzaffarpur, Darbhanga and Katihar, there are more than one neighbourhood shopping areas which are either linear or nuclear in form, depending on the local geographic conditions. Mirzapur and Bakerganj in Darbhanga, Kalyani in Muzaffarpur, Mangal Bazar and M.G. Road markets in Katihar, Station Road market in Hajipur, D.B. Road market in Saharsa and shops along Gudari Road in Dalsinghsarai can be cited as examples of neighbourhood shopping areas or centres.

The importance of these shopping centres has increased with the growth of these towns. It is noted that the business turnover is usually high in shopping areas, which lie along major roads and are easily accessible from the residential areas. This also accounts for ribbon-like development of these shopping areas. In general, these areas are avoided by the wholesale trade. But recently, a few shops specialising in trades, like, cycle and cycle-spares, auto and auto-spares and various repair services, have come up. These centres also have shops dealing in hardware and machinery, electrical goods, books, stationery and drawing materials, bangles, watch repair, draping, hair-dressing, tailoring, grocery and provisions, besides cheap eating places, restaurants, betel and tea stalls. The speciality, appearance and character of the neighbourhood shopping centre differs from town to town as also between various centres in the same town.

There are three important neighbourhood shopping centres in Darbhanga, namely, Mirzapur, Bakerganj and the Station Road market. The shopping area of Mirzapur serves a large part of the population of Darbhanga and caters to the specialised trade in hardware, machinery and automobile parts. It also has a large number of general stores, grocery shops and road-side eating places. In contrast, the shopping centre of Bakerganj, located in the administrative zone of Laheriasarai, has experienced a nucleated growth. It serves the elite of the town and has modern shops with beautiful show-cases, displaying cloth, ready-made garments, photographic aids, jewellery, radio and electrical appliances. Besides, there are drug stores, cycle, general merchants and gift shops, barber's saloon and tailoring houses (Fig. 7.2). The general appearance of this market is attractive. There is no traffic congestion as the roads are wide. Movement of heavy vehicles is also quite frequent.

In Hajipur, the neighbourhood shopping centre has developed, along Sonpur-Muzaffarpur highway, between Anwarpur Chowk and the Railway Station. It specialises in hardwares, machinery, agricultural inputs, including seeds, and automobile parts. Besides, there are a few groceries and general stores. The D.B. Road shopping centre of Saharsa, located between Mahabir Chowk and the City Police Station, is elongated in shape. It has a variety of decorated shops with beautiful show-cases.

The neighbourhood shopping centre of Mangal Bazar, in Katihar, is triangular in shape. Both wholesale and retail trade is carried here in narrow and congested streets which are liable to water-logging in the rainy season (Plates 15 and 16). It deals in essential commodities of daily life, from groceries to luxury goods. The streets are so narrow that the customers have to walk for several hundred metres to reach the shops which are usually small-sized. Another shopping ribbon is emerging along the M.G. Road between Thana Chowk and the Water Tower. A mixture of commercial function with residential land-use characterises this highway area.

Plate 15: A view of the shopping area of Mangal Bazar at Katihar.

Plate 16: A view of shopping street during the rainy season in Katihar.

Muzaffarpur, like Darbhanga, also has more than one neighbourhood shopping centres. These are located at Kalyani, Motijheel and along the Station Road. They provide all sorts of shopping facilities, besides amenities for recreation, like, cinema, theatres and club. The shops here are generally decorated with neon lights and the shopping streets are wide.

In Gopalganj a neighbourhood shopping centre has developed in an elongated shape along the Siwan-Barauli Road. It has a concentration of general stores and several repair shops, including automobiles.

The neighbourhood shopping centres have not developed fully in smaller towns. The shops in these centres carry on retail trade in various commodities and provide service facilities. A few wholesalers, sometimes, also put up retail shops in the neighbourhood shopping centres to take advantage of lower rentals and easy accessibility. Customers prefer to visit these markets because of concentration of specialised services, like, watch, cycle, automobile and radio repairs, at these places. Besides, there are utensil shops, tea stalls, betel shops, barber's saloon and vegetable vendors.

Isolated Shopping Nucleation

This isolated shopping centre is important for the local customer, who purchases the needs of daily life, fairly regularly, from shops located at vantage points in his locality. These shops are usually set-up at the intersection of streets in the residential colony or near the bus or railway station or religious centre. They meet the demands of a local or casual nature only. The shops deal in groceries and provisions, drugs, shoes, sweet-meats, eatables, confectionary, ready-made garments and *bidi-paan*. In addition, some shops also provide services, like, cycle repair, tailoring, hair-cutting, laundering and supply of green vegetables.

It is noted that the railway and bus stations are some focal points which promote the development of isolated shopping nucleations. Later, with the growth in town size, shopping nucleations may emerge into neighbourhood shopping arcades. But this development is dependent upon the volume of trade and the purchasing capacity of the customers. The shops, dealing in specialised goods, are generally located at vantage points. For example, a ribbon-like cluster of medical shops, dealing in drugs and pharmaceutical materials, has come up along Belta Road in Laheriasarai. But other stores, selling general merchandise, also occur side by side in this area. Likewise, there is a large concentration of book and stationery shops near C.M. College at Darbhanga. This has also favoured the establishment of other shops. Similar developments are noted in other towns as well.

Religious places or spots also promote nucleation of shops. For instance, Garib Nath Temple in Muzaffarpur, Durgasthan in Katihar, Kalibari in Forbesganj, Konharaghat in Hajipur, Brahmasthan in Mairwa have promoted nuclei of shopping concentrations. Besides, a few grocery or general merchandise shops or tea stalls or vegetable shops may be found in each *Mohalla* of the town. The quality of goods offered, in these shops, is generally poor and the range of materials available is extremely limited. These clusters occur in a scattered manner in Muzaffarpur, Darbhanga and Katihar. Intensification of some of these clusters might take place with the growth of the town in the near future.

Specialised Market

Analysis of the commercial structure of sample towns reveals that the location of the wholesale trade in agricultural products and perishable items, like, vegetables, meat and fish, is not bound by specific criteria.

Agricultural products form an important item of trade and commerce in the towns of North Bihar. The region has marketable production of rice, sugarcane, jute, tobacco, chillies, oilseeds and turmeric which are collected by *mandis* in smaller towns. These *mandis* are located at convenient points on the open side of towns, so that they may avail of bulk transportation facilities (Plates 17 and 18). Though the bullock-cart is the chief mode of transport in rural areas, these commodities, for purposes of wholesale trade, are moved either by rails or trucks. The towns of Forbesganj, Jainagar, Purnea, Katihar and Dalsinghsarai have well-developed *mandis*, locally known as *Gola* or *Chatti* where bulk trade is carried on.

Green vegetable and fruit markets have developed in the inner parts of town, like, Hajipur, Madhubani, Darbhanga and Laheriasarai (Gudari Bazar). These markets have open spaces, along which lie tin-roofed shops, constructed by the town committee, which sell meat, fish and fruits. Besides, there are a few shops doing retail trade in foodgrains. These markets are easily accessible to most of the town-dwellers. But the shops doing business in perishable items, in Gudari Bazar of Laheriasarai, are located in unhygienic and filthy conditions.

Plate 17: A view of an open-air food-grain and jute mandi at Forbesganj.

Plate 18: A view of Gudari Bazar of Dalsinghsarai.

The future growth pattern of commercial areas in the towns of North Bihar will depend largely on the development of the transport network. It is expected that the number of small-size shops will fall while that of larger businesses will increase. There has been no planned development of commercial centres in these towns, except a few *Katras* (square-sized shopping area) consisting of 10 to 40 shops. The pace of the development of individual shopping centres is not only dependent on the rate of economic growth and industrial expansion in individual towns but also on government policy and municipal laws.

REFERENCES

Alexander, J.W. (1954): The Basic — Non-Basic Concept .f Urban Economic Functions, *Economic Geography*, XXX, pp. 246-61.

Beaujeu-Garnier, J. and G. Chabot (1971): *Urban Geography*, Longmans, London.

Dickinson, R.E. (1964): *City and Region : A Geographical Interpretation*, Routledge and Kegan Paul Ltd., London.

Hoyt, Homer (1958): "Classification and Significant Characteristics of Shopping Centres", In H.M. Mayer and C.F. Kohn (Eds.) (1967): *Readings in Urban Geography*, Allahabad, pp. 454-61.

Jefferson, Mark (1931): "The Distribution of the World's City Folk : A study in Comparative Civilisation", *Geographical Review*, XXI, pp. 446-65.

Maher, C.A. (1979): The Changing Residential Role of the Inner City : The Example of Inner Melbourne, *Australian Geographer*, 14, 2, pp. 112-22.

Murphy, R.E. (1966): *The American City : An Urban Geography*, McGraw Hills Inc., New York.

Murphy, R.E. and J.E. Vance, Jr. (1954): Delimiting the C.B.D., *Economic Geography*, XXX, pp. 189-222.

Muth, R.F. (1975): *Urban Economic Problems*, Harper and Row Publishers, New York.

Proudfoot, M.J. (1937): City Retail Structure, *Economic Geography*, XIII, pp. 425-28.

Ratcliff, R.E. (1949): "Demand for Non-Residential Space", In H.M. Mayer and C.F. Kohn (Eds.) (1967): *Readings in Urban Geography*, Allahabad, pp. 399-417.

Vaughan, T.D. (1960): "Dromore: An Urban Study in Country Down", *Irish Geography*, 4, 2, pp. 130-37.

Webb, J.W. (1959): "Basic Concept in the Analysis of Small Urban Centres of Minnesota", *Annals of the Association of American Geographers*, 49, pp. 55-72.

8

MORPHOLOGY OF OTHER FUNCTIONAL AREAS

MORPHOLOGICAL ANALYSIS of functional areas other than those under residential and commercial uses is also desirable in view of their influence on the general layout plan of towns. In fact, parts of the urban space devoted to industrial, administrative, educational, medical, recreational, transportational and religious uses are equally important since they represent the city's dwindling growing space (Murphy, 1966, p. 396). These morphological areas are well-knit and inter-related. An industrial unit attracts men and materials, that result in housing demands and movement of raw materials and finished products. Parks and playgrounds function as places of recreation, where the industrial workers and other urban communities relax and get themselves relieved of their boredom. Similarly, the administrative and educational areas have important say in shaping the urban morphology. The religious, cultural and medical services also promote urban sprawl and each one has its own sphere of influence.

A town may be compared to a living organism; its different functional areas are like various parts of this organism. The roads and streets form its circulatory system, which, by permitting traffic-flow, bring life to its various functional areas and to various parts of its umland. However, these functions cover much smaller areas than the residential use. Initially, most of the towns have been greatly affected by the administrative function. The other functional areas, it may be noted, have also favoured the growth and development of commercial and residential areas.

Industrial Areas

Industries play a significant role in urbanisation. While industries give rise to towns, towns also create industries. The evolution of industries at a particular place leads to the growth and expansion of the urban pattern, because it favours concentration (Beaujeu-Garnier and Chabot, 1967, p. 148). Though North Bihar has a predominantly agricultural economy, a few industries have sprung up in the area. But their contribution in the overall urbanisation of the region is still very limited. A few consumer goods industries have been set up in a number of towns, which provide facilities, like, raw material, labour and capital goods. Large-scale industries are a few only; these appear as discrete phenomena and are alien to the existing townscape. The small-scale and household industries, however, occur in a scattered manner, even in residential areas of most of the towns. These industrial units do not form a distinct zone.

Evolution of Industrial Structure

Historical evidences suggest the occurrence of a well-developed set of service industries, both in villages and towns. These industries catered to the local and regional demands. At present, also, the industries in the towns of North Bihar are rural-oriented in character (Singh, 1956, p. 21). These are scattered in almost all the towns and include wood-work, smithy, leather-work, weaving, bangle-making, pottery and various other crafts, like, idol-making. Manufacture usually takes place in small household industrial units, which have sprouted in and around the towns. Some of the manufacturing units have, in fact, functioned as magnets which have helped to bring transformation in the existing urban landscape. Dickinson (1964, p. 66) notes that agglomeration of industries takes place in order that there may be an efficient sharing and exchange of produce and services between the industries. This principle is popularly known as the economy of scale. It is noted that, even at the primitive or handicraft stage, these industries have contributed towards the emergence of the industrial landscape in the towns of North Bihar. The early industrial units were mostly hand-operated. The use of steam or diesel engines first came into vogue due to the enterprise of the indigo planters in the British period (Chaudhury, 1963, p. 233).

The industries in the towns of North Bihar have passed through several stages. In the beginning, the industrial landscape consisted of cottage and household industries, manufacturing utility articles, like, cutlery, agricultural implements, leather goods, *durries*, metal products, besides *gur* making, spinning and weaving, carpentry, smithy. These small units occurred in a scattered manner in the residential areas of almost all the towns. The agriculture-based indigo industry flourished until the discovery of the synthetic dyes. Thus, towns, like, Lalganj, Revelganj and Mahnar Bazar declined in importance as the indigo industry was ruined. Among the artisan crafts, making of *Bidri* ware was most important of Purnea and Katihar; these products had country-wide market. But this household industry completely vanished with the decline of the aristocracy (Chaudhury, 1963, p. 232).

The second phase of industrial development took place with the introduction of power-driven machines and metal-based manufacturing in larger towns, like, Muzaffarpur, Darbhanga, Chapra, Katihar and Purnea, resulting in the development of steel fabrications, particularly agricultural implements, trunks and suit-cases and other utility articles, auto-repairing, hosiery and soap-manufacturing, printing presses, ice-factory and cold storages.

The third phase has been marked by the growth of large-scale industries, mostly on the outskirts of towns. This development was largely favoured by the expansion of rail and road transports and with the availability of electric power. Thus, Arther Butler & Co., producing various kinds of steel products and machinery parts, came to be established at Muzaffarpur. Similarly, large-scale agro-based industries, like, sugar mills, paper mills, jute mills, jute bailing presses, engineering works, rice, oil and flour mills, were developed in various towns, including Gopalganj, Siwan, Samastipur, Darbhanga, Katihar, Forbesganj, Banmankhi and Jainagar. A large number of sugar refineries were also installed on the outskirts of some towns (Plate 19). The expansion in town-size of Siwan and Gopalganj particularly took place following the establishment of the sugar refinery and distillery at these places. Establishment of rice and oil mills led to similar developments at Nirmali and Bairagania. Recent construction of the road-cum-rail bridge at Mokamah and establishment of the oil refinery and fertiliser factory at Barauni have produced a modern industrial landscape, which has also engulfed Begusarai.

Plate 19: A view of an open-air market along the Station Road in Forbesganj.

Impact of Industries on Town Morphology

It is evident from the preceding discussion that the patterns of location and evolution of industries are very much linked to the economy of various towns and to the requirements of people living in their respective umlands. Quite often, the locational pattern of industries is reflected in the building fabric of towns. Some categories of industries are found distributed in residential and commercial areas. But the industrial units, in general, occupy a very small proportion of the urban space. Small industrial units, like, bangle- and *bidi*-making, are found at street corners in almost all the towns. These units occupy the ground floors of buildings often in conjunction with other functional uses. The market-based producing units, like, printing press, bakery and soap-making, are found in the business-area, whereas weaving and spinning are located in indigenous parts.

In general, the small workshops prefer road-side locations because of easy accessibility, but larger industries exhibit a preference for areas in close proximity to railway stations on the outer periphery of towns, like, Katihar, Begusarai, Barauni and Muzaffarpur. There is little impact of small industrial units on the townscape of smaller towns, like, Mairwa, Dalsinghsarai and Birpur. But large industrial units have produced segregated morphological patterns, characterised by high tin-roofed buildings with steaming chimneys, large godowns, officers' quarters and labour colonies, at Barauni, Begusarai and Katihar. Recently planned industrial estates, housing small industrial units, have developed in a segregated manner from other uses in towns, like, Murliganj, Forbesganj, Darbhanga, Muzaffarpur and Sitamarhi.

The industrial units do not form a zone but occur as pockets in the townscape. But even a small unit produces its impact on the town's morphology, often creating morphological problems. For instance, the location of Arther Butler & Co. in the central part of Muzaffarpur has created problems for its future expansion and constraints on other uses. The industrial units also act as gravitational foci for concentration of population. This has resulted in congestion, including emergence of slums, urban vices and crimes in areas close to industrial units. The industrial complexes in Barauni-Begusarai belt and at Katihar illustrate this aspect in large measure.

Educational Areas

All urban functions are not economic. Towns inevitably exercise a cultural role in shaping the social life both within and without the urban organism (Beaujeu-Garnier and Chabot, 1967, p. 407). Services, like, education and recreation, attract exotic population which also promote urban growth. Educational facilities, particularly college and university education, cannot be made available at the village level. Thus, to cater to the social and cultural needs of the tributary population, almost all the towns have developed some educational and recreational functions which have brought diversity in their morphological character. The distributional pattern of educational institutions of various levels vary according to the size of towns.

Locational Pattern of Educational Institutions

Schools are generally found in the midst of residential areas. Sometimes, these may be situated in mixed functional areas. The primary schools occur in a highly scattered manner in different *Mohallas* so as to meet the requirements of child education. The middle and high schools are generally located at the main road foci in the middle zone, so that these institutions are within easy reach of residents in the inner and outer zones. Sometimes, these schools are housed in residential buildings due to lack of space. The degree colleges, requiring larger space in terms of buildings, hostel facilities and playgrounds, are often located on the outskirts of the town; they draw students not only from the town where the college happens to be located but also from the neighbouring rural areas and other towns. As the infrastructure required for university education is much greater in terms of teaching, hostel and playground facilities, its location is preferred in the outer parts of the town.

Morphological Pattern of Educational Areas

Almost all the towns of North Bihar have at least one degree college. These institutions cater to the educational needs of the town population as also those living in their umlands. In larger towns the educational function tends to concentrate in pockets or a zone, because the number of primary, middle and high schools happen to be large. But this is not true in case of smaller towns where the facilities are limited.

There is a lot of variation in facilities available in government and privately-managed schools. The government schools generally have a walled campus with *pucca* buildings, hostel, library and playground facilities, whereas the private schools lack most of these privileges. The latter, with the exception of the missionary schools, are generally housed in either dilapidated or half-done buildings, quite close to residential areas. The *Zila* schools (owned by the government), in particular, occupy ideal locations which are free from the din and bustle of the town. The layouts of primary and middle schools, either public or private, are generally deplorable. The situation and building pattern of colleges also vary from town to town, of course, depending upon the quality of management and extent of philanthropic support.

The pull factor of these institutions varies in proportion to the facilities available in them.

The technological institutes and universities form a distinct morphological area in Darbhanga, where two universities, K.S.D. Sanskrit University and L.N. Mithila University, have been established in the former Raj Compound. A special feature of these universities is that lecture rooms, laboratories, libraries and administrative offices are located in palatial buildings which are set in a garden complex with ponds and playgrounds. The concrete roads of these campuses are lined with ornamental and shady trees. A separate study centre of Mithila University has come up at Kilaghat on the outskirts of the town. As these universities are seats of higher learning, they attract students from the whole of North Bihar and, sometimes, also from outside. The development of Bihar University at Muzaffarpur has also been in a haphazard and unplanned manner. It does not have a walled campus like the one at Darbhanga. In fact, the university area at this place is sandwiched between L.S. College in the north and R.D.S. College in the south; the two colleges now form an integral part of the university. The Institute of Technology, located on the western outskirts of the city, however, has a walled campus with ample residential facilities.

Towns having higher educational institutions have functional problems of a different nature. A continuous increase in the student population over the years has led to shortage of residential accommodation in the neighbourhood of educational areas. Consequently, there has been a mushroom-like growth of poor quality houses, often under unhygienic conditions, in and around these institutions. Subhankarpur and Kadirabad *mohallas* in Darbhanga, Domuchak and Kalambagh areas in Muzaffarpur, Gupta Para in Katihar, Sapta and Laheriaganj in Madhubani and Masjid Chowk in Hajipur are examples of areas with poor quality houses, mostly inhabited by the student population. This has resulted in escalation of land values of prestigious sites near educational institutions. Thus, we can conclude that the educational function makes demands on the town in exactly the same way as certain industries (Beaujeu-Garnier and Chabot, 1967, p. 173).

Administrative Areas

The towns of North Bihar, large or small, old or new, have an area where administrative functions are concentrated. This may be called the administrative zone, which is usually located on the outskirts of town at some distance from the main residential areas. The larger towns, in particular, have developed well-delineated areas for the use of the local administrative and government organisations so that they can function smoothly and in a co-ordinated manner (Dube, 1976, p. 88). The administrative area, with its office complex, possesses the advantage of monopoly, as it hardly faces any competition from other land-uses (Singh, 1959, p. 86). Its location is determined by accessibility of ample vacant space. Consequently the administrative zone, in the towns of North Bihar, occupies peripheral sites, sometimes far from other functional zones.

Evolution of Administrative Areas

In the medieval period, North Bihar formed a part of *Subah* Bengal and Tirhut. The region was divided into *Sarkars* (division), *Dastur* (district) and *Mahal* (sub-division) for administrative purposes. The location of administrative headquarters of various orders was guided mainly by defence considerations. Thus, a number of towns had emerged primarily for revenue collection during the medieval times. Hajipur then happened to be the regional capital; other administrative centres were Tughlaqpur and Samsuddinpur (*Sarkar* Tirhut) and Purnea (*Sarkar* Purnea) (Chaudhury, 1963, 1964). The administrative offices, of this period, were confined to the fortresses or four walls of the ruler's residences.

In the British period a remarkable change took place in the administrative set-up and in the form, size and location of the administrative area. The Britishers, with their European style of living, required spacious bungalows with attached gardens which could be constructed only on the periphery of towns. Isolation of their homes from those of the native population was made with a view to ensure their security and comfort (Rimsha, 1976, p. 10). Thus, the administrative zones, developed during the British period, known as the Civil Lines came to be located on the outer margins of the pre-existing towns.

In free India, the size of the administrative zones in the towns of North Bihar varies according to the position occupied by individual town in the administrative hierarchy, i.e., divisional, district, sub-divisional or block headquarters. Large cities, like, Darbhanga and Muzaffarpur, incorporate administrative headquarters from block to divisional level, whereas small towns, like, Murliganj and Mairwa, have only block offices. Sometimes, offices of semi-government autonomous bodies, like, River Valley Projects, Lateral Road Project, Kosi and Gandak Canal Projects, are located in towns. Birpur, Saharsa, Murliganj, Mairwa and Jainagar have assumed additional administrative functions due to the location of one or more of these semi-autonomous bodies at these towns. Thus, it is noted that the administrative areas in the towns of North Bihar have expanded considerably during recent times. These areas have also fostered further growth of commercial activity and the residential function in their neighbourhood.

Morphology of Administrative Areas

From the above discussion, it is quite evident that administrative areas have developed on the outskirts of towns. There is, however, striking difference between the Civil Lines, founded by the Britishers, and the administrative areas, developed in the post-independence period. The administrative areas of larger towns, having diversity of administrative functions, are quite extensive. In these areas are located divisional offices, district collectorate, judiciaries and police offices, housed in suitably spaced single-storeyed *pucca* or tiled-roof buildings. This is typical of the administrative areas of Darbhanga and Muzaffarpur, where the circuit house, the dak-bungalow and the inspection bungalow lie in close proximity to the older Civil Lines and the newly-developed administrative areas (Fig. 8.1). The housing pattern and the general appearance of the newly-developed administrative areas in the recently constituted divisional and district headquarters of Saharsa, Gopalganj, Katihar and Hajipur are quite different. The morphological character of administrative blocks in these towns is dominated by multi-storeyed buildings making vertical use of space.

Rapid outward expansion of the residential area has removed the former spatial separateness of the administrative zone in older towns, like, Muzaffarpur, Darbhanga, Chapra and Motihari. Additional constructions to meet the increasing requirements of administration, from time to time, have also created congestion in this zone. A large number of road-side eating places, restaurants and shops, dealing in court stationery and other articles, have sprouted. This has led to overcrowding and suffocating congestion. In contrast, the administrative areas in small and newly-grown towns are located quite

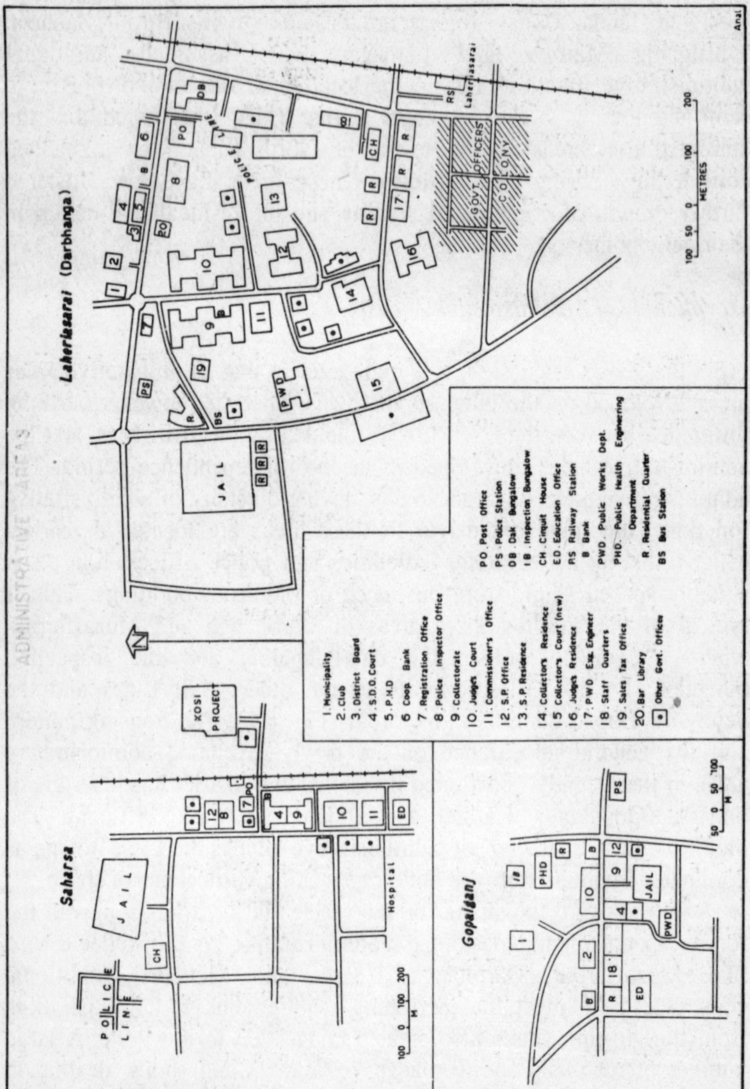

Fig. 8.1: Administrative areas: Saharsa, Laheriasarai (Darbhanga) and Gopalganj.

far from the town area. Consequently, these are free from congestion and overcrowding. In these towns, independent offices, like, the police station, post-office, municipal office, N.A.C., P.W.D. electric-supply office, etc., are, however, located in the middle zone. These offices, housed in medium-size buildings, render various services to the town-dwellers.

Medical Areas

Almost all the towns of North Bihar provide medical facilities in large or small measure. These facilities are utilised by the town-dwellers and residents in their respective umlands. In smaller towns, the medical facility occurs as pockets, but, in larger towns, it usually forms a zone comprising hospital buildings, dispensary, primary health and family welfare centres, residences of doctors, nurses and other auxiliary staff, besides medicine shops. This zone, like the administrative function, also occurs on the outskirts of towns. Recent expansions of the residential and other functions, resulting in encroachments on the medical zone, have been noticed in cities, like, Darbhanga and Muzaffarpur. The older medical establishments are usually found in the congested parts of these cities, whereas the newer medical facilities have been developed on their periphery. The unhealthy conditions prevailing in the heart of towns has resulted in the shifting of a few medical facilities from the inner areas towards the outer periphery.

Though the medical zone covers a relatively much smaller area than other functional uses, it still acts as a pull factor in urban expansion, bringing together various professional services related to health-care and attracting trade and commerce.

The medical zone forms a centre of gravity whose significance cannot be measured in economic terms. A distinct medical zone is found at Darbhanga with D.M.C. Hospital, having about 1,000 beds for male and female patients, as its nucleus. There are 10 units functioning in this hospital, namely, medical, surgical, gynaecological, ophthalmalogical, blood-bank and glucose saline laboratory, clinical pathology, radiology, dental, anaesthetic, radium therapy and pediatrics. Besides, a few research centres have been also developed. Thus, the D.M.C. Hospital has a large sphere of influence not only in North Bihar but also in the contiguous Nepal Tarai. It is a highly popular medical institution and remains overcrowded throughout the year. A large part of the medical and para-medical staff hospital, which is settled in the town, has been drawn from rural areas of both North and South Bihar. Establishment of the medical zone, at Laheriasarai in Darbhanga, has resulted in concentration of hotels, rest-houses, drug stores and groceries along Betta Road and in Rahamganj. In addition, a high class residential area, mostly inhabited by doctors, traders, etc., has developed in close proximity to this zone.

The medical facility is not well-developed in smaller towns. It occurs only in pockets rather than zones. The medical facility in smaller towns may include a small hospital or dispensary with a few medical staff and drug stores around. This is true of towns, like, Jainagar, Murliganj and Dalsinghsarai. In spite of the inadequacy of medical facilities available at these centres, the out-door patient ward remains over-crowded. A scattered growth of nursing homes, clinics and dispensaries by private medical practitioners, however, has taken place in Class II and III towns, namely, Katihar, Hajipur, Samastipur, Chapra, Madhubani, Saharsa and Forbesganj.

Recreational and Cultural Areas

Parks, playgrounds, cinemas, clubs and open spaces act as recreational spots and provide amusement to the urban-dwellers. The parks and playgrounds, in particular, show a maximum humanisation of the natural landscape and serve as the lungs of the city community as a whole (Singh, 1955, p. 95). Open spaces are equally important for all towns, because a residential area without open spaces, like, gardens, court-yards and playgrounds, is almost inconceivable. Similarly, a religious place without its open spaces, a shopping centre without its plaza and a school without its playground cannot be imagined (Dhar, 1969, p. 34). Unfortunately, the towns of North Bihar suffer from inadequacy of recreational facilities, which are considered essential for healthy living.

Parks are equally important for healthy living. But in most of the towns, the parks either do not exist or are too few or quite inadequate in size. This is also true of the newly-grown towns, except in townships, like, Birpur and Barauni.

The playgrounds are quite common in almost all the towns. These are generally attached to colleges and schools but are, sometimes, also used by the general public. Poor maintenance of the playgrounds is responsible for their unattractive look in general. There is a race-course and a polo-ground, both at Muzaffarpur and Darbhanga, but these are mostly used for public meetings, occasional gatherings and as sites of open-air theatre. The open-air theatre is very popular in the towns of North Bihar, particularly at occasions, like, Durga Puja, when drama and musical arrangements are also made. There is provision for stadium at Gopalganj, Darbhanga and Muzaffarpur only. But the towns of North Bihar have ample open spaces, mostly in the form of shallow-water ponds in almost all the functional areas, which reduce congestion and the overall population density. These ponds and tanks have multi-functional uses, including fishing, bathing and cultivation of *Makhana* and *Singhara* (water berries). As these water-bodies constitute a considerable part of the urban space at Darbhanga, the town is called a city of tanks.

Cinema is the most popular and cheapest form of commercial recreation available in the towns of North Bihar. The cinema halls are usually situated along important roads in the middle zone of the town so that these could attract large number of cine-goers from the surrounding areas. Though cinema houses do not form a zone, their siting at convenient locations produces congestion, particularly overcrowding of the main thoroughfares at the beginning and closing of different shows. Organisations, like, officers' club, youth club, etc., occur in larger towns. They cater to the recreation of a small clientele, the educated elite of the towns.

Religious Areas

All the towns of North Bihar possess some places of worship, like, temple, mosque, church, *samadhi, mazar* and mounds of religious significance. These places of worship do not form a zone, but often occur in segments having distinct religious identity. For example, the mosques are usually located in *mohallas* having a large proportion of Muslim inhabitants. Similarly, the temples are generally located near principal concentrations of the Hindu community. The churches lie close to the Christian localities.

Sometimes, temples or mosques have acted as nuclei for the initial growth of towns or *mohallas* within a town. Consequently, these religious places have greatly affected their town plans. Places of worship, having replicas or idols of Lord Shiva, Rama, Hanuman and the Goddess Durga and Kali, are the foci of human congregations on auspicious occasions. In a large number of towns, important shopping enclaves have come up near road-crossings or along roads leading to important temples. Sometimes, these shopping enclaves are also named after the concerned deity, such as the Shankar Chowk in Saharsa, Ram Chowk in Darbhanga, Mahabir Chowk in Dalsinghsarai, Durgasthan in Madhubani and Kali Bari in Forbesganj.

There are also simpler religious places or spots, like, the Konhara Ghat in Hajipur, Janki-asthan in Sitamarhi, Garibasthan in Muzaffarpur and Hariramdih in Mairwa. These are sacred spots of great ritual significance which come to life once in a week. An enormous influx of local pilgrims is noted at these places on Sundays. This presents problems of hygiene and sanitation for the urban-dwellers. Sometimes, temporary shops, as off-shoots of the business area, are set up at these locations to cater to the needs of the devotees.

Cemeteries and burning grounds or *ghats* are other forms of socio-religious expressions. These are generally located at the outer margin of the town, somewhat segregated from residential areas.

REFERENCES

Beaujeu-Garnier, J. and G. Chabot (1971): *Urban Geography*, Longmans Group Ltd., London, p. 470.

Chaudhury, P.C.R. (1963): *Bihar District Gazetteers, Purnea*, Secretariat Press, Patna, pp. 64-113.

Chaudhury, P.C.R. (1964): *Bihar District Gazetteers, Darbhanga*, Secretariat Press, Patna, pp. 3-36.

Dhar, H.K. (1969): Role of Open Space in Residential Area, *Urban and Rural Planning Thought*, XII, pp. 34-52

Dickinson, R.E. (1964): *City and Region*, Rautledge and Kegan Paul, London, pp. 64-7.

Dube, K.K. (1976): *Use and Misuse of Land in Kaval Towns*, N.G.S.I., Varanasi.

Murphy, R.E. (1966): *The American City: An Urban Geography*, McGraw Hill Book Co., New York, p. 464.

Rimsha, A. (1976): *Town Planning in Hot Climate*, Mir Publishers, Moscow, p. 287.

Singh, R.L. (1955): *Banaras and its Umland: A Study in Urban Geography*, N.K. & Bros., Varanasi.

Singh, R.L. (1956): Mirzapur: A Study in Urban Geography, *Geographical Outlook*, I, pp. 16-27.

Singh, U. (1959): Functional Regions of Allahabad, *National Geographical Journal of India*, VII, pp. 67-90.

9

PROBLEMS AND PLANNING

THE TOWNS of North Bihar have been confronted with a large number of problems following an unprecedented growth in their dimensions. This has resulted in overcrowding, congestion, poor housing facilities, encroachment on open spaces and agricultural land, abnormal increase in traffic flow and accidents, poor water supply, deterioration in health and sanitary conditions and increase in crimes. Even, development of slums has taken place in a number of towns. The unprecedented growth of urban areas and incessant migration of rural-folk to urban areas have assumed such alarming proportions that they require immediate attention of the urban planners and other concerned authorities. Hoselitz (1959, p. 231) has, therefore, asked for an early application of rehabilitation and development plans to Indian cities, particularly in view of their heterogeneous character.

It is an established fact that the larger towns have more problems than the smaller ones. But the smaller towns have some problems typical of their own group. Preparation of a town development plan requires consideration of former growth trends, existing conditions and probable future requirements. In this context, Wilson (1974, p.12) has noted three basic ingredients of planning, namely, policy, design and analysis.

In the present study, a model conceptual frame-work has been proposed for a systematic study of the problems of urban areas so that a comprehensive town development plan could be prepared (Fig. 9.1). Emphasis has been laid here not only on further expansion but also on the renovation of existing areas under residential, commercial and industrial uses, besides improvements in transportation facilities and street network, adoption of flood preventive measures and a variety of other public works. After an elaborate analysis of the problems associated with various land, uses, a design has been provided for formulating town reconstruction, and specific suggestions have been made in this regard. These steps are intimately related and supplementary to each other. The capital required for urban reconstruction and the need for municipal and government legislations, in this regard, have been also considered. Thus, a comprehensive plan for the development of North Bihar towns has been proposed. As most of the towns of North Bihar are small in size, their planning has to be attempted at grassroot level.

The major problems, confronting the towns of North Bihar, relate to their morphological structure. Consideration of these problems will form a prelude to the preparation of a comprehensive plan for town development.

Problems

All towns of the region have experienced a tremendous growth of population during the last three decades. This gain in population is attributable to natural increase, migration from rural areas and, to some extent, the influx of refugees from East Pakistan (now Bangladesh). Population migration from rural to urban areas has been an important phenomenon throughout the historic times, as is evident from various records. This town-ward migration has been particularly in evidence in the last few decades because of attractions of higher standard of living and better social life in towns. Villages in close proximity to towns, like, Begusarai-Barauni, Samastipur, Katihar and Hajipur, have witnessed the recent impact of urbanisation and soon these will be engulfed in the overall urban landscape.

The pace of population rise and urbanisation, during recent times, has varied from town to town. In the last 30 years, towns, like, Jainagar, Dalsinghsarai, Motihari, Khagaria, Chapra, Bettiah and Purnea, have witnessed moderate increases in population and urban growth, while Forbesganj, Barauni and Katihar have shown very rapid growth. Natural increases in town population and urban migration have created a variety of problems related to housing, education, health and employment. Consequently, most of the towns have experienced phenomenal increases in their residential areas. The problems of residential, commercial, industrial and other morphological areas have been considered separately. These towns also suffer from floods and experience various traffic and transport problems.

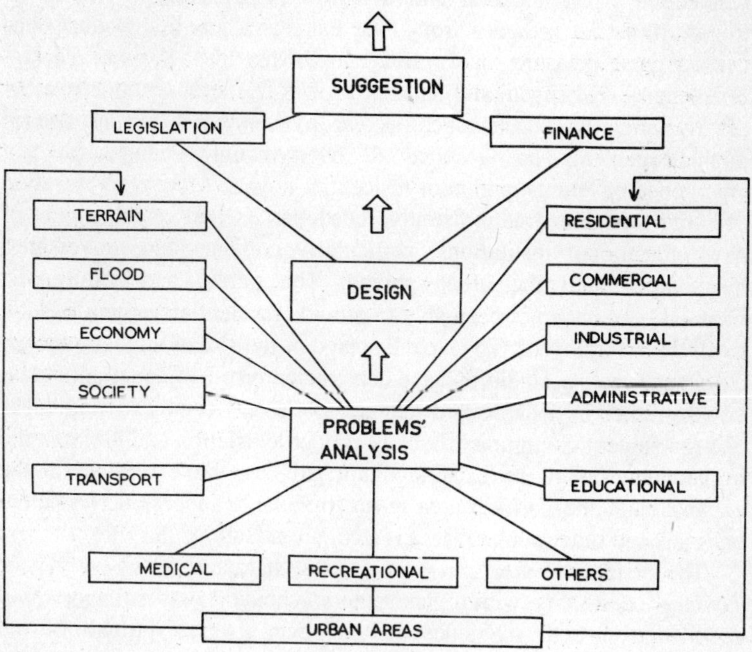

Fig. 9.1: Model for comprehensive planning.

Problems of Residential Areas

The residential area is the largest component of the built-up area in the towns of North Bihar. It consists of various types of houses, arranged along streets of weird design. Changes in the built-up area have caused a number of problems in the physical fabric of residential areas. Immense increase in population has resulted in an acute shortage of residential accommodation and overcrowding, particularly in larger towns. Influx of refugees from East Pakistan (now Bangladesh) has caused great pressure on dwellings in towns, like, Katihar, Purnea, Forbesganj, Kishenganj and Saharsa. However, increase in the number of dwellings has been much slower as compared to the rise in population. This has resulted in overcrowding, congestion and emergence of 'slums' and poor residential-hovels. Moreover, elevation of some towns into administrative headquarters and establishment of new educational institutions, particularly colleges and universities, have accelerated the urban sprawl. The public and semi-public organisations have not been able to provide residential accommodation to all their employees. To take advantage of the situation, the moneyed class and wealthy landlords have constructed profit-oriented poor class houses rather in a haphazard manner to fleece over these employees and the student community. Lack of proper legislation and laxity in the implementation of the existing municipal laws have resulted in the expansion of the built-up area in an irregular manner. Encroachment on roads and other public places is a common feature.

The residential areas, in general, are characterised by very poor sanitary conditions with open gutters, choked with sullage, often occurring on both the sides of the street. Recent growth of the *jhugi-jhumpri bustee* in some towns provide instances of extreme congestion, over-crowding and insanitary living.

Problems of Commercial Areas

It has been noted earlier that the main shopping area of the town is generally located along the main road or at road-crossings, locally known as *chauraha* in the older and central parts of the town. It forms the focal point of commercial activities and is, sometimes, known as the 'Gudari Bazar', where retail establishments or general stores dealing in convenience goods cater to the day to day needs of the town population. There is considerable variation in the intensity and distributional pattern of commercial land-uses from town to town. However, a very high degree of commercial nucleation, including extreme congestion and overcrowding of commercial establishments, is noted in the central parts of almost all the towns. The pattern of shopping is often old-styled and appalling congestion prevails on the roads and pavements as well. A few shopping areas occur in narrow and winding lanes where congestion and overcrowding have become too glaring phenomena to be ignored. In fact, the inhabitants in the commercial core are confronted with health hazards due to congestion and overcrowding. Reeve (1917, p. 286) holds commercialism responsible for congestion. The centripetal force of commercial activities, resulting in a high degree of congestion in the central business area (C.B.A.) or the commercial core, also accounts for overflow of traffic — a feature most inconvenient for both buyers and sellers. Also an acute shortage or spacious commercial premises is found in this area.

The location of 'Gudari Bazar' in the central business area presents special problems. Footpath vendors, selling fruits and vegetables, meat and fish, etc., obstruct the smooth flow of traffic, both vehicular and pedestrian. Some shops display their saleable goods on the pavement also aggravating the problems of congestion. Road-side restaurants and tea-stalls, in the commercial area, throw their kitchen refuse on the pavements and road-sides, thus making the area filthy and dirty.

Problems of Industrial Areas

Industrial establishments and workshops also add to the complexity of problems in towns. It has been noted that small industrial establishments generally occur in residential areas inhabited by working class people. For example, in Muzaffarpur, Arther Butler & Co. is located in the residential area along the Station Road. Rice, flour and oil mills also occupy similar locations at Darbhanga, Jainagar, Forbesganj and Katihar. Small industries, including metal works, saw mills and furniture making, often occur in residential and commercial segments. This creates a host of problems, including noise nuisance due to tapping of metal-beaters or blacksmiths, grinding and vibration of flour milling and oil crushing, dust pollution due to saw milling and foul odours of the soap factory. The problems of noise, dust and chemical pollutions prevail in almost all the larger towns of North Bihar.

Bullock-carts and hand-driven *thellas* generally used to bring in raw materials and send out finished products, create traffic congestion and transport bottlenecks, particularly when the industrial establishments happen to be located in the inner and middle zones of towns. Sometimes, the roads get so chocked with traffic that even pedestrian movement becomes sluggish and hazardous.

Problems of other Morphological Areas

Each town has a certain proportion of land, under public or semi-public uses, designed to serve the town-dwellers and residents in its umland. Areas providing educational, medical, recreational and administrative functions have problems of their own. The problems of these areas are enumerated separately.

Problems of educational institutions: Field observations reveal an uneven distribution of educational institutions in the towns of North Bihar. Though the Government has taken over the management of primary and secondary schools, there is still a lot of variation in the amenities available in public, private and missionary schools. Keeping in view the large size of the student population, the number of nursery, primary, middle and high schools is insufficient. Some of these schools are located in noisy, over-crowded and unhygienic conditions prevailing in the heart of the town. Consequently, these schools cannot provide for the basic needs, like, playgrounds and lawns. Though the colleges, universities and technical institutes, catering to the needs of higher education, are situated on the periphery of towns, they still lack in facilities like well-equipped laboratories, libraries, hostels and playgrounds. As a few universities are housed in residential buildings, they do not even provide some of the basic facilities that are usually available in other universities of the country.

Problems of medical institutions: Though the towns of North Bihar are provided with hospitals and dispensaries, the facilities available therein are quite inadequate. Consequently, a large number of town-dwellers are deprived of the medical aid. The endemic nature of malaria and other tropical diseases in North Bihar calls for special preventive and curative measures. There are, however, large hospitals with specialised services only at Darbhanga and Muzaffarpur. In other towns, the medical facilities available are either inadequate or of poor quality.

The hospital complex at Darbhanga, situated in the midst of residential area, has created environmental pollution due to discharge of hospital refuse through open drains. This practice is a grave menace to public health. Similarly, the hospital area at Muzaffarpur, also, suffers from overcrowding and poor sanitary conditions.

Problems of administrative units: The structure of the towns in North Bihar varies mainly in accordance to their administrative status. Though largely managed by Government agencies, the administrative areas have problems of their own. In smaller towns, the administrative areas are neither well-planned nor suitably developed. Housing of various government offices in rental buildings without requisite amenities, particularly in larger towns, creates problems both for the employees and the public. Thus, some of the offices are located far from the administrative areas. Their location in residential areas is also not desirable. Landlords also do not want to spare their houses for this purpose.

Problems of parks and recreational areas: Town-dwellers need recreational facilities to relieve the drudgery of urban living. People can breathe fresh air in parks and playgrounds. Other recreational facilities, like, cinema, theatre, club and picnic spots, help to re-invigorate the town-dwellers. The towns in North Bihar provide these facilities in limited measure only. However, most of these towns have large open spaces under orchards, ponds and vegetable gardens.

Playgrounds occur attached to colleges and schools, located on the periphery of towns only. The general public is not supposed to make use of them. Most of these playgrounds and parks are poorly maintained and badly used.

Traffic and Transportation Problems

From traffic point of view, the arrangement and lay-out of roads, their relative position and means of inter-communication are matters of fundamental importance (Singh 1961, p. 112). The towns of North Bihar, in general, have narrow roads, incapable of bearing heavy traffic. In fact, not a single town has good quality roads that can be considered suitable for bearing heavy urban traffic. Their existing condition is far from satisfactory. Several roads are unmetalled and many without pavements for pedestrian traffic, which create congestion and traffic hazards.

Most of the roads in the central parts of towns, like, Muzaffarpur, Darbhanga, Katihar, Hajipur and Samastipur, were designed a long time ago when the traffic was too meagre. These roads are no longer able to cope with heavy increases in both pedestrian and vehicular traffic as a consequence of phenomenal rises in population and number of vehicles on the road. Consequently, the traffic problem in the commercial areas of towns has assumed alarming proportions during business hours. Besides, modern modes of transport, like, automobile, including trucks and motor-bikes, compete for road space with slow-moving *rickshaws*, bullock-carts and *tongas*, that are generally driven by untrained rural-folk. As the cyclists and pedestrians also do not care for traffic rules, road jams and accidents take place quite frequently. In the last 30 years, there has been also a phenomenal increase in heavy traffic of trucks, buses and tankers on major district roads and State highways. Consequently, when this traffic passes through a particular town, it creates traffic congestion and jams. Poor observance of traffic rules by vehicle drivers and the public in general also make the situation worse.

Flood Problem

The towns of North Bihar suffer damages from floods quite frequently. It is noted that 25 out of a total of 49 towns in the region are located on the river banks and rivulets. Some of these towns suffer from floods almost every year, while others are affected only occasionally or marginally. The towns of Muzaffarpur, Darbhanga, Sitamarhi, Barauni, Begusarai, Katihar, Bairgania, Gogri, Naugachhia, Bagaha, Nirmali, Chapra, Revelganj and Khagaria are affected by floods almost every year. The floods, apart from paralysing the activities of the town-dwellers, also cause damages to buildings and human life.

Planning

It is apparent from the preceding analysis that the towns of North Bihar are confronted with a variety of problems, which can be solved only by evolving suitable strategy in a planned way. Planning, in fact, is a process to maximise or optimise the usefulness of a given institution (Singh, 1972, p. 449).

Through planning, an attempt can be made to solve the problems being faced by the towns of North Bihar and their urban communities. We expect the towns to provide not only modern amenities but also decent living. For this, an integrated approach in town development is required in which the geographer has to play an important role in the physical, planning and development of town areas for residential, commercial, industrial and other purposes. Keeping this in view, need has been felt for preparing a comprehensive plan which may provide the general guidelines for urban development. This will also help to provide viable solutions for the different problems confronting the towns of North Bihar.

Suggestions for the Improvement of Residential Areas

As the residential area happens to be the largest component of the urban fabric in North Bihar, its problems of obsolete dwellings, congestion, overcrowding and insanitary conditions require urgent consideration. True, a better living environment with less land per dwelling has become an essential ingredient of town planning, both in physical and structural terms. A sound developmental planning is required to improve the living conditions in towns by providing ample facilities for better roads and other civic amenities. Thus, keeping in view the social and economic background of the towns in North Bihar, the following measures are proposed for the improvement of their residential areas:

(i) First, all haphazard or unplanned construction of dwellings in various sections of the town should be stopped through proper municipal legislation. Obsolete and dilapidated buildings, occurring mostly in the older parts of the town, have to be demolished and modern buildings should be constructed in their place by providing financial assistance, at a reasonable rate of interest, to the house-owners;

(ii) Bihar Urban Ceiling Act of 1961 should be implemented without any further delay. Thus, the surplus urban land could be acquired for the development of residential complexes, particularly for poor people in the middle and lower-income groups. The lay-out plan, allocation of plots, and approval of building plans have to be made by the town development authority, which could also supply building materials at approved rates;

(iii) Formation of a small town planning unit is suggested so that it could assist the Municipality and N.A.C. in town development. At present, none of the towns of North Bihar, except Muzaffarpur, has either improvement trust or any other town planning organisation;

(iv) As the towns of North Bihar lie in the seismic zone of India, the vertical expansion of buildings has to be restricted, preferably, to two storeys only;

(v) Low-lying, marshy and waste lands, lying in the urban areas of Darbhanga, Katihar, Jainagar, Saharsa, Purnea, Supaul and Madhepura, could be reclaimed for development of residential colonies and other uses. In doing so, due consideration has to be given to the economy of space, provision of public utility services and the expenditure involved;

(vi) The slum areas in towns, like, Muzaffarpur, Katihar, Hajipur and Darbhanga, need immediate attention. It is proposed that the slum-dwellers, at present residing under unhygienic conditions in the densely populated parts of these towns, may be re-habilitated at alternative sites on the outskirts of the town and the slum-cleared areas can be developed into parks and playgrounds.

Suggestions for the Improvement of Commercial Areas

The recent population explosion and increase in the size of towns have resulted in phenomenal growth of commercial activities, particularly in larger towns. This has caused an overlap of functional uses in most of the towns. Hence, to relieve congestion and overcrowding in the C.B.A., a proposal is made to shift the residences to other areas and the space vacated may be renovated into shops, show-rooms and other commercial establishments. This can be done by pursuasion, legislation and provision for financial assistance. The 'Gudari Bazar', located in the heart of towns, needs also to be moved to some other convenient location so as to ease congestion. The space so vacated can then be allotted for retail business on hire-purchase basis. Thus, the wholesale and retail trade may function at separate locations. Big godowns and warehouses may be established either in close proximity to the railway station or at entry points of important roads into the towns, wherever ample open space is available. These will provide cheap and convenient storage facilities for bulky goods, like, jute, and other agricultural produce at towns, like, Forbesganj, Purnea and Katihar. Thus, the congestion in the central business area, where some of the warehouses are at present located, can be relieved. Pavement shops need not to function in the commercial core of the town and all encroachments on road have to be stopped.

Provision for a municipal market, selling general merchandise and perishable goods, has to be made in each ward. This will also contribute to the easing of congestion in the central business area. Paved foot-ways for pedestrian traffic have to be constructed in the commercial areas of, at least, larger towns. This will increase street capacity in towns, like, Darbhanga, Muzaffarpur and Katihar. Provision for bypass roads has to be made so that inter-town traffic need not touch intermediate stations. There is also need for developing suburban markets to cater to the needs of expanding towns.

Suggestions for the Improvement of Industrial Structure

The existing industrial establishments are not necessarily suitably located in most of the towns. It has been noted that the small-scale and household industries usually occur in residential areas. Barber (1969, p. 147) has observed that the object of industrial planning is to provide suitable space and facilities for industry and to integrate industry into the community in such a manner that it will thrive and result in economic advantages to the community, with a minimum of adverse effects. Keeping this in view, the household industry may be retained in the residential area but both the small-scale and large-scale industries, which produce a lot of noise, have to be shifted to areas distinctly allocated for the purpose. For example, Arther Butler & Co., sited in the midst of residential area at Muzaffarpur, needs immediate shifting.

Industries emitting objectionable dirt, fumes, odours and noise have to be sited far from the residential areas so that the pollutants may not endanger the health of the town-dwellers. Establishment of industrial estates, like the one at Barauni and Begusarai, is suggested for this purpose. Some of the existing industries at Katihar, Forbesganj and Darbhanga may have to be moved to such an industrial estate. There is ample scope for the development of fruit and food processing industries in the region.

Suggestions for the Improvement of Other Morphological Units

Educational Institutions

Educational institutions, catering to the needs of school and higher education, occur in various parts of the towns. There is an imperative need to provide for more primary and nursery schools at suitable locations in the residential areas of almost all the towns. The high schools should be located, preferably, close to the main road in the peripheral parts of residential areas so that these could be easily approachable. Special attention is to be given to privately-managed high schools which usually suffer from lack of facilities and suitable staff. Measures have to be taken to improve the academic facilities available in degree and P.G. colleges; these fill the gap between the school and the university education. The locations of C.M. College and K.S. College in the central residential area of Darbhanga have been responsible for creating a lot of congestion. Similarly, Bihar University campus, located in the middle parts of Muzaffarpur, is also confronted with the problem of space. A more rational use of the existing space is suggested or alternatively the university may be shifted to a more spacious area on the periphery of the town.

Medical Centre

The number of hospitals and dispensaries in the towns of North Bihar is quite insufficient to cater to the health-care of the town-dwellers and the rural-folk. These facilities are also unevenly distributed. There is an urgent need for having a female hospital, equipped with maternity home, in almost all the towns of North Bihar. The size and facilities available in these hospitals, may be in keeping with the size of the town's population. Care has to be taken in the selection of site for the hospital. For example, T.B. clinic, sanitorium and veterinary hospitals have to be located on the outskirts of the town. Provision for the specialised treatment of cancer, polio, malaria, veneral and quarantine diseases, etc., is highly desirable. These units have to be equipped with sensitive and sophisticated instruments. Needless to mention, the ambulance facility will further enhance their efficiency.

Administrative Units

A number of public and semi-public buildings, meant for

accommodating government offices, occur in all the towns of North Bihar. The most important among these are the municipal town hall, post-office, P.W.D. office, police station, auditorium, museum, public library and administrative courts, etc. It is suggested that various administrative offices may be grouped together, as far as possible, in one area so that these can render more efficient service. The administrative area, in fact, needs a planned development so that new attractive structures may be constructed with extensive set-backs and parking facilities and lawns. Such an elaborate landscape can be had only on the outskirts of towns.

Parks and Playgrounds

In true sense, parks and playgrounds do not exist in any town of North Bihar. However, there are a few sports grounds, but these are mostly uncared for and in deplorable state. Recent increase in literacy has brought in a new consciousness among the town-dwellers for having recreational facilities, including parks and playgrounds. Development of parks and playground on suitable vacant land is desirable with a view to maintaining the physical and mental health of town-dwellers, prevention of delinquency and crime and promotion of safety-measures (Goetsch, 1969, p.168). Thus, each town should have at least three parks, viz., Children Park, Municipal Park and Railway Park. The location of parks and educational institutions of higher learning may be put close together.

The low-lying swampy lands in towns, like, Darbhanga, Muzaffarpur and Katihar, can be reclaimed and used for laying parks and playgrounds. There are a large number of tanks and ponds in these towns, which could be used for recreational purposes by putting up flower gardens on their banks and providing angling facilities. Besides, these tanks and ponds can be also used for aquaculture and fish farming.

Suggestions for the Improvement of the Transport System

Efficient mobility within the town is, indeed, essential for the continued vitality of the multitude of activities that the town must support. It can be possible with the help of a well-designed network of roads and streets, as also by having an efficient mode of transport for both men and materials. Narrow and winding roads in most of the towns of North Bihar create traffic congestion and overcrowding on roads. Widening of the existing roads and streets, removal of encroachment on the pavement by shopkeepers and check on unauthorised parking of *rickshaw*, *tonga* and other vehicles will go a long way to increase traffic mobility. There is also need for providing suitable sites for parking of vehicles near spacious *chauraha*. Construction of carriage-ways with footpaths on both the sides of main roads in towns, like, Darbhanga, Muzaffarpur, Chapra and Katihar, are immediately required. In Katihar, Motihari, Samastipur and Madhubani, bypass roads are yet to be constructed so that the movement of through vehicular traffic may be speeded up. At present, this traffic passes through the main shopping areas of the towns concerned, thus adding to traffic congestion. Observance of traffic rules and restriction on the movement of heavy vehicles during peak business hours will also help to relieve the pressure. All towns should be connected with State highways, lateral roads and national highways so that there can be better interaction among the towns of the region.

Measures for Flood Protection

The towns of the region suffer from floods in varying degrees almost every year. Though the floods cannot be prevented altogether, yet their severity can be minimised and damages reduced in an effective way. The State Government has already executed several schemes under which protective 'bunds' have been constructed, particularly to protect the larger towns. However, flood protection measures have not been implemented in case of smaller towns which still suffer from the severity of floods. Afforestation in upper catchment areas, construction of storage reservoirs and protective embankments, strengthening of natural levees, besides dredging of river channels and inundation canals are some of the important flood-control measures recommended for the region. The protective embankments along rivers, bordering towns, have to be made of concrete to avoid seepages. Towns more susceptible to floods can be provided with ring embankments. Arrangements will have to be made to pump out the drain-water and surface drainage into rivers, wherever such ring embankments are constructed.

Saharsa: A Sample Study in Town Planning

Saharsa is a recently grown town of the region. It has a number of problems which can be considered as typical for most of the towns of the region. Consequently, its problems have been analysed in detail and a Master Plan has been prepared for its development. This plan attempts to provide the geographical perspective in town development.

The present urban space of Saharsa is surrounded by a number of low-lying *chaurs*, which generally dry up in the winter and summer seasons. This urban space gradually slopes down towards the south. A relatively upland area in the west, comprising Saharsa *Basti*, forms its oldest site. Other *mohallas*, like, Mirtola, Kayasthatola, Gangzala and Nayabazar, make its later developments. The growth of the town has been somewhat restricted by the occurrence of lowlands in the south and south-east. Consequently, its expansion has taken place recently along Madhepura Road in the east and Bangaon Road in the west. Administrative buildings occupy the town space in the north-west. The residential area occurs primarily in the western, eastern and north-central parts and along the main roads where it is mixed up with commercial uses (Figs. 6.5 & 7.3). The commercial establishments are usually housed in *pucca* buildings along the D.B. Road and in Kaprapatti. A considerable part of the urban space, in the south-central part, is under the use of the railways, such as the yard, station, goods-shed, engine-shed, ware-house and the employees' residential colony. The functional uses in other parts are of a mixed nature.

Keeping the above-mentioned facts in view, a comprehensive plan for the future development of Saharsa has been prepared (Fig. 9.2). It envisages maximum possible adjustments with the present town structure so that there is a minimum of demolition. Consequently, creation of an outer zone has been proposed, because the existing inner zone of the town, comprising its commercial core, is structurally very compact and congested. No further construction or extension of buildings has to be permitted in the inner zone. A renovation plan has been suggested compartment-wise so that obsolete residential buildings could be demolished and commercial establishments made to shift to the newly developed residential areas for neighbourhood shopping sites in the outer zone. The plan also takes into consideration the present and future requirements of residential space both within and outside the municipal limits.

An industrial area has been provided in the north-east along the proposed railway track in Haskpara. This area may also have a residential colony with shopping facilities. Provision has been made for having an educational institution, a dispensary and a community

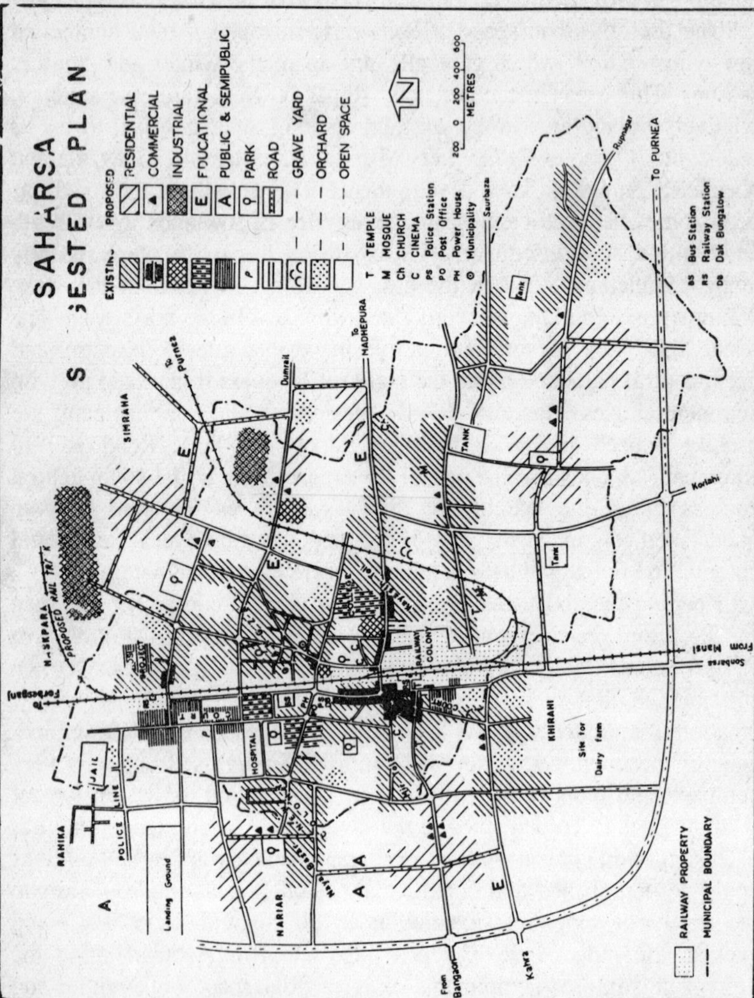

Fig. 9.2: Saharsa: suggested plan.

centre in all the residential areas to be developed in future. The type and level of these institutions may be determined according to the density of population in the wards concerned. The Law College and Manohar School, at present located in the congested inner zone of the town, need to be shifted beyond the railway crossing in the east. A few parks and playgrounds have been also provided in the areas to be renovated and proposed to be developed in future.

The town has a few tanks, along which flower gardens may be laid so that these could be used as recreation spots. Horticulture can be developed profitably as a large part of the town space is still under agricultural uses. Dairying and poultry farms can be located at Khirahi in the south.

The existing air-strip at Nariar in the west may be converted into civil lines and a new air-strip can be constructed farther north, at a distance of about 10 km from the town. Thus, public and semi-public buildings can be constructed at Nariar.

The existing roads and footpaths need to be widened and encroachments thereon to be removed. In this regard, special attention has to be given to Station Road and Dahlan Chowk area. Construction of a bypass road has been suggested in the south-west so that Purnea-bound heavy vehicles need not pass through the town. A few link-roads have been also proposed. Construction of an overbridge, across the railway track near Mahabir Chowk, will relieve congestion and lead to a smooth flow of traffic. Moreover, linking of the neighbouring rural settlements with the town of Saharsa will mean reciprocal growth for both the town and the neighbouring villages.

Thus, the main objective of the proposed plan has been to make the town of Saharsa clean, beautiful, fulfilling and prospective so that a decent living can be made possible there.

At the end, it may be said that the future of the urban-dwellers of North Bihar is full of trials, thrills, problems, promises and opportunities. Successful implementation of a town development plan depends upon a multitude of factors, including appropriate leadership — both at political and expertise levels — with a high degree of vision and imagination, co-operation and co-ordination at various levels, besides application of sound planning principles through workable techniques. Attempt has to be made to minimise, if not eliminated, the negative aspects of urban living. Similarly, the mistakes of the past have to be avoided so that a high degree of excellence in plan execution may be achieved.

Planning for development or re-development of towns is, in fact, a multi-disciplinary exercise in which the geographer has to play an equally important role as the architect or the sociologist or the economist or the civil engineer. A team, comprising the above-mentioned specialists, can be formed to formulate viable and ideal plans, particularly for our newly developing towns, so that the urban-dwellers can enjoy at least the minimum facilities of residence, work, rest and recreation.

REFERENCES

Barber, J. Byron (1969): "Industrial Land Planning", in Wm. H. Claire (Ed.): *Urban Planning Guide*, ASCE M & R, 49, New York, pp. 147-62.

Goetsch, Herbert A (1969): "Community Facilities Planning", in Wm. H. Claire (Ed.): *Urban Planning Guide*, ASCE M & R, 49, New York, pp. 163-94.

Hoselitz, B.F. (1959): The Cities of India and their Problems, *Annals of the Association of American Geographers*, 49, pp. 223-31.

Reeve, S.A. (1917): Congestion in Cities, *Geographical Review*, 3, pp. 278-93.

Singh, R.L. (1972): *Rural Settlement in Monsoon Asia*, N.G.S.I., Varanasi.

Singh, U. (1961): Allahabad: A study in its Planning and Development, *National Geographical Journal of India*, VII, II, pp. 99-115.

Wilson, A.G. (1974): *Urban and Regional Models in Geography and Planning*, John Wiley & Sons, London.

10

SUMMARY AND CONCLUSION

NORTH BIHAR (25° 10′N to 27° 31′N; 83° 58′ E to 88° 17′ E) measures about 53,796 sq km and accounts for about one-fourth of the total area of the State of Bihar. Physiographically it is a featureless plain; the only exception is a small hilly tract comprising the Sumeshwar range and Ramnagar Dun in the north-west. Its elevation is less than 75 m above the mean sea level. The monotony of its landscape is broken by the existence of a large number of stream channels — some discarded ones, others active round the year and some only during the floods. These streams generally flow in southerly or south-easterly direction until they meet the Ganga, whole channel elevation is 60 m at the point of entry and 30 m at the point of exit in Bihar. A large number of swamps and marshes occur scattered in this plain. The most fertile parts of this region are the areas adjoining the *chaurs* and *tals* and the *diara* tracts.

Geologically North Bihar, with the exception of the Sumeshwar range in the north-west, is made up of Pleistocene and later sediments. The Sumeshwar range, composed of sandstone and conglomerate, forms a part of the Siwalik system of fresh water deposits of late tertiary times.

The Ghaghra, the Gandak, the Burhi Gandak, the Kosi and the Mahananda, all draining into the Ganga, are the trunk streams of the region. They have not only helped to build-up the North Bihar plain by the process of alluviation but have also guided the evolution of urban settlements along them since the historic times. Unfortunately, some of these streams are notorious for causing flood havocs.

Climatically the region lies in a zone of transition between the comparatively moist West Bengal in the east and drier Uttar Pradesh in the west. Hence, the heat in the summer is generally not as intense as in the drier west. Truly speaking, the region is devoid of forest vegetation, except a small wooded patch in the north-west. But orchards and groves are commonly met near the rural habitations.

Agriculture is, by far, the most dominant sector of the economy of North Bihar. About 66.8 per cent of the region is devoted to agriculture. Variations in surface relief, soil and moisture conditions have resulted in variation in the distribution of cultivated area. There are three main harvests, namely, the *Aghani*, the *Bhadai* and the *Rabi*. Rice is the principal food crop of the region, followed by wheat, maize, barley and sugarcane. Other cereals include pulses such as 'Arhar', 'Moong', 'Masoor', 'Khesari', 'Kelai', 'Urad' and 'Gram'. Among the non-food crops, the more important are jute, tobacco, chillies, turmeric and oilseeds.

Three is a complete lack of heavy industry in the region. Though a few industries have been established recently in the region, it still has a predominantly agricultural economy. Sugar and jute, the two agro-based industries, with large employment possibilities have been established in the region in the past several decades. A recent addition to this list is paper manufacture, based on bagasse. Establishment of Indian Oil Refinery at Barauni has fostered the development of petro-chemical and a few other industries in its neighbourhood. The bulk of the industrial employment is, however, provided by the household sector, which accounts for about 56 per cent of the workers engaged in industries. Recently, there has been some significant advances in agricultural production, but developments in industries are not equally matched. Nevertheless, construction of the rail-cum-road bridge over the Ganga near Patna, conversion of the metre-gauge railway line into broad-gauge and establishment of the super-thermal power station at Muzaffarpur are expected to activate industrial growth at a rapid pace in the future. There is scope for further development of petro-chemical industries in the Barauni-Samastipur industrial belt.

Existence of a large number of streams with capacity to inundate large areas during floods have greatly affected the layout of the transport network in the area. It is, therefore, evident that the railways and roads generally run along the flood-free natural levee or the divide zone between the streams. The total length of the railways is 2,400 km; these are mostly aligned N-S or W-E. Similarly, the total road length is about 40,340 km. Of this, about 7,720 km is metalled and 32,650 km unmetalled. Large stretches of the village and district roads are generally submerged under the floodwater in the monsoon season and they get partly washed away almost every year.

As river transport was quite significant in this region before the coming of the railways, the growth of towns initially took place at ferry points located on river banks. However, development of rail and road transports, particularly after 1900, not only led to the decline in importance of towns solely dependent on river transport but also stimulated growth of new towns along the rail and road tracks. As the cost of both the rail and road haulage has increased recently, there is a lot of scope for the development of river transport, as a few rivers remain navigable throughout the year.

North Bihar in 1971 had a population of 2,63,04,409 persons which gave it an average density of 507 persons' sq. km. Thus, the density of population in North Bihar is nearly double the average density for the whole State. The distribution of population even within the region is uneven. For example, the areas, adjoining the main rivers, which are liable to inundation in the rainy season, have comparatively lower density of population. The growth rate of population is also high with the result that it has doubled itself during 1931-71 and, by 2000 A.D., it is expected to increase to 43.65 million. The rate of increase in the urban population has been rather slow during 1901-31, but fairly rapid thereafter. In 1971, there were a total of 49 towns in North Bihar and the urban-dwellers accounted for only 5.2 per cent of the region's population. The towns of the region are mostly small-sized; these are usually located along the rail routes. A greater concentration of urban centres is noted in the central part of the region but there has been no distinct development of urban zones because of the dominant agrarian economy. The urban centres mostly occur as islands or pockets in the otherwise pre-dominantly rural milieu. Nevertheless, it has been possible to define the zones of least, low, medium and high urban concentrations, based on the percentage values of urban to total population.

Considering the growth of total urban population during 1901-71, the year 1931 stands as a great divide. The pre-1931 period, in fact, is characterised by negative growth by as much as 5 per cent, whereas the post-1931 period is marked, firstly, by a sharp rise and, then, by phenomenal growth until 1961. The pace of rapid growth in urban population in the post-independence period had been as much as 63.20 per cent during 1951-61; this had somewhat slowed down during 1961-71, when the increase was only 29.9 per cent. The rapid increase in urban population is largely due to the steady stream of migration from villages to towns in pursuit of business, occupation, education, trade and various kinds of employment. This migration has been fostered by increasing pressure of population on agriculture in the country-side.

Developments in transport, expansion of commerce and industries and re-organisation of administrative set-up have greatly affected the rank of various towns in North Bihar. It has been noted that the Class I towns exhibit higher growth rates than the smaller towns, which seem to be more evenly distributed in the region. Considering the nature of dispersion, the towns of the region are categorised into three groups:

(i) loosely clustered (Rn 0.4 to 0.8),
(ii) random (Rn 0.8 to 1.2), and
(iii) low uniformity (Rn 1.2 to 1.6).

The two Class I towns exhibit loosely clustered distribution. Random nature of dispersion characterises the 22 Class IV towns. All other classes of towns (Categories II, III, V and VI) exhibit distributional patterns of low uniformity. The development of latter pattern has taken place largely due to the physical attributes of the terrain, including existence of a large number of streams causing floods, besides insufficient development of the transport network and industries.

Though most of the towns of North Bihar owe their origin to medieval times, they have experienced considerable expansion during the modern times, particularly with the development of the rail and road transports, trade and commerce and various professional and administrative services. The location of older towns has been mostly guided by the considerations of defence, administrative needs and political strategy. These towns have been generally located on the banks of the rivers, which not only provided trade outlets, but also affected their morphological patterns. Religious and cultural factors have also, sometimes, fostered the growth of towns in the past, like, Nandangarh, Sitamarhi and Hariharkshetra (now Sonpur).

Like developmental biology, the general morphological characteristics of towns have been examined under three aspects, namely, histogenesis, pattern formation and morphogenesis. These processes are influenced by sets of centripetal and centrifugal forces; the former favours the development of concentric growth pattern while the later leads to expansion in the peripheral zone. Keeping these aspects in view, the growth characteristics of 11 sample towns, namely, Darbhanga, Katihar, Hajipur, Saharsa, Forbesganj, Gopalganj, Murliganj, Dalsinghsarai, Birpur, Jainagar and Mairwa, have been examined in detail. The internal plan and the external form of these towns have been also analysed.

Roads and streets constitute the skeletal frame-work of a town. Their formation, in case of planned development, often precedes town growth, but in case of unplanned development, their formation often takes place in the post-nucleation stage. The street plan also affects the internal morphology of town, including the nature and character of its various functional zones. The size of various functional zones varies from town to town, depending on the size-class and special characteristics of the town concerned. Thus, four morphological zones, namely, the inner, the middle, the outer and the suburban, have been identified in almost all the towns of North Bihar on the basis of the ground plan and the intensity of the usage of built-up land.

Various physical and cultural factors have acted in unison to give the towns of North Bihar the following forms:

(i) elongated,
(ii) triangular,
(iii) rectangular,
(iv) circular, and
(v) amorphous.

Examination of the urban profile or the sky-line of built-up area of a few towns, from vintage point, reveals that the old commercial areas usually have multi-storeyed buildings in contrast to the one-storey buildings in other areas. The spires and domes of temples and mosques often abruptly rise or fall in this urban profile.

The spatial shape, population-size and functional structure of the sample towns seem to have been greatly affected by their situation. There is also a wide variation in the occupational structure of the working population in these towns. The working population in smaller towns is largely engaged in primary production, particularly agriculture, but in larger towns it is largely employed in secondary and tertiary occupations.

Analysis of the land-use of the sample towns shows that, on an average, the residential, commercial, industrial, educational and administrative areas use 54.08 per cent, 2.25 per cent, 2.38 per cent, 5.8 per cent and 3.7 per cent of the developed urban space, respectively. The functional land-uses vary from town to town, depending upon their size and nature of functions.

The most important component in the morphology of North Bihar towns is the residential area. It is noted that the residential sites, during the medieval times, were selected in close proximity to some religious nuclei, namely, a temple or mosque, but during modern times, these have been largely developed in the neighbourhood of the work-place. The extreme compactness of some old residential areas may be explained as a consequence of the defence requirements of the medieval times, when houses were huddled together in a small space. Segregation of residential areas, in the past, was sometimes also based on communal or cultural considerations. These cultural or communal enclaves or 'Mohallas' can even now be identified by the style of architecture and the pattern and design of buildings.

A rapid expansion in the residential areas of the towns of North Bihar took place during the British period. Thus, the civil lines, the railway colonies and the cantonments were developed distinctly apart from the pre-existing residential areas. Moreover, expansion of the residential area also took place towards the outer margins of the town as a consequence of the construction of railways and the development of roads which fostered the growth of trade, commerce and industry. Three classes of residential areas — low, middle and high — have been identified on the basis of the type and style of the residential structure. The low class residential areas are either characteristics of the older sections of the town or have recently developed as isolated nucleations in the peripheral zone. This area is marked by congestion, high density of population and poor sanitation. People tend to flock here, as they prefer to reside close to their place of work. The middle class residential areas have largely developed a little away from the central zone towards the periphery of the town. Double-storeyed houses, standing along wide roads, are characteristic of middle class residential areas which predominate in the towns of North Bihar. The high class residential areas have generally developed on the outer margins of the town, particularly in the civil lines and planned residential colonies. Isolated cluster of high-class residences have been, sometimes, also noticed along the main roads.

Development of slums has taken place particularly in the larger towns of North Bihar, either due to poor economic condition of the people inhabiting it or as a result of large scale migration of poor job-seekers from rural areas. The high cost of living in other residential areas and abject poverty of the residents have forced them to live in congested and insanitary conditions.

Slums are generally located in ill-drained areas. The residential structures in the slums usually have mud walls with roofs of anything from straw to mutilated tins and rotten pieces of sackings for doors or windows.

In the central business area, there is an inter-mingling of residential function with commerce, education and household and other small scale industries.

The quality of buildings, in the towns of North Bihar, is generally poor. Walls made of burnt-brick predominate in almost all the towns, but those of mud and grass or reed are also found in good proportion. Recently, the construction of modern bungalows or apartment-type buildings is on the increase. But the rapid growth in urban population, through natural increase and by immigration from rural areas, has more than off-set the accommodation available from new constructions, so that there is an acute shortage of residential accommodation in these towns. This is also reflected by the density of houses, which has increased from 406/sq. km in 1961 to 633/sq. km in 1971. It is noted that about 55 per cent of the urban dwellings have one to two rooms, 17 per cent three rooms, 15 per cent four rooms and 10 per cent five rooms.

The commercial structure of sample towns is largely related to the location and growth characteristics of the respective towns. The advantage of the location of commercial activity on most favourable sites, initiated in the medieval towns, has in some cases continued to pay dividends even to this day. In general, there is concentration of commercial activity in the older parts of the towns. Development of the rail and road transports not only favoured the growth of new commercial areas but also led to some shift in commercial activity from the older commercial areas located near the river banks. The newly developed commercial areas, occurring near transport nodes or in close proximity to the main commercial areas, act as tributary to the latter. Planned marketing centre is a recent new-comer and is found in the newly established townships only.

Both wholesale and retail trades generally occur side by side in almost all the towns of North Bihar. Considering the price range and the variety of commodities sold, there are three distinct hierarchical levels of commercial areas, namely, the central business area, the neighbourhood shopping centre and the isolated shopping nucleation or local markets. The lower order shopping units are often dependent on the higher order commercial areas, which specialise in wholesale trade. The physical attributes of site often has dominating influence on the shape and pattern of shopping streets. Establishment of industrial units on the outskirts of towns has, sometimes, led to a partial shift in commercial activity.

Though the industrial establishments occupy a small proportion of the urban space, these have, nonetheless, played an important role in the economic structure and the urban pattern of towns. Household industries predominate in the towns of North Bihar. Consequently, they occur in an inter-mingled manner in the working class housing colonies or commercial or other residential areas. Sometimes, important industrial establishments, located on the outskirts of the town, act as a magnetic force in transforming the urban land-use pattern. Proximity of market is, by far, the most important factor in affecting location of these units. Recently, a few large scale industries have been developed mostly on the outskirts of the towns, like, Barauni, Katihar, Samastipur and Muzaffarpur. The location of these units has been favoured by easy access to rail and road transports and availability of electric power. Some small scale units, which depend on the main establishments for the supply of raw materials, have also come up on the outskirts of the town.

Recent establishment of industrial estates on the outskirts of some towns has not only led to the setting up new industrial establishments but also to the shifting of some of the older units from residential and commercial areas to the newly developed estates.

Almost all towns, whether large or small, have a well developed educational zone. The educational institutions, particularly schools, are generally located in the older parts of the towns. However, the universities and colleges, which require larger built-up area and playgrounds, generally occur in the outer zones of the towns. It is noted that the smaller centres of learning such as the kindergarten, primary or other schools do not form any compact morphological unit as is often the case with institutions of higher learning, like colleges and universities.

The administrative areas also occupy distinctly separate sites, generally towards the periphery of the town. But in some towns, the growth of built-up area has been so fast that these have been engulfed by other land-uses. The administrative zone, in the medieval times, used to be confined to the four walls of the ruler's fort. Its development as a separate zone, in the form of civil lines on the outskirts of the town, was initiated during the British period. This was considered necessary to ensure security and comfort of the foreign rulers.

The medical zone has developed only in big towns. In towns, like, Darbhanga and Muzaffarpur, the older medical zone happened to be situated in the densely populated and congested parts of these towns, whereas the newer ones have come up on their outer periphery. Planned development of the medical zone on the outskirts of the town has not only promoted town expansion but has also attracted other services and facilities.

There is insufficient provision for parks, playground and other recreational facilities in the towns of North Bihar. A few parks and playgrounds, occurring in some towns, are in deplorable condition because of poor maintenance and lack of civic sense among the urban-dwellers. Commercial recreation is available in cinema halls, which are generally located in the congested residential or commercial areas.

Religious centres, like, temples, mosques or churches, do not form a distinct zone, as they occur as discrete units in various community enclaves.

Almost all the towns of North Bihar face the problems of floods, traffic congestion, unplanned expansion, insanitary conditions largely engineered by poor drainage, lack of civic sense and recreational facilities such as parks and playgrounds. Lack of drive and foresight in the functioning of the local self-government, including municipalities, N.A.C. and town development boards and corruption rampant in these bodies have been largely responsible for the unplanned growth of the town. There is urgent need to formulate a comprehensive plan for town development, including expansion and beautification, with the help of a team of experts consisting of urban geographers, architects, town planners, sociologists, civil engineers and economists.

Considering the various functional and morphological problems of the towns, allocation of new areas for the development of residential, commercial, recreational and other functions have been suggested. Establishment of compact residential colonies on the outskirts of the town, with provision for public utility services, can be had at a reasonable cost. Cultural centres, like, hospitals, colleges, parks and playgrounds and cinemas, should be located at convenient places, taking into account the size of the town's population. The town development authority also needs to educate the town-dwellers about the proper use of civic facilities provided by them.

GLOSSARY

Aghani	..	Crops harvested in winter
Arhar	..	Pigeon Pea (*Cajanus indicus*)
Bandh	..	Embankment
Bazar	..	Market
Bhadai	..	Autumn crops
Bidri	..	Delicate carving work on metal articles
Chowk	..	Cross-road
Chauraha	..	Cross-road
Chaur	..	A water pool
Dhar	..	A new course of a river
Diara	..	Sandy stretches thrown out of the river bed
Ghat	..	A landing place, ferry
Gola	..	Grocery centre
Kans	..	A kind of wild grass (*Saccharum spontaneum*)
Katha	..	A unit of the measure of area of the land
Khesari	..	A kind of pulse (*Lathyrus sativus*)
Kirana	..	Merchandise, mainly grocery
Loo	..	Very hot dusty wind
Mandi	..	Market, generally a wholesale grain market
Masur	..	A kind of pulse (*Lens esculenta*)
Mohalla	..	A ward of town
Moong	..	A kind of pulse (*Phaseolus mungo*)
Pucca	..	Brick-built
Rabi	..	Spring crop
Tal	..	A natural depression filled with rain water or by overflow of a stream
Tarai	..	The moist plain

APPENDIX

LIST OF TOWNS WITH AREA, DENSITY AND POPULATION (1971)

S. No.	Name of Town	Area in sq.km.	Population per sq.km.	Total population
Class I (1,00,000)				
1.	Darbhanga	19.18	6,885	1,32,059
2.	Muzaffarpur	15.57	8,117	1,26,379
Class II (50,000-99,999)				
3.	Chapra	16.96	4,900	83,101
4.	Katihar	16.56	4,838	80,121
5.	Purnea (U.A.)	44.00	1,285	56,484
6.	Bettiah	7.55	6,757	51,018
Class III (20,000-49,999)				
7.	Begusarai (U.A.)	9.60	4,587	44,084
8.	Barauni	19.31	2,170	41,912
9.	Hazipur	19.64	2,133	41,890
10.	Motihari (U.A.)	14.30	2,824	40,352
11.	Kishenganj	29.46	1,252	36,893
12.	Siwan	3.14	10,561	33,162
13.	Madhubani	2.52	13,063	32,919
14.	Samastipur	3.45	9,150	31,566
15.	Sitamarhi (U.A.)	6.60	4,091	27,123
16.	Bagaha	28.41	892	25,344
17.	Saharsa	14.09	1,648	23,217
18.	Supaul	22.37	1,008	22,558
19.	Araria	30.97	724	22,425
20.	Khagaria (U.A.)	6.00	3,715	22,329
21.	Forbesganj	10.42	2,034	21,198
Class IV (10,000-19,999)				
22.	Mahnar Bazar	10.02	1,991	19,953
23.	Teghra	7.29	2,721	19,837
24.	Gopalganj	9.26	1,863	17,253

Contd.

Contd.

S. No.	Name of Town	Area in sq.km.	Population per sq.km.	Total population
25.	Gogri	8.47	1,918	16,247
26.	Narkatiaganj	7.28	2,203	16,041
27.	Lalganj	7.86	2,010	15,798
28.	Bihariganj	17.75	878	15,581
29.	Madhepura	7.22	2,134	15,407
30.	Revelganj	12.50	1,226	15,300
31.	Rosera	1.03	14,357	14,788
32.	Murliganj	14.07	902	12,688
33.	Ramnagar	10.75	1,170	12,579
34.	Chanpatia	7.57	1,610	12,189
35.	Sugauli	11.59	1,049	12,154
36.	Raxaul Bazar	5.82	2,073	12,064
37.	Mirganj	5.48	2,200	12,056
38.	Mahrajganj	7.60	1,565	11,894
39.	Bairgania	8.24	1,428	11,767
40.	Pupri	5.59	1,977	11,052
41.	Dalsinghsarai	2.94	3,655	10,747
42.	Birpur	13.44	752	10,103
Class V (5,000-9,999)				
43.	Jainagar	1.55	6,398	9,917
44.	Naugachhia	4.36	2,189	9,544
45.	Banmankhi Bazar	3.27	2,835	9,272
46.	Jogbani	15.12	584	8,824
47.	Nirmali	5.30	1,306	6,921
48.	Mairwa	4.37	1,548	6,766
Class VI (less than 5,000)				
49.	Chakia	0.77	3,857	2,970

Source: Census of India 1971, Series 4, Bihar Part II-A, General Population Tables.
U.A.: Urban Agglomeration.

BIBLIOGRAPHY

Adams, John S. (1970) : Residential Structure of Mid Western Cities, *Annals of the Association of American Geographers*, 60, pp. 37-62.

Ahmad, E. (1965) : *Bihar: A Physical Economic and Regional Geography*, Ranchi University, Ranchi.

——— (1976) : *Some Aspects of Indian Geography*, Central Book Depot, Allahabad.

Ahmad, K.S. (1966) : Urbanisation Trends in West Pakistan, *Pakistan Geographical Review*, 21, (1), pp. 1-20.

Ahmad, Nafis (1963) : The Landscape of the Dacca Urban Area, *The Oriental Geographer*, VII, (1), pp. 1-18.

Ahmad, Qazi S. (1967) : Distribution Pattern of Urban Centres in Pakistan, *Pakistan Geographical Review*, 22, (1), pp. 1-8.

Alam, S.M. (1965) : *Hyderabad-Secunderabad (Twin Cities): A Study in Urban Geography*, Bombay.

Anal, A.K.S. (1972) : Begusarai: A Study in Urban Morphology, *The Deccan Geographer*, X, pp. 1-8.

Applebaum, William (1952) : A Technique of Constructing a Population and Urban Land-Use Map, *Economic Geography*, 28, pp. 240-43.

Arunachelum, B. (1955) : Bombay City Stages of Development, *Bombay Geographical Magazine*, 3, pp. 34-9.

Aspinall, P.J. and J.W.R. Whitehand (1980) : Building Plans: A Major Source for Urban Studies, *Area*, 12, (3), pp. 199-203.

Aurousseau, M. (1924) : The Recent Contribution to Urban Geography — A Review, *Geographical Review*, XIV, pp. 444-55.

Bagchi, K. (1966) : The Howrah Conurbation: A Study in Urban Sprawl, *Geographical Review of India*, XXVIII, pp. 16-31.

Balchin, P.N. and J.L. Kieve (1977) : *Urban Land Economics*, Macmillan, London.

Barkley, R.E. (1958) : *Technique of Population Analysis*, John Wiley and Sons, New York.

Bartholomew, H. (1955) : *Land-Use in American Cities: Harvard City Planning Studies*, Cambridge.

Basak, T.N. (1976) : Bochum—A Study of Urban Growth, *Geographical Review of India*, 38, (1), pp. 60-77.

Berry, B.J.L. (1959) : Ribbon Development in the Urban Business Pattern, *Annals of the Association of American Geographers*, XLIX, pp. 145-55.

Berry, B.J.L., J.W. Simmons and R.J. Tennant (1963) : Urban Population Densities, Structure and Change, *Geographical Review*, 53, pp. 389-405.

Bird, James (1958) : Billingsgate — A Central Metropolitan Market, *Geographical Journal*, 124, pp. 464-75.

Bonine, M.E. (1979) : The Morphogenesis of Iranian Cities, *Annals of the Association of American Geographer*, 69, (2), pp. 208-24.

Bore Gowda, P. (1979) : Urban Sprawl in Bangalore, *National Geographical Journal of India*, XXV, (3 & 4), pp. 194-99.

Bourne, L.S. (1976) : Urban Structure and Land-Use Decisions, *Annals of the Association of American Geographers*, 66, pp. 531-47.

Boyce, R.R. and W.A.V. Clark (1964) : The Concept of Shape in Geography, *Geographical Review*, LIV, pp. 561-72.

Brand, Richard R. (1972) : The Spatial Organisation of Residential Areas in Accra, Ghana, with particular Reference to Aspects of Modernisation, *Economic Geography*, 48, pp. 284-98.

Brodsky, Harold (1973) : Land Development and the Expanding City, *Annals of the Association of American Geographers*, 63, pp. 159-66.

Brush, J.E. (1953) : The Hierarchy of Central Places in South-western Wisconsin, *Geographical Review*, 43, pp. 380-402.

——— (1961) : "The Morphology of Indian Cities in Roy Turner" (Ed.) *India's Urban Future*, Bombay.

Bull, G.B.G. (1964) : Fieldwork in Towns: A Review of Technique, *Geography*, 49, pp. 206-21.

Carter, H. and S. Wheatley (1980) : Residential Segregation in Nineteenth Century Cities, *Area*, 12, (1), pp. 57-62.

Carruthers, Ian (1957) : A Classification of Service Centres in England and Wales, *Geographical Journal*, 123, pp. 371-85.

Chakravarty, A.K. (1959) : Floods in Himalayan Rivers of Ganga Plain: Causes and Control, *Geographical Review of India*, 21, pp. 33-42.

Chambers, W.T. (1931) : Geographic Areas of Cities, *Economic Geography*, VII, pp. 171-88.

Chatterjee, A.B. (1964) : Cultural History of Howrah City, *Geographical Review of India*, XXVI, pp. 23-34.

——— (1965) : Ecological Structure of Calcutta's Twin, *National Geographical Journal of India*, XI, (2), pp. 59-62.

Chatterjee, A.B. and P.N. Roy (1973) : A Spatial Analysis of the Changing Livelihood Structure Around Calcutta, *National Geographical Journal of India*, XIX, (2), pp. 92-7.

Childe, V. Gordon (1979) : "The Urban Revolution", In G.L. Possehl (Ed.) *Ancient Cities of the Indus*, New Delhi, pp. 12-17.

Claire, Wm. H. (Ed.) (1969) : *Urban Planning Guide* — ASCE M & R, 49, ASCE, New York.

Chang, Sen-Dou (1970) : Some Observations on the Morphology of Chinese Walled Cities, *Annals of the Association of American Geographer*, 60, pp. 63-91.

Clarke, C.G. (1974) : Urbanisation in the Caribbean, *Geography*, 59, pp. 223-32.

Clarke, W.A.V. and James E. Burst (1980) : The Impact of Work Place on Residential Relocation, *Annals of the Association of American Geographer*, 70, (1), pp. 59-67.

Cohen, S.B. and G.K. Lewis (1967) : Form and Function in the Geography of Retailing, *Economic Geography*, 43, pp. 1-42.

Colby, C.C. (1933) : Centrifugal and Centripetal Forces in Urban Geography, *AAAG*, XXIII, pp. 1-20.

Conzen, M.R.G. (1960) : Alnwick, Northumberland: A Study in Town-Plan Analysis, *The Institute of British Geographer*, Transaction, 27, pp. 27-81.

——— (1960) : The Plan Analysis of an English City Centre. In K. Norborg (Ed.) (1962) : *Proceeding of the I.G.U. Symposium in Urban Geography*, pp. 383-414.

Dutt, A.K. (1966) : Evolution of Jamshedpur City: A Historical Approach to Urban Study, *Indian Geographical Journal*, 41, pp. 19-28.

Davis, Kingsley (1951) : *The Population of India and Pakistan*, Princeton.

Davis, Kingsley and H. Hertz (1959) : *The Pattern of World Urbanisation*, New York.

Davis, J.T. (1965) : Middle Class Housing in the Central City, *Economic Geography*, 41, pp. 238-51.

Davis, S.G. (1964) : The Rural-Urban Migration in Hong Kong and its New Territories, *Geographical Journal*, 130, pp. 328-33.

Dayal, P. and B. Thakur (1976) : Commercial Ribbons in Patna: Spatial Growth and Functional Structure, *National Geographical Journal of India*, XXII, (3 & 4), pp. 164-77.

Deshmukh, P.W. and C.T. Pawar (1977) : Occupational Characteristics of New Towns in Maharashtra, *The Deccan Geographer*, XV, (1), pp. 235-49.

Dhar, H.K. (1969) : Role of Open Space in Residential Area, *Urban and Rural Planning Thought*, 12, pp. 34-52.

Dickinson, R.E. (1932) : The Distribution and Function of the Small Urban Settlements of East Anglia, *Geography*, 17, pp. 19-28.

——— (1934) : The Town Plans of East Anglia: A Study in Urban Morphology, *Geography*, 19, pp. 37-50.

——— (1945) : The Morphology of the Medieval German Town, *Geographical Review*, 35, pp. 74-97.

——— (1951) : *The West European City*, London.

Diwakar, R.R. (Ed.) (1959) : *Bihar Through the Ages*, Orient Longmans, Bombay.

Dixit, K.R. (1961) : The Concept of Functional Zones, *National Geographical Journal of India*, VII, (3), pp. 191-205.

Doeppers, D.F. (1974) : Ethnic Urbanism and Philippine Cities, *Annals of the Association of American Geographers*, 64, pp. 549-59.

Doran, M.F. and R.A. Landis (1980) : Origin and Persistence of an Inner-city Sum in Nassau, *Geographical Review*, 70, (2), pp. 182-93.

Dwyer, D.J. (1974) : *The City in the Third World*, Mcmillan, London.

Dwyer, D.G. (1979) : Urban Geography and the Urban Future, *Geography*, 64, (2), pp. 86-95.

Edward, L.I. (1962) : The Geographer in Planning, *Professional Geographer*, XIV, pp. 84-98.

Epstien, Bart, J. (1971) : Geography and the Business of Retail Site Evaluation and Selection, *Economic Geography*, 47, pp. 192-99.

Falk, T. (1980) : Retail Change and Downtown Commercial Viability: The Case of Norrkoping, Sweden, *Geografiska Annaler Series B, Human Geography*, 62B, (1), pp. 21-4.

Foster, A.S. and E.M. Gifford (Eds.) (1967) : *Comparative Morphology of Vascular Plants*, Bombay.

Ford, L.R. (1974) : The Urban House Type as an Illustration of the Concentric Zone Model: The Perception of Architectural Continuity, *Journal of Geography*, 140, pp. 29-39.

Freeman, T.W. (1958) : *Geography and Planning*, London.

Geddes, P. (1955) : *Cities in Evolution*, London.

Ghosh, S. (1950) : The Urban Pattern of Calcutta, *Economic Geography*, XXVI, pp. 51-8.

Goodall, Brian (1972) : *The Economics of Urban Area*, Pergamon Press, London.

Green, F.H.W. (1950) : Urban Hinterlands in England and Wales: An Analysis of Bus Services, *Geographical Journal*, 116, pp. 65-88.

Guha, M. (1953) : The Morphology of Calcutta, *Geographical Review of India*, XV, pp. 20-8.

Gupta, D.N. (1959) : The Community its Plan and the Planner, *Geographical Review of India*, 21, pp. 51-60.

Griffin, T.L.C. (1965) : The Evolution and Duplication of a Pattern of Urban Growth, *Economic Geography*, 41, pp. 133-56.

Gwynne, R.N. (1978) : City Size and Retail Prices in Less-Developed Countries: An Insight into Primacy, *Area*, 10, (2), pp. 136-40.

Hagget, P. (1965) : Locational Analysis in Human Geography, London.

Harris, C.D. (1945) : The Cities of the Soviet Union, *Geographical Review*, 35, pp. 107-21.

Hartman, George W. (1950) : The Central Business District : A Study in Urban Geography, *Economic Geography*, 26, pp. 237-44.

Hartshorne, R. (1932) : The Twin City District. A Unique Form of Urban Landscape, *Geographical Review*, 22, pp. 431-40.

Hatt, Paul K. and Albert J. Reiss Jr. (1963) : *Cities and Society*, The Free Press of Glencoe, Inc., New York.

Heght, Alfred (1977) : Exploring the Urban Industrial Relocation Process, *The Journal of Geography*, 143, pp. 15-8.

Hiltner, J. and B.W. Smith (1974) : Intra-urban Residential Location of the Elderly, *Journal of Geography*, 140, pp. 23-33.

Halford, W.G. (1952) : Geography and Town Planning, *Geography*, 37, pp. 191-98.

Hort, J.F. (1976) : Urban Encroachment on Rural Areas, *Geographical Review*, 66, pp. 1-17.

Hudson, F.S. (1977) : *Geography of Settlements*, Macdonald and Evans, Plymouth.

Hughes, R.H. (1951) : Hong Kong: An Urban Study, *Geographical Journal*, 117, pp. 1-23.

Huff, D.L. and James M. Lutz (1979) : Ireland's Urban System, *Economic Geography*, 55, (3), pp. 196-212.

Hurst, M.E. Eliot (1970) : An Approach to the Study of Non-residential Land-Use Traffic Generation, *Annals of the Association of American Geographers*, 60, pp. 153-73.

Husain, Irshad (1980) : Urban Encroachment on Rural Lands — A Case Study of Bulandshahr City in India (1950-73), *Philippine Geographical Journal*, XXIII, pp. 155-65.

Jain, J.L. (1979) : Spatial pattern of Urbanisation in Madhya Pradesh Application of Composite Index, *National Geographer*, XIV, (1), pp. 17-33.

Jain, N.G. and Lakshmi Iyer (1980) : Urban Spatial Pattern in Maharashtra, *The Deccan Geographer*, XVIII, (2), pp. 839-45.

Jauhari, A.S. (1957) : Trend of Urbanisation in the Punjab Plains During the Twentieth Century, *National Geographical Journal of India*, III, (3 & 4), pp. 125-36.

——— (1962) : Growth of Urban Settlements in the Sutlej-Yamuna Divide, *National Geographical Journal of India*, VIII, (1), pp. 1-24.

Jefferson, Marks (1931) : Distribution of the World's City Folk: A Study in Comparative Civilisation, *Geographical Review*, 21, pp. 441-65.

Johnso, James H. (1977) : *Urban Geography: An Introductory Analysis*, Pergamon Press, London.

Johnston, R.J. (1977) : Regarding Urban Origin Urbanisation and Urban Pattern, *Geography*, 62, pp. 1-8.

Jones, Emrys (1960) : *Social Geography of Belfast*, London.

Kar, N.R. (1962) : Pattern of Urban Growth in Lower West Bengal, *Geographical Review of India*, XXIV, pp. 1-4.

Karan, P.P. (1957) : The Pattern of Indian Towns: A Study in Urban Morphology, *Journal of American Institute of Planners*, XXIII, pp. 70-5.

Karimi, S.M. (1967) : Urbanisation of Bihar Plain, Aligarh Muslim University, Aligarh.

Karennvar, M.F. (1976) : A Quantitative Analysis of the Pattern of Urban Settlements in Karnataka State, *Geographical Review of India*, 38, pp. 78-84.

Kayastha, S.L. (1958) : Kangra—A Himalayan Town, *national Geographical Journal of India*, IV, (2), pp. 39-94.

Kenyon, James B. (1968) : Land-Use Admixture in the Built-up Urban Waterfront: Extent and Implications, *Economic Geography*, 44, pp. 152-77.

Khan, F.K. and N. Islam (1964) : High Class Residential Areas in Dacca City, *The Oriental Geographer*, VIII, pp. 1-41.

King, L.J. (1961) : A Multivariate Analysis of the Spacing of Urban Settlements in the United States, *Annals of the Association of American Geographers*, 51, pp. 222-33.

Kirk, W. (1978) : Town and Country Planning in Ancient India According to Kautilya's Arthasastra, *Scottish Geographical Magazine*, 94, (2), pp. 67-75.

Konge, G.H. (1978) : Functional Classification of Large Towns of Karnataka, *The Deccan Geographer*, XVI, (2), pp. 450-60.

Krishan, Gopal and S.K. Agrawal (1973) : Commercial Pattern of a Planned City: Chandigarh, *National Geographical Journal of India*, XIX, (2), pp. 83-91.

Leigh, Roger (1969) : Analysis of the Factors Affecting the Location of Industries within Cities, *The Canadian Geographer*, XIII, pp. 28-33.

Lentnek, B., M. Charnews and J.V. Colter (1978) : Commercial Factors in the Development of Regional Urban System: A Mexican Case Study, *Economic Geography*, 54, pp. 291-313.

Litovka, O.P. (1980) : Urbanisation in the USSR: Problems of Spatial Differentiation, *Soviet Geography: Review and Translation*, XXI, (1), pp. 30-6.

Locke, Michael (Ed.) (1966) : *Major Problems in Developmental Biology*, Academic Press, New York.

Mabogunji, Akin L. (1964) : Evolution and Analysis of Retail Structure of Lagos, Nigeria, *Economic Geography*, 40, pp. 304-23.

Mahadeva, P.D. and D.C. Jayasankar (1969) : Concept of a City Region: An Approach with a Case Study, *Indian Geographical Journal*, 44, pp. 15-26.

Maher, C.A. (1974) : Spatial Patterns in Urban Housing Markets: Filtering in Toronto 1953-71, *The Canadian Geographer*, XVIII, pp. 108-24.

——— (1979) : The Changing Residential Role of the Inner City — The Example of Inner Melbourne, *Australian Geographer*, 14, (2), pp. 112-22.

Majumdar, R.C., H.C. Raychaudhuri and K.K. Dutta (1963) : *An Advanced History of India*, Macmillan & Co. Ltd., London.

Malik, R.A. (1965) : Cities of the Upper Indo-Gangetic Plain, *Pakistan Geographical Review*, 20, (1), pp. 61-72.

Mason, Greg (1979) : The Deregulation of Urban Land Markets: A Note on Alternatives to Zoning, *The Annals of Regional Science*, XIII, (2), pp. 54-66.

Mathur, R.B. (1974) : Urban Spatial Planning in India: Some Misconceptions, *National Geographical Journal of India*, XX, (4), pp. 236-45.

Muth, R.F. (1975) : *Urban Economic Problems*, Harper & Row, Publishers, New York.

Mayer, Harold M. and Clyde F. Kohn (1967) : *Readings in Urban Geography*, Central Book Depot, Allahabad.

McGovern, P.D. (1968) : The new Towns of Scotland, *Scottish Geographical Magazine*, 84, pp. 29-44.

Medvedkova, O.L. (1980) : Components in the Evolution of Urban Systems: Theory and Empirical Testing, *Soviet Geography: Review and Translation*, XXI, (1), pp. 15-29.

——— (1980) : Structural Characteristics of Cities as Multifunctional Centres, *Soviet Geography: Review and Translation*, XXI, (5), pp. 263-83.

Misra, H.K. (1975) : The Size and Spacing of Towns in the Umland of Allahabad, *The Geographer*, XXII, (1), pp. 45-55.

Mookerjie, D. (1969) : Urbanisation Pattern in India (1951-1961), *The Professional Geographer*, 21, pp. 305-14.

Mukherjee, M. (1966) : Functions and Functional Classification of Towns in Bihar. Unpublished Ph.D.Thesis, Patna University, Patna.

Muller, Edward K. (1976) : Selective Urban Ohio, Valley (1800-1860), *Geographical Review*, 66, pp. 178-99.

Mumford, Lewis (1961) : *The City in History*, London.

Munsi, S.K. (1972) : Spatial and Temporal Disparities of Urban Growth in West Bengal, *Geographical Review of India*, 32, pp. 339-53.

Murphy, R. (1964) : The City in the Swamp: Aspects of the Site and Early Growth of Calcutta, *Geographical Journal*, 130, pp. 241-55.

Murphy, Raymond E. (1966) : *The American City: An Urban Geography*, McGraw-Hill Book Company, New York.

Newling, B.E. (1969) : The Spatial Variation of Urban Population Densities, *Geographical Review*, 59, pp. 242-52.

Nigam, M.N. (1960) : Evolution of Lucknow, *National Geographical Review of India*, VI, (1), pp. 30-46.

——— (1964) : Functional Regions of Lucknow, *National Geographical Journal of India*, X, (1), pp. 35-52.

Pacione, Michael (1980) : Redevelopment of a Medium-sized Central Shopping Area: A Case Study of Cydebank, *Tijdschriff Voor Economische on Sociale Geografie*, 71, (3), pp. 159-68.

Pal, S.K. (1970) : Changing Role of Urbanisation of Central Cities in India, *Geographical Review of India*, 30, pp. 97-112.

Palm, S. (1978) : Spatial Segmentation of the Urban Housing Market, *Economic Geography*, 54, pp. 210-21.

Pandey, M.S. (1963) : *The Historical Geography and Topography of Bihar*, Motilal Banarasidas, Delhi.

Pandeya, p. (1970) : *Impact of Industrialisation on Urban Growth (A Case Study of Chota Nagpur)*, Central Book Depot, Allahabad.

Possehl, Gregory L. (Ed.) (1979) : *Ancient Cities of the Indus*. Vikas Publishing House Pvt. Ltd., New Delhi.

Pownall, L.L. (1957) : The Retail Potential of Some Representative New Zealand Towns, *Economic Geography*, 33, pp. 163-70.

——— (1960) : Low Value Housing in two New Zealand Cities, *Annals of the Association of American Geographers*, 50, pp. 439-60.

Pred, Allan (1975) : Diffusion, Organisational Spatial Structure and City-System, *Economic Geography*, 51, pp. 252-68.

Preston, R.E. (1966) : The Zone in Transition : A Study in Urban Land Use Pattern, *Economic Geography*, 42, 3, pp. 236-60.

Pyare Ram (1980) : Functional Classification of Towns of Bundelkhand, *National Geographer*, XV, (1), pp. 53-66.

Raheja, B.D. (1973) : *Urban India and Public Policy*, Somaiya Publications Pvt. Ltd. Bombay, New Delhi, pp. 1-323.

Ramesh, A. (1964) : Origin and Evolution of Ootacmund, *National Geographical Journal of India*, V, (1), pp. 1-11.

——— (1965) : *The Tamilnad Deccan: A Study in Urban Settlements*, Banaras Hindu University.

Rao, V.L.S.P. (1962) : Macro Urban Analysis, Geographer's Contribution, *Bombay Geographical Magazine*, 10, pp. 5-12.

Raporort, A. (1977) : *Human Aspects of Urban Form: Towards a Man Environment Approach to Urban Form and Design*, Pergamon Press, London.

Reddy, N.B.K. (1970) : Urban Evolution, Growth Pattern and Urbanisation in the Krishna Godavari Deltas, *National Geographical Journal of India*, XVI, (3 & 4), pp. 270-87.

Reeve, S.A. (1917). Congestion in Cities, *Geographical Review*, pp. 278-93.

Renner, George T. (1935) : Cities of Puget Basins, *Economic Geography*, 11, pp. 280-83.

Rimsha, A. (1976) : *Town Planning in Hot Climates*, Mir Publishers, Moscow.

Robson, B.T. (1975) : The Urban Environment, *Geography*, 60, (2), pp. 184-88.

Rowland, D.T. (1977) : Theories of Urbanisation in Australia, *Geographical Review*, 67, pp. 167-76.

Rowland, Richard H. (1980) : Declining and Stagnant Towns of the USSR, *Soviet Geography: Review and Translation*, XXI, (4), pp. 195-218.

Roy, B.K. (1977) : Urban Landuse Maps for Towns and Urban Agglomerations in Census of India, *National Geographical Journal of India*, XXIII, (3 & 4), pp. 160-65.

Sanders, Ralph A. (1976) : Bilevel Effects in Urban Residential Patterns, *Economic Geography*, 52, pp. 61-70.

Sargent, C.S. Jr. (1972) : Toward a Dynamic Model of Urban Morphology, *Economic Geography* 68, pp. 357-74.

Sarkar, S.C. (1969) : Economic Condition of North Bihar, *Modern Review*, CXXIV, (2), pp. 121-28.

Savigear, R.A.G. (1965) : A Technique of Morphological Mapping, *Annals of the Association of American Geographers*, 55, pp. 514-21.

Saxena, Sudha (1970) : *Trends of Urbanisation in Uttar Pradesh*, Satish Book Enterprise, Agra.

Scott, P. (1955) : Cape Town: A Multi-Racial City, *Geographical Journal*, 121, pp. 149-57.

Sen, A.K. (1959) : City Regions of India, *Geographical Review of India*, XIX, pp. 32-42.

Sharma, A.K. (1974) : System Analysis Technique A Tool for Transportation Location Decision, *Urban and Rural Planning Thought*, 17, pp. 214-25.

Sharma, J.P. (1978) : A Note on the Evolution and Functional Morphology of a Temple Town of Himachal Pradesh: Chamba, *National Geographical Journal of India*, XXIV, (1 & 2), pp. 77-85.

Skeldon, Ronald (1980) : Recent Urban Growth in Papua New Guinea, *Australian Geographer*, 14, (5), pp. 267-77.

Singh, H.H. (1972) : *Kanpur: A Study in Urban Geography*, Varanasi.

Singh, J.P. (1977) : Residential Use of Land in Shillong, *Geographical Review of India*, 39, pp. 232-40.

Singh, K.N. (1957) : Morphology of the Twin-Township of Dehri-Dalmianagar, *National Geographical Journal of India*, III, (3 & 4), pp. 169-79.

——— (1959) : Functions and Functional Classification of Towns in U.P., *National Geographical Journal of India*, V (3), pp. 121-48.

——— (1961) : Barhaj: A Study in the Changing Pattern of a Market Town, *National Geographical Journal of India*, VII, (1), pp. 21-36.

Singh, Onkar (1967) : The Trend of Urbanisation in Uttar Pradesh, *National Geographical Journal of India*, XIII, (3), pp. 141-57.

——— (1969) : Towns of Uttar Pradesh, Unpublished Ph.D.Thesis, Banaras Hindu University.

Singh, O.P. (1969) : *A Study of Central Places in U.P.*, Banaras Hindu University, Varanasi.

Singh, R.L. (1955) : *Banaras: A Study in Urban Geography*, N.K. Bros., Banaras.

——— (1955) : Gorakhpur: A Study in Urban Morphology, *National Geographical Journal of India*, 1, (1), pp. 1-10.

——— (1956) : Ballia: A Study in Urban Settlement, *National Geographical Journal of India*, II, (1), pp. 1-6.

——— (1963) : Origin of Medieval Towns in the Saryupar Plain of U.P., *National Geographical Journal of India*, IX, (1), pp. 1-11.

Singh, R.L. (Ed.) (1973) : Urban Geography in Developing Countries, *Proceedings* of I.G.U. Symposium No. 15, Varanasi, *N.G.S.I.*, Varanasi.

Singh, R.N. and Sahab Deen (1979) : Occupational Structure of Urban Centres of Uttar Pradesh Household Industry: A Case Study, *National Geographer*, XIV, (2), pp. 159-74.

Singh, U. (1961) : Allahabad: A Study in Its Planning and Development, *National Geographical Journal of India*, VII, (2), pp. 99-115.

——— (1966) : Changes in the Built-up Area of 'KAVAL' Towns in the Ganga Plain (India), *National Geographical Journal of India*, XII, (4), pp. 203-17.

Sinha, B.N. (1965) : Urban Land Policy in India, *National Geographical Journal of India*, XI (3 & 4), pp. 131-43.

Sita, K. (1980) : Some Aspects of Urbanisation in South Konkan, *Geographical Review of India*, 42, (3), pp. 238-44.

Simmons, J.W. (1968) : Changing Residence in the City: A Review of Intra-Urban Mobility, *Geographical Review*, LVIII, (4), pp. 622-51.

Smailes, A.E. (1953) : *The Geography of Towns*, London.

Smith, P.J. (1962) : Calgary: A Study in Urban Pattern, *Economic Geography*, 38, pp. 315-29.

Smith, R.H.T. (1965) : Method and Purpose in Functional Town Classification, *Annals of the Association of American Geographers*, 55, pp. 539-48.

Solomon, R.J. (1966) : Procedures in Townscape Analysis, *Annals of the Association of American Geographers*, 56, pp. 254-68.

Stafford, Howard A. (1963) : The Functional Basis of Small Towns, *Economic Geography*, 39, pp. 165-75.

Stanislawski, D. (1946) : The Origin and Spread of the Town Grid Pattern, *Geographical Review*, 36, pp. 105-20.

Sumner, C.R. and J. Oliver (1978) : Early North Queensland Housing as Response to Environment, *Australian Geographer*, 14 (1), pp. 14-21.

Sundaram, K.V. and C.S. Chandrashekhar (1968) : Urban Morphology and Internal Structure of Indian Towns, *National Geographical Journal of India*, XIV, (1), pp. 55-64.

Swaminathan, E. (1979) : A Quantitative Approach to the Study of the Spatial Distribution and Functional Hierarchy of Shopping Centres in Coimbatore City, *National Geographical Journal of India*, XXV, (3 & 4), pp. 231-53.

Taylor, G. (1945) : Towns and Townships in Southern Ontario *Economic Geography*, XXI, pp. 86-96.

——— (1951) : *Urban Geography*, London.

Thakore, M.P. (1962) : *Aspects of Urban Geography of New Delhi*, Ph.D. Thesis, London University.

Thakur, B. (1980) : *Urban Settlements in Eastern India*, Concept Publication, Delhi.

Tiwari, P.S. (1969) : Urban Patterns in Madhya Pradesh, Banaras Hindu University, Varanasi.

Tuppen, John (1977) : Redevelopment of Lyon City Centre, *Scottish Geographical Magazine*, 93, pp. 150-58.

Turner, Roy (Ed.) (1962) : *India's Urban Future*, Bombay.

Verma, L.N. (1966) : Some Forms of the Town Sites in the Aravallis, *Indian Geographical Journal*, 41, pp. 52-63.

Verma, N.R. and Gopal Krishan (1980) : Site Analysis of Hill Towns, *Transactions Institute of Indian Geographers*, 2, (1), pp. 101-10.

Weaver, D.C. (1969) : Changes in the Morphology of Three American Central Business Districts 1952-1966, *The Professional Geographer*, 21, pp. 406-10.

Whitehand, J.W.R. (1977) : The basis for historico-geographical theory of urban form, *The Institute of British Geographers, Transaction New Series*, 2, pp. 400-16.

Willatts, E.C. (1971) : Planning and Geography in the Last Three Decades, *Geographical Journal*, 137, pp. 311-38.

William-Olsson, W. (1940) : Stockholm: Its Structure and Development, *Geographical Review*, XXX, pp. 43-57.

Wilson, A.G. (1974) : *Urban and Regional Models in Geography and Planning*, John Wiley & Sons, London.

Winid, B. (1967) : Problems of Towns: Patterns in Developing Countries, *The Professional Geographer*, 19, pp. 15-16.

Wolch, J.R. (1980) : Residential Location of the Service-Dependent Poor, *Annals of the Association of American Geographers*, 70, (3), pp. 330-41.

Wood, W.F. (1955) : Use of Stratified Random Samples in a Land Use Study, *Annals of the Association of American Geographers*, 45, pp. 350-67.

Young, W.J. (1975) : Distance Decay Values and Shopping Centre Size, *The Professional Geographer*, 27, pp. 304-9.

Young, Paulin V. (1973) : *Scientific Social Survey's and Research*, Prentice Hall, India, New Delhi.

Zierer, C.M. (1942) : Land Use Differentiation in Sydney, Australia, *Annals of the Association of American Geographers*, 32, pp. 255-308.

——— (1941). Melbourne as a Functional Centre, *Annals of the Association of American Geographers*, 31, pp. 251-88.

GOVERNMENT PUBLICATIONS

Bihar Statistical Handbook (1978) : Directorate of Statistics an Evaluation, Govt. of Bihar, Patna.

Chaudhury, P.C.R. (1958) : *Bihar District Gazetteers, Muzaffarpur*, Patna.

——— (1960) : *Bihar District Gazetteers, Champaran*, Patna.

——— (1960) : *Bihar District Gazetteers, Saran*, Patna.

——— (1963) : *Bihar District Gazetteers, Purnea*, Patna.

——— (1964) : *Bihar District Gazetteers, Darbhanga*, Patna.

——— (1965) : *Bihar District Gazetteers, Saharsa*, Patna.

Das, B.L., *Census of India 1971*, Series 4, Bihar, Part 11.A, General Population Tables.

———, *Census of India 1971*, Series 4, Bihar, Part 11.B (i & ii), General Economic Tables.

———, *Census of India 1971*, Series 4, Bihar, Part IV, Housing Report and Tables.

———, *Census of India 1971*, Series 4, Bihar, Part VI-A, Town Dictionary.

Indian Agricultural Atlas (1958) : Ministry of Food and Agriculture, Govt. of India, New Delhi.

National Census of Small Scale Industrial Units in Bihar 1972-73 (1975) : Directorate of Industries, Bihar, Patna.

Prasad, S.D., *Census of India 1961*, IV, Bihar Part 1.A(i), General Report on the Census.

Registered Factories in Bihar (corrected up to 31st August, 1972), Secretariat Press, Bihar, Patna.

Season and Crop Reports, Bihar, 1971-72; Statistics and Evaluation Department, Patna.

Statistical Analysis and Projections for Small Scale Industries in Bihar 1973-74 (1978) : Directorate of Industries Bihar, Patna.

DAILY NEWSPAPERS

The Economic Times, April 12, 1965, Bombay.

The Indian Nation, October 29, 1978, Patna.

——— August 15, 1979, Patna.

——— August 15, 1980, Patna.

——— October 17, 1980, Patna.

The Searchlight, September 2, 1964, Patna.

——— April 24, 1965, Patna.

INDEX